BEAUTYSCAPES

Manchester University Press

BEAUTYSCAPES

Mapping cosmetic surgery tourism

Ruth Holliday, Meredith Jones and David Bell

Manchester University Press

Published by Manchester University Press
Altrincham Street, Manchester M1 7JA
www.manchesteruniversitypress.co.uk

British Library Cataloguing-in-Publication Data
A catalogue record for this book is available from the British Library

ISBN 978 1 5261 3425 7 hardback
ISBN 978 1 5261 5581 8 paperback

First published 2019

Typeset by
Servis Filmsetting Ltd, Stockport, Cheshire

In memory of Debra Gimlin, Jane Sherratt and Brian Wilmot

CONTENTS

PLATES

Acknowledgements

We would like to thank the Economic & Social Research Council (grant reference: RES-062-23-2796) for funding this research. Elspeth Probyn was a co-investigator on the project, conducting interviews in Malaysia and contributing to a number of articles and presentations emerging from it. Olive Cheung was central to the project's success, remaining with it for the duration, organising and conducting many parts of the fieldwork and contributing subtle and informed understandings of the Chinese patient experiences in Korea, while Ji Hyun Cho accessed and interviewed Korean patients and surgeons. Emily Hunter conducted interviews and ethnography in Australia, Thailand and Malaysia, and assisted in writing up early publications, as did Kate Hardy in the UK, Spain, Tunisia and Poland. Additional interviews were undertaken in Poland by Marcela Kościaśczuk and in Spain by Almudena Casas and Jackie Sanchez Taylor. Rowan Savage and Hannah Lewis assisted with data coding. Matthew Wilkinson was our excellent project administrator and events coordinator.

We would also like to thank Laurence Vick, Legal Director at Enable Law, Graeme Perks, chair of the Professional Standards Committee and former president of the British Association of Plastic, Reconstructive and Aesthetic Surgeons (BAPRAS), Christopher Stone, former Clinical Director of Specialist Surgery at the Royal Devon and Exeter NHS Foundation Trust and director of Medical and Legal Ltd, Keith Pollard, director of Intuition Communication Ltd, Ki Nam Jin, Professor of Health Administration at Yonsei University and Nada Al-Hadithy, plastic surgeon at the Royal Devon and Exeter NHS Foundation Trust, all of whom at different points acted as advisors to the project. We are grateful to Dr Ilaria Vanni Accarigi for helping us find a crucial piece of misplaced fieldwork.

We are grateful to Anne Kerr and an anonymous reader for comments on a draft of the book, and to reviewers and organisers, editors and interlocutors for previous publications and presentations too numerous to list here. We thank Thomas Dark at Manchester University Press for commissioning this book and for his patience and encouragement, David Appleyard for seeing the book through production, Joe Haining at Blenheim Editorial for his fantastic copy editing and Martin Hargreaves for compiling the index. Our biggest thanks go to our participants – the patient-consumers, drivers, translators, nurses, hoteliers, agents, international medical travel facilitators and surgeons who gave up their time and stories to make this research possible.

The material presented in this book builds on and extends previous publications from the project, especially the following:

Ruth Holliday, David Bell, Olive Cheung, Meredith Jones and Elspeth Probyn (2015), Brief encounters: assembling cosmetic surgery tourism, *Social Science & Medicine*, 124, 298–304.

Ruth Holliday, Olive Cheung, Ji Hyun Cho and David Bell (2017), Trading faces: the 'Korean Look' and medical nationalism in South Korean cosmetic surgery tourism, *Asia Pacific Viewpoint*, 58 (2), 190–202.

Meredith Jones, David Bell, Ruth Holliday, Elspeth Probyn and Jacqueline Sanchez Taylor (2014), Facebook and facelifts: communities of cosmetic surgery tourists, in Garth Lean, Russell Staiff and Emma Waterton (eds), *Travel and Transformation*, Aldershot: Ashgate, 189–204.

Further information about the research project can be found at www.ssss. leeds.ac.uk.

1

CLINICAL TRAILS:

RESEARCHING COSMETIC SURGERY TOURISM

When we began the research project on which this book is based, we were all too aware of the criticisms of international medical travel (IMT) and of cosmetic surgery. In the mainstream media IMT is largely represented as personally and socially selfish and reckless, especially when it involves cosmetic procedures. The stereotype is one of patients travelling abroad for procedures on the cheap, carried out by unqualified 'cowboy' medics who make big profits based on the promise of magical results that can never be achieved. Added to this are recurrent narratives of returning patients being patched up back home by domestic healthcare services after bungled surgeries, often at the taxpayers' expense. On UK television screens, popular shows like Channel 5's *Botched Up Bodies Abroad* vividly recount such horror stories. IMT is usually referred to in media and popular discussion as medical tourism – a term we both utilise and complicate in this book.

In most Western countries, at least, most people assume that doctors in their home country are qualified and belong to recognised and trusted institutions and professional organisations; whereas doctors abroad are imagined as underqualified, uncaring and only out to make a profit. The Western media is full of shocking stories of British or Australian (and subsequently Chinese) patients dying or being left disfigured as a result of these reckless journeys – to the point of moral panic. Meghann Ormond (2013a) conjectures that this, like all moral panics, betrays a deep anxiety: in this case about the neoliberalisation and globalisation of healthcare and the breakdown of the post-war consensus that health is an individual human right provided for citizens by their nation-state. IMT speaks to this fear of the end of national healthcare. This narrative, however, is flipped when international medical tourists come 'here': then they are represented as seeking to steal our own hard-won healthcare and access our excellent medical facilities without making social or fiscal contributions.

Those who seek cosmetic surgery, meanwhile, are most often represented in mainstream media in two different but interconnected ways. Firstly, there is the vanity model: rich (or seeking a rich husband), self-obsessed women who aspire to the goal of ultimate beauty and eternal youth. Secondly, there is the victim model: the hapless cultural dopes, victims (ironically) *of* the media, who are so unduly influenced by it that they aspire to emulate those 'perfect' celebrities that fit the first, vanity, model. The story goes that these TV viewers and consumers of advertising mistake Photoshopped perfection for normal bodies and are left feeling inadequate and lacking (Jones 2013). This line was taken to its logical conclusion in the UK in 2014 by the Conservative MP (and GP) Sarah Wollaston in an online comment piece for a British newspaper published the wake of the discovery that 50,000 women in the UK (and 400,000 in Europe) had been fraudulently sold faulty breast implants made from mattress filler instead of medical grade silicone. While questioning the profit motives of the businesses that made and sold the implants (and that refused to replace them when their toxic nature was uncovered), Wollaston also revealed her personal disgust at these women's preferred bodily aesthetics, claiming they looked like 'grotesque dolls' (Wollaston 2012). Further, she suggested that

> perhaps in future women who wish to undergo cosmetic breast enlargement should have to pay an additional premium to cover the costs of removal in the event that they regret their decision or the implants fail; it could also cover the cost of maintaining a national register. (Wollaston 2012)

Thus, Wollaston laid the responsibility for fraud and deception by a private company pursuing inflated profit margins firmly at the feet of the victims of these crimes. This Poly Implant Prosthèse (PIP) scandal, discussed in more detail in chapter two, was initially blamed on medical tourism by the British Association of Aesthetic Plastic Surgeons (BAAPS), who mobilised their press and PR leverage to point the finger at cheap breast augmentations performed in central and Eastern Europe (BAAPS 2011; Holehouse 2012), despite it later becoming clear that the vast majority were implanted in the UK. So, here we begin to see some of the interests at work in various media discourses – and via figures of authority and powerful institutions – impacting on how cosmetic surgery tourism is perceived. The discourses surrounding it are based on xenophobic, misogynistic and classed notions, and are also deeply protectionist.

In contrast, in much of the academic literature we read as we embarked on our research, IMT was viewed through the lenses of postcolonialism, critiques of orientalism or as neoliberalisation, resulting in the asset-stripping and exploitation of 'less developed' populations – as a 'reverse subsidy for the elite', as one paper's title bluntly put it (Sengupta 2011). Often read as a manifestation of 'bad globalisation', IMT is characterised as an elite practice whereby wealthy patients (whether from the Global North or South) off-shore their own healthcare, abandoning health systems at home in search of better care or a better deal. While literature from a tourism management perspective

largely sidesteps these ethical dimensions of IMT in favour of developing business models, much of the critical literature is grounded in an ethical position
that begins from the assumption that IMT is a dubious practice. Of further
worry to us was the fact that much of this literature is based around and very
much influenced by readings of the media discourses we have sketched above.

Cosmetic surgery has itself been the subject of a long lineage of academic
work, and today is often interrogated via feminist approaches to demonstrate
the gendered power relations that disproportionately value women in terms
of their bodies, or seek to extract value from women's bodies, and also in
terms of neoliberal attempts to make the self into a project (Shilling 2012).
From de Beauvoir ([1949] 2011) to Bordo (1993), women's investments in
their bodies have been seen variously as symptoms of false consciousness or
subjugation to patriarchal discourses of women's beauty, whether they be
circulated in person, in advertising and the media or via the Internet. Such
is the dominance of this understanding that not only are the feminist frames
through which cosmetic surgery is viewed limited but they also offer very
little room for male patients of cosmetic surgery to be investigated (Holliday
& Cairnie 2007).

However, it is important to note that when feminists began to write about
cosmetic surgery – some thirty years ago – 'the conglomeration of global,
media, technological, and aesthetic conditions [that now make up cosmetic
surgery tourism] was the stuff of science fiction' (Heyes & Jones 2009: 1), and
that while the dominant feminist discourse has presented cosmetic surgery as
damaging and disempowering, some feminist scholars have 'always evinced
a certain flexibility and curiosity about what cosmetic surgery might mean
to individuals' and their social contexts (7). How we think about cosmetic
surgery now requires acknowledgement that local fashions and logistics intersect in complex ways with an ever-changing global landscape. Later in this
chapter we outline the more nuanced (but less popular) feminist theoretical
approaches to cosmetic surgery that we are building upon, and we also discuss
this in more detail in chapter two. First, however, we provide a brief overview
of cosmetic surgery tourism as a phenomenon, before moving on to discuss
the way we approached researching it.

Cosmetic surgery tourism: the basics

Cosmetic surgery tourism can be defined as travel to access procedures that
enhance appearance. It is a distinct segment of IMT with a distinctive patient
profile, a particular set of geographies and a set of drivers (or motives) that
share some commonalities with other forms of IMT but which in other ways
diverge from them. It is a phenomenon made up of diverse actors, including those we focus on in *Beautyscapes*: patients, surgeons, facilitators and

intermediaries, hospitals, governments, health systems, airlines, hotels, websites, social media and many more. As we show in chapter three, these diverse actors are assembled in particular places and times – and that assemblage is what we know as cosmetic surgery tourism.

As we also discuss in chapter three, the 'cosmeticness' of cosmetic surgery tourism positions this group of patient-travellers as distinct from those travelling out of medical necessity – and this shapes both discourses and practices that surround the journeys patients undertake. As we recount in this book, the patients we met were ordinary people, propelled for various reasons to seek treatment abroad. They came from particular places and they travelled to particular places. While extrinsic factors such as exchange rates and airline flight paths have a role to play in shaping this map, as do policy decisions made by governments and healthcare providers, the map of patient flows for cosmetic surgery tourism can partly be understood by looking at the drivers that are behind these journeys, principal among those being cost, quality, access and availability (Holliday & Bell 2015). Price differentials between home and abroad can be substantial, and cost is especially significant for patients who are paying out of pocket for treatment – as cosmetic surgery patients are. In IMT marketing, the cost savings of treatment are a major selling point – patient-travellers (and their travelling companions) can add travel and a holiday and still be paying less than they would at home for treatment alone.

Yet not everyone we met was looking to save money. Sometimes the quality of either the procedure or the medical care was more important. While quality and cost might be wrapped together, we also found cases where quality mattered more: Chinese patient-travellers going to Seoul were willing to pay more than they would at home, and their decision-making was driven by quality (Holliday *et al.* 2017). Access as a driver here means physical access – proximity or ease of travel – but it can also mean cultural proximity: the attraction of going somewhere that is familiar enough to lessen the estrangement of travel. Availability is also a driver when procedures and treatments are unevenly distributed around the world. Experimental treatments in particular might be concentrated in particular places, while certain treatments may be illegal or heavily restricted in some countries, making travel necessary for citizens wishing to access them. In the broader IMT field this can range from assisted conception to assisted dying, and from stem cell treatments to xenotransplantation.

A vexed question in all work on IMT concerns patient volume: how many people are travelling for treatment? This issue is complex because data sources are uneven and at times unreliable, not least because data are collected and disseminated with particular motives at work – for example, those with commercial interests wanting to maximise the numbers apparently travelling in order to boost business. The most widely reported figures for IMT are also the most contested (Horsfall & Lunt 2015a). In *Beautyscapes* we do not claim to be able to say how many people are undertaking these journeys; we focus instead on the stories told to us by those people who we met and talked with.

Research, selves and investments (a sort of epistemology)

The two discourses of medical tourism and cosmetic surgery outlined above unite to form a powerful prohibition against cosmetic surgery tourism – and, unsurprisingly, the cosmetic surgery tourists we spoke to were acutely aware of this. To comprehend the phenomenon of cosmetic surgery tourism we needed to find an approach that navigated the different investments and interests at work for patients, for IMT industry workers and for 'home' cosmetic surgery organisations and professional associations, and which could respond critically to dominant media and academic discourses. *Beautyscapes* represents this navigation, embedded in the extensive empirical work that this project is centred upon.

At the outset we want to discuss two issues that frame our analysis in this book. Firstly, our patient-consumers were aware, from media discourses, of the negative associations attached to their desire for cosmetic surgery and their choice to seek it abroad.[1] Adapting Hollway and Jefferson's (2009) work on 'defended subjects' we show that our participants are responding to a discourse in which they are embedded, rather than offering a disinterested account of their surgical journeys. This made them, to some extent, 'defensive subjects'. On the other hand, unlike Hollway and Jefferson, we also think about the unconscious investments of researchers in such a politically fraught field and attempt to position ourselves 'nearby' our participants (Trinh 1989), understanding things from their perspective (albeit that this attempt is doomed to fail) rather than playing the 'god trick' of judging them from our own (often distant) locations (Haraway 1988). While this understanding can never be transparent, and we can only access knowledge that is situated by our own identities and theoretical preferences, we try to avoid the privilege of 'partial perspective' invested in us as middle-class white people whose jobs and relationships require little attention to embodied appearance. Secondly, given that so much work on cosmetic surgery – partly because it mostly comes from a feminist perspective – focuses only on women's experiences, we also wanted to interview and follow male patient-consumers in order to avoid focusing on what Robyn Wiegman (2012) calls 'identity knowledges' (we elaborate on these key terms below).

Defensive subjects

In their investigation of fear of crime, Wendy Hollway and Tony Jefferson (2009) argue that an interviewee's answers should not be accepted at face value as automatically representing that person's truth. Rather, they suggest that interviewees are not at all 'transparent to themselves' and are instead 'defended' (298): motivated by unconscious anxieties, not least about what they think the interviewer would like them to talk about. To circumvent this problem, Hollway and Jefferson recommend that interviewers keep the number of questions to a minimum and maximise the openness of questions to make more room for interviewees' own understandings, narratives and affective associations.

While there is certainly plenty of food for thought in Hollway and Jefferson's free association narrative interview technique, our participants were not *defended* against their own fears, rather we found that they were *defensive*, given their acute awareness that the practice in which they were involved is so maligned in public consciousness. In a sense, then, their answers to interview questions represented a defence of their choice to undertake cosmetic surgery tourism against what they presumed would be accusations of irresponsible vanity, rather than uncomplicated and transparent accounts of the facts. That is not to say that the whole of each interview progressed according to this pattern, but defensiveness nevertheless emerged recurrently in interview beginnings, with statements such as 'I didn't do this because I wanted to look like a celebrity ...'; 'I tried to live with my [faulty body part] for many years before taking the decision to have cosmetic surgery'; 'I just wanted to be normal'; 'I spent a very long time researching my surgeon'; and, perhaps most tellingly, 'I'm not like those girls who go to [perceived unsafe destination] and get a boob job on a whim to look like Jordan'.[2] On one occasion we were talking to a surgeon in a hospital waiting area about how long people waited before they had surgery, and afterwards a patient approached us and said:

> I heard you saying that people take a long time to decide whether to have surgery. I got your email about being in the project and decided not to get in touch because I know what university professors say about us, but when I heard you talking just now I changed my mind and I want to speak to you, [because] it took me seven years to make up my mind to come here. (Mary, UK to Poland)[3]

So, our participants were defensive subjects because of the huge weight of negative discourse in which they were entangled and that they had to tackle before telling their stories.

While Debra Gimlin (2012) rightly demonstrates the importance of healthcare systems in shaping cosmetic surgery narratives in different national contexts, we might also see IMT itself as a context in which cosmetic surgery narratives are shaped. Thus, we do not read our participants' responses as 'transparent to themselves', but we do see them as important contributions to an understanding of cosmetic surgery tourism, the discourses around it and the ways that those discourses are negotiated by participants.

Identity knowledges and cosmetic surgery research

We must also note that researchers are not without their unconscious attachments to the disciplinary practices of their fields, which brings us to our second point: that our approach breaks with more familiar accounts of cosmetic surgery because it does not begin with dominant feminist approaches. This is not to say that we fail to apply gender theories to our data or that we do not employ feminist approaches to our research when those analyses are appropriate, but this study does not begin and end with feminism. The majority of studies of cosmetic surgery take as their starting point the fact that the vast majority of its patients are women. This is problematic because while many surgeons' organisations put the proportion of women patients at 90 per cent or higher, they fail to include procedures like hair transplants and cosmetic dentistry – in which more men participate – in their figures. In addition, many breast reduction procedures are performed on men, yet these surgeries are not manifest in the figures in the same way as women's (see Holliday & Cairnie 2007). Added to this, prominent writers in the field, such as Kathy Davis (2003), have theorised that men will never be consumers of cosmetic surgery in significant numbers because as active subjects they cannot succumb to the passive role of patient.

As a result, most feminist studies begin within the following frame: the vast majority of cosmetic surgery patients are women, and cosmetic surgeons are largely men. This requires an exploration of women's experiences and theoretical explication through a feminist lens. The role of feminist research on cosmetic surgery is often to uncover the power relations between female patients, male surgeons and the male gaze more generally, and in exposing them to public scrutiny, eradicate the violence of cosmetic surgery against women's bodies. So, while there is much insightful investigation into the causes of cosmetic surgery, assumptions that cosmetic surgery is largely a feminist issue remain unchallenged. This leaves male patients' and surgeons' perspectives uninvestigated, and the relationship between surgeons and patients presumed to be one of unequal power with the surgeon in a dominant position. By including male cosmetic surgery tourists, and surgeons as well as patients, we have attempted to interrogate rather than presume power relationships.

From the outset we were determined to avoid what Wiegman (2012: 5) terms 'identity knowledges'. Identity knowledges are the 'political investments and aspirations' of those authorised (for example, as credentialed academic researchers) by speaking *as* as well as *for* the subjects they claim to represent. Identity knowledges imagine that simply raising consciousness of inequality and injustice will result in their eradication. Feminist researchers, for example, often seek out injustice and invariably find what they are looking for; in speaking as and speaking for those who face injustice, a researcher's authority, as well as political and disciplinary investments, remain intact. But identity knowledges forget that there are other ways of looking (all gazes produce only 'situated knowledges'), so that looking in a different place, or in a different way, produces different results. In addition, even if we find injustice in the world, changing it is an entirely different matter. As we have shown, the mass media are well versed in a form of mainstream feminist critique of cosmetic surgery. We very much doubt that these critiques have worked to prevent a single woman who wanted cosmetic surgery from having it (although they may have made her more guarded about who she told and how she justified her decision).

In this study, then, we deliberately rejected a starting point where we saw cosmetic surgery tourism as only a feminist issue. We attempted to use many lenses, and started instead by asking: what is cosmetic surgery tourism as it is understood from the point of view of the women and men who consume it, the surgeons who perform it and the other workers who make up this industry? When we looked through these different lenses we found many surprising things, not least that without specifically seeking them out, almost a third of the cosmetic surgery tourists we encountered were men.

The stories that unfold throughout this book reflect our shared commitment to approaching the topic of cosmetic surgery tourism with open minds. Although almost every time we gave a presentation on the project we were asked to state our own ethical position (a question we became adept at fending off), in both academic and non-academic outputs from our project we always endeavoured to present the experiences we encountered, the stories we were told, in ways that did not simply feed off or into the dominant media and academic discourses of either IMT or cosmetic surgery. Indeed, that was our ethical position.

In *Beautyscapes* we discuss cosmetic surgery tourism as an always mediated and mediatised, always networked assemblage that lends itself to feminist interpretations. However, we complicate many mainstream feminist readings of it and argue – indeed advocate – that patient-consumers must not be seen as dupes of patriarchy or as unenlightened subjects. Rather, we note that reasons for seeking cosmetic surgery tourism are most often deeply considered and have as much to do with class as with gender, and we argue for a subtle or nuanced position that includes analyses of men's cosmetic surgery tourism practices. In this way, we do not position ourselves as separate from feminist critique: rather, we attempt to understand the processes and people described in this book from both inside and outside of feminist knowledges and standpoints, including (at times) a materialist approach which attempts to privilege the 'view from below' of the participants rather than the 'view from above' of those doing the critique. We elaborate on this approach in chapter three.

This approach shaped how we engaged with our participants. In addition to more formal interviews, in our research we involved ourselves in casual conversations with and between multiple agents in cosmetic surgery tourism, sharing our own histories when it seemed fitting. Working in this open way – not expecting anything in particular, trying to listen and observe and converse in ways that allowed us to discover things that might be totally unexpected – led to many insights. Below and at the end of this chapter we offer vignettes, each describing a researcher's shifting place in the site of discovery, her personal and academic perceptions, and how these discoveries unfolded.

Itineraries

About our first field trip of the project, Ruth wrote:

Waking in the dark, even in the relative warmth of my budget airport hotel room, I feel the chill of the pre-dawn air oozing in from the window under the curtain. It's 5 a.m. and we are catching an early flight from the UK's East Midlands Airport.

I feel both excited and apprehensive. It will be great to get this leg of the fieldwork started after what have seemed like endless negotiations and preparations. I'm wondering anxiously: what will it be like? What will the patients be like? Will we be welcomed at the hospital, or will we be in the way, viewed with suspicion? How will I build research relationships with patients and surgeons alike? How will the flight be? I hate flying at the best of times! Drawing back the curtains I find something new to worry about – the hotel carpark is covered in a thick blanket of snow. Will the plane even take off?

After a quick continental breakfast with research assistant Olive – who is taking all this in her stride – we take a taxi to the airport. The roads are quiet and all sounds are muted – why does noise disappear into snow? We are travelling to Poland on a budget flight alongside a small group of cosmetic surgery tourists who we will meet for the first time at the departure gate.

The airport is predictably chaotic – people are lying on benches waiting for delayed flights or passing on stories about inconveniences or rumours of cancellations, but as yet there is no actual information on the departure boards. Navigating the airport we attempt to meet our patients, liaising via text with the Surrey-based agent who had arranged our trips and those of our fellow travellers. Finally, we meet Janet, a patient in her late fifties or early sixties (I'm guessing), in a chain cafe near the departure lounge. She is visibly nervous, monosyllabic and profoundly impervious to our best early morning efforts at charm. Her surgery – a facelift – is scheduled the day after tomorrow with Dr J, who she has 'met' only through a small number of Skype and email consultations.[4] After five minutes she shakes us off and heads for the bar to 'steady her nerves'.

Half an hour later among a wave of stranded passengers we lunge towards the airline desk as the tannoy confirms the cancellation of our flight. In the queue we encounter three more of our party. Two have been offered a taxi to Stansted Airport by the agent who had arranged their trip – they had the VIP package – while a third, Lisa, had not planned in advance to travel and must, like us, make her own arrangements. Lisa is visiting her partner, Jason, whose surgery has not gone according to plan. Jason has experienced what the agent, on her Facebook page, is calling a 'little bleed' after a 'tummy tuck' (figure 1.1b). Lisa is concerned because she has not heard from Jason directly, and annoyed because Jason's agent posted about his problem on her Facebook page before she spoke directly to Lisa about it. We would later discover that Jason's 'little bleed' meant he needed three blood transfusions to survive his surgery.

There is no Poland flight from East Midlands Airport for three more days, but our fieldwork is meticulously scheduled, so we decide to leave the following morning from Liverpool instead. No transfer to Liverpool is offered by the budget airline. We are back out in the snow and hoping to find a working train. The inconveniences of 'no frills' airlines, we would discover, are familiar to cosmetic surgery tourists. Some patients cannot afford to travel to London on the train for their consultations, while a £60 return flight on a low-cost carrier to a private clinic in a country they have never previously visited, and whose language they cannot speak, offers them the best option of restarting their futures free from the problematic part of their body that has been holding them back.

On the way out, we bump into Janet again. Her surgery had been cancelled, as arriving a day late would leave no time for pre-surgery tests. She is already transformed from our earlier meeting – now warm and smiling, her relief palpable, where earlier she had seemed cold, forbidding and cross. It is 7.30 a.m. and she is a little bit drunk. I ask if she will think again about her surgery given that she was obviously so apprehensive, and she explains she is determined to re-book. When she is not smiling, she says, her look becomes what her niece calls her 'resting bitch face' – she has always been such a warm and friendly person and now people say she looks angry and treat her accordingly. She will definitely go ahead with her facelift. I think I see what she means.

Another night in a different airport hotel and a flight with Lisa at 6 a.m. En route she explains how Jason ended up in Poland. She had met him only ten months previously on a dating website. They had both been sporty in their youth: Jason was a keen rugby player, Lisa had been a swimmer. As time went on jobs and children took up all their time *while their eating habits remained the same and they had put on 'a lot of weight'. Three years ago, after a health scare, Jason decided to lose weight and went to the Czech Republic for a gastric band, while Lisa joined a popular weight-loss scheme. Both had lost fat quickly, but for Jason this resulted in the breakdown of his marriage because, he recounted, his wife liked 'big' men. Lisa had been single for a while and when they met online they immediately felt a strong connection. While Lisa didn't mind having some loose skin after losing weight, Jason didn't like his, especially as it hung down on top of Lisa while they were making love. Lisa was against the idea of surgery, but Jason had already decided to rid himself of what she called his 'apron', and he had booked surgery in Poland through the agent before he'd started dating Lisa. The only problem was that as he booked it before he met Lisa, he assumed he'd be going alone, and although he'd booked the VIP package it didn't cover a new partner going along. So, Lisa had to make her own way out after hearing on the agent's Facebook that Jason had had a 'little bleed'. She didn't know what to expect. And then there was the snow ...*

Still with Lisa, we arrive in Poland and are collected from the airport by Jarek, our convivial, English-speaking driver. Clearly Jarek excels in putting nervous patients at ease, and lightens our anxious ride to the hospital. As we pull under the clinic's covered entrance, a bang on the roof makes us all jump. Jason is standing outside the car in the snow, wearing only a hospital gown, thick overcoat and slippers. In one hand he is holding an IV stand and in the other, with which he has given our car roof a friendly knock, he is holding a cigarette. We all breathe out.

Journeys such as this were at the heart of our research method. We travelled alongside patients – or patient-consumers, as we might more properly call them – to destinations in Spain, Poland, Tunisia, South Korea, Malaysia and Thailand, sharing some of their experiences of travel, surgery, recovery and return home, though not of surgery directly. We accompanied patient-consumers on flights, through airports, in clinics and hospitals, and in hotels and apartments. Alongside patient-consumers we visited tourist attractions, went shopping and had waxes; we also spoke to them on their return home, generating copious field notes. Supplementing these journeys, we interviewed people who had visited a broader range of destinations including India, Belgium and the Czech Republic, conducting a total of 105 qualitative interviews with patient-consumers. In addition to this, we sat in on surgical consultations, spoke with medical staff at work and in social spaces, interviewed patient managers in clinics and visited agents – or medical travel facilitators (MTFs) – in offices, restaurants and homes. In all, we conducted 110 interviews with people working in the international medical travel industry, including 36 surgeons, 29 MTFs/agents, 11 marketing staff and 34 other workers including nurses, patient managers, hoteliers, drivers, lawyers, interpreters and hospital owners.

These investigations offered us a fairly comprehensive picture of cosmetic surgery tourism across Europe and parts of Asia, and, importantly, its variations across different sending and destination countries. We explored the journeys of patient-consumers from China travelling to South Korea, from Australia travelling to Thailand and Malaysia, and from the UK travelling to Spain, Poland and Tunisia, as well as other destinations picked up as our research progressed. While the research team was fairly large, and people joined and departed from it as contracts commenced and terminated or better employment offers than the precarity of the 'contract researcher' were gratefully accepted, a core of investigators and a lead research assistant remained for the two-and-a-half-year duration of the project.

All our data was held on a central database and regular project meetings ensured we developed shared understandings and approaches (for the most part). There were logistical problems, of course – when the UK and Australian teams met (via Skype) at least one country team was exhausted and in their pyjamas. Yet interview schedules were jointly developed in advance and codes agreed and similarly applied, albeit on opposite sides of the globe, facilitated by the same technologies our participants used to navigate their own transnational connections. Coding was conducted via InVivo software and, given the large number of interviews, some basic statistical data and a broad-brush picture emerged. In writing up we revisited the interviews and field notes for each country again to capture more of a flavour of each destination and journeys made to it. Different members of the team foregrounded different concerns or theories and nearly all were able to agree on the account presented here. It should be noted, however, that not everyone agreed all the time, and that researchers who had developed strong frameworks through previous research on different specialisms, particularly when they had undertaken relatively little empirical work, sometimes tended towards understandings of cosmetic surgery tourism that diverged markedly from the rest of the team. The account in this book therefore represents primarily the views of the authors and the majority but not all of the research team.

Well-trodden paths

Much of the academic writing on IMT originates in North America and foregrounds North–South journeys. As we will show in chapter seven, this frequently results in a very specific set of power relationships being described: wealthy westerners going south or east to secure high-quality care at bargain prices predicated on low-wage economies. However, none of the journeys documented in this book exactly follows that model. In South Korea, for instance, Chinese patients pay more for surgery than they would back home because quality and health scares are key push factors against having procedures in China. In addition, the regional flows of both patients and cosmetic surgery cultures between China and South Korea are cross-border relationships as opposed to the postcolonial ones most often reflected in the North American literature (e.g. Ackerman 2010). While most of the patient-consumers we spoke to from Australia and the UK could be thought of as travelling to less-developed countries, they were most certainly not the foot-loose, jet-setting cosmopolitans invented in Anthony Elliott's (2008) *Making the Cut*. Far from fitting cosmetic surgery tourism into their already globalised lifestyles, stopping off for a nip and tuck between business meetings, the patient-consumers we spoke to were ordinary people on modest incomes – taxi drivers, receptionists, sales assistants, hotel porters, nurses, prison officers, purchasing managers, oil rig workers – who could not afford surgery in the private sector back home.

The people we encountered travelled for facelifts, abdominoplasties, breast augmentations and uplifts, body recontouring, liposuction, hair transplants and dental veneers. All told us stories of the many years they had tried to live with their problematic body part before choosing surgery. They did not want to look like celebrities, only to feel 'normal' or regain something of themselves that they felt they had lost over the years or through successive childbirths; or through 'wear and tear' or weight loss that had left them with unsightly excess skin, which one of our participants, Neil, referred to as his 'mushroom' (figure 1.2); or maybe simply to become the 'real me'. In chapter two we will explore these motivations in more detail.

Cosmetic procedures are rarely covered by either nationalised healthcare or medical insurance. They are paid for out of pocket (often literally, in cash) with small inheritances, savings or credit cards. These expenditures compete with newer cars, family holidays or home improvements. They are rare financial outlays, especially to spend so much all on oneself, but they are ultimately mundane rather than exceptional, seen by our interviewees as being on a par with other forms of self-improvement. Cosmetic surgery tourism is also an expanding phenomenon. Though statistics are notoriously hard to come by, it is estimated by the UK's International Passenger Survey that around sixty to eighty thousand international medical tourists leave the UK each year and that 60–70 per cent of these are sourcing cosmetic procedures including cosmetic dentistry and hair transplants. We estimate, based on numbers supplied from MTFs, that MTFs and agents assist around twenty thousand Australians to leave the country annually for cosmetic surgery. However, this number does not take into account people who organise their own trips and surgeries and those who undertake incidental operations during holidays.[5]

The patient-consumers we spoke with shared other characteristics too. They all researched surgeons and destinations thoroughly, a difficult task since surgeons' qualifications can be baffling even to the initiated, and there are no independent registers of how many times or how well a surgeon has performed a particular procedure. Patients were very aware of the ways in which websites can be manipulated, with rival clinics posting negative reviews, for example. Most people we spoke to were more likely to trust word-of-mouth recommendations than surgeons' websites. Social media sites were therefore the information sources of choice since they provided direct access to other patients. This is explored more thoroughly in chapter six. Making the right choice of surgeon, clinic, recovery place and so on is vital since cosmetic surgery is often highly under-regulated and there is little legal recourse for patients in their own countries, let alone across national borders, if things go wrong. Getting advice at home is hard, too, since GPs are reluctant to recommend surgeons for fear of sharing liability. And should complications develop once a patient has returned home, the social sanctions for accessing aftercare in public healthcare are significant – especially for complications from surgeries that might be considered vain or trivial. This means that the choices and risks associated with the 'consumption' of cosmetic surgery must be borne by the patient-consumer, who is subsequently blamed if things go wrong. Our participants were well aware of this: while cosmetic surgery tourism is often depicted as a 'burden on the NHS' in intertwined discourses of the media and academic research shaped by the same vested interests (Jeevan & Armstrong 2008; Miyagi *et al.* 2012), our participants' own practices before, during and after surgery revealed how they had taken on responsibility for this burden and sought to minimise its impact. Cosmetic surgery tourism was not a choice taken lightly.

Unlike the horror stories so often reported in the media, 97 per cent of our patients claimed they were delighted with the outcome of their surgeries and would return to the same surgeon if necessary, or recommend them to a friend.[6] We return to this issue in the concluding chapter. Patients contrasted the brusque manner or obvious sales pitch of surgeons they had consulted in their own country with the 'genuine care' of the surgeons they travelled abroad to see (as we discuss in chapter five). They regularly commented on the cleanliness of hospitals and the cleaning work they saw being undertaken, contrasting this with hospitals back home. Despite travelling on tight budgets, currency differentials between the UK and Poland or Australia and Thailand enabled working-class patients to access up-market facilities; this was often their first experience of private medicine. Despite their low incomes, they nevertheless 'lived rich' in the countries they visited.

Surgeons, meanwhile, often commented positively on the care work they were able to undertake with these patients since moving into the medical tourism sector. This was contrasted with either the care they had been able to provide within beleaguered public healthcare or the difficulties of wrangling with health insurance bureaucracy. Some did express a slight defensiveness, usually about how their profession was portrayed, and sought to justify cosmetic surgery as equally medically valid as specialisms such as oncology. Some worried about their role in the perceived 'brain drain' of surgeons trained in public institutions moving to work in private healthcare. And they often articulated the positive contributions of the industry to both healthcare and to the national economy and reputation of their country, which was discussed in an earlier article through the framing of 'medical nationalism' (Holliday *et al.* 2017).

It is perhaps easy to think about cosmetic surgery tourism as a transaction between patient and doctor, but it is in fact a series of complex networks, incorporating medical staff based in a clinic or hospital (permanently, or having flown in temporarily to work in rented space); MTFs (who are usually former patients: trailblazers who discover their intrepid surgical journeys can be capitalised by showing others the way); concierges, whose primary task is the emotional labour of soothing pre-operative patients' nerves and making post-operative patients feel cared for in hospitals as well as in the hotels and apartments where their recoveries are completed; and drivers, translators and others who work to facilitate international medical tourists' surgical journeys. Hoteliers and landlords, as well as airlines, local tourist attractions and shopping centres also benefit from the packages offered to cosmetic surgery tourists. These networks of patients and businesses, sometimes fixed, sometimes temporary or mobile, might more usefully be thought of as assemblages: bringing together different kinds of things, people and services in a globalised relationship (Chee *et al.* 2017; Holliday *et al.*, 'Brief encounters', 2015). We discuss this framework in more detail in chapter three.

In our fieldwork we often became entangled in these networks and their associated labour, especially the emotional labour of caring for patients. We translated their concerns, intervened on their behalf, fixed communication apps or Internet connections for them so they could call loved ones back home, or simply entertained and cheered them up, allayed fears, soothed ragged nerves and so on, all the while collecting stories of lives and of the material and emotional journeys of medical tourism and cosmetic surgery.

The road less travelled

The emotional labour of fieldwork was nowhere more heightened than in observing surgeries, and we recognise the need to acknowledge our quite difficult and emotional experiences of watching surgery. Here we describe two very different surgical encounters: one description is by Ruth, documenting an encounter at a high-end clinic in Seoul frequented by Japanese film stars and K-pop celebrities, and the second, by Meredith, describes a procedure at a budget clinic in Bangkok, known locally as the 'Abattoir'. In many ways these accounts capture the diversity of our experiences as 'witnesses' of cosmetic surgery tourism in action, but they also give a flavour of its varied formations: a wealthy Chinese patient who travels for safe, high-quality, cutting-edge technology and pays a premium, compared to two patients from Laos who, despite their relative poverty, have found enough cash to travel to Thailand to undergo gender reassignment surgery.[7]

Ruth describes a trip to Seoul:

We arrive at the clinic in Gangnam on a sticky afternoon in July. Met by the clinic's marketing manager, we stand in the lobby while he talks about the history of the clinic in what feels like a carefully rehearsed sales pitch. The main surgeon and owner of the clinic was trained by the first Korean cosmetic surgeon, he tells us, and that surgeon in turn received his training in the United States. This original surgeon learned cutting-edge skills in the US, but claimed that many procedures were unsuitable for the Asian body. The clinic owner and his contemporaries had to re-write the textbooks on cosmetic surgery to make them appropriate to their new context.

The lobby is clad in marble, cooling in the city heat, and a front desk is arranged with an array of international flags and staffed by two women in immaculate uniforms. Our guide explains that the clinic layout is designed so that clients never meet each other in hallways or lobbies. Instead, a series of interconnecting rooms ensure the absolute anonymity of their clients – mostly film and pop stars and members of wealthy elite from Korea and Japan. The conversation turns to the industry, and we hear a number of complaints that would become familiar to us in our fieldwork here. We are told, for example, that small clinics do not always register their patients, thus avoiding government taxes, but that this is more difficult in larger more respectable clinics. We hear that during the Seoul Olympics hotels were given tax breaks to host international visitors, but there is no government support for cosmetic surgery, despite the fact that it is such an important industry for Korea. And we are reminded that Korea, and this clinic in particular, is at the forefront of technology in this area, which means that the government should be proud of and do more to support this growing industry. This conversation is interrupted by Dr P, who guides us swiftly down a corridor and furnishes us with scrubs and sterile slippers that lie neatly folded on an oak gym bench. We wash our hands and follow him further down the corridor to the last room – the operating theatre – where he hands us over to the clinic owner, Dr K, who is in the middle of performing a breast augmentation.

Dr K is a man in his fifties, professional and slightly avuncular. He is neatly turned out but not flashy. At this moment he is in full scrubs with a face mask. As the door opens, music fills the corridor. It is the J. Geils Band's 'Centrefold' – a song about a man who finds his ex-girlfriend spread naked over the centre pages of a pornographic magazine. I later ask him – via research assistant Ji Hyun's translation – about his choice of music, but he explains it's just the radio (coincidence?). In the middle of the room is a high bed surrounded by high-tech lighting and equipment. The marble flooring and abundant technology gleam under the brilliant lights. A slim woman in her thirties or early forties with a body that by most standards would be called beautiful shifts uncomfortably, from lying to sitting and lying again, on the bed, held in place/comforted by two nurses who grip her hands, and stroke her arms, hair and forehead. I had expected her to be unconscious! But here she was sitting and lying and shifting around to facilitate the procedure and aware – though perhaps dimly under the local and twilight anaesthetic – of the ongoing surgery to her body.

The music is soon outdone by the sound of the woman's heartbeat echoing through the theatre, amplified by her heart monitor. Dr K inserts a lipo needle into her abdomen, pumping it roughly, withdrawing a whitish, yellowy, blood-streaked mass through its thick metal stem and trapping it – this unseen, internal component of the body made visible in the transparent plastic barrel, growing larger through a series of withdrawals and reinsertions. This is my first experience of watching cosmetic surgery.

When he is satisfied with the quantity, Dr K beckons us to follow him across the corridor to another room where he inserts the fat collected into what I assume is a kind of giant centrifuge. He turns it on and over the din of the machine he explains that it separates fat cells from stem cells and then recombines them with the stem cells in much higher concentration. The advantage of this process is that the stem cells grow a blood supply to the transplanted fat, preventing necrosis and anchoring the fat to its new location in the breast. He explains, through Ji Hyun, that the risk of infection is very high in the first twenty-four hours but after that the risks of the procedure are much lower than conventional ones and the patient's own fat is more permanent and less 'foreign' than a manufactured implant. The body has been 'sculpted' rather than 'augmented' and the increased ratio of stem cells allows a larger quantity of fat to be moved from one part of the patient to another. I feel excited at the ingenuity of this imaginative technological solution and slightly awestruck by the power and scale of the equipment involved.

We return to the operating theatre where Dr K inserts the reconstituted fat into the patient's breasts in a procedure that is the inverse of the earlier one. Again, the recipient, tended by the nurses and all the while spoken to gently by Dr K, begins to move uncomfortably as her breasts swell. She has clearly been administered some kind of twilight medication, and despite having given consent for researchers in scrubs to stand and watch this most intimate of processes she does not seem fully aware of our presence. Her heartbeat booms loudly from the monitor. I feel like crying but I'm not really sure why.

Dr K moves with us into the corridor, becoming visibly relaxed now the surgery is over, having checked carefully for breast volume and symmetry, and assessed the patient's vital signs. He tells us the biggest problem is that patients don't really appreciate this technology, they don't care if it's an implant or his new and advanced methods. They often don't want to pay the necessary premium. He also laments that despite his training with South Korea's first and pioneering cosmetic surgeon, patients now look for younger surgeons, thinking they are better placed to deal with their youthful requirements. Like many of the patients included in this study, Dr K is feeling his age.

Researchers' emotions are still too rarely encountered in academic writing. And yet we came to understand that part of the labour we were conducting as researchers – who were at times intimately entwined with our research subjects – was 'emotion work' (Hochschild 1983; see also chapter four).

Meredith writes about fieldwork in Bangkok:

Early on in the research for this book I followed five Australian women for three weeks in Bangkok, interviewing them before and after their surgeries, accompanying them to appointments, eating and drinking with them, staying in their hotel, interviewing the nurses and other workers around them. I saw the patients bruised and swollen, bandaged and groggy with painkillers. After three weeks my research in Thailand was done, the interviewees had all gone home and I had scheduled a couple of days to have fun in Bangkok – I got out my guidebooks and made a list of places I wanted to see. Then I got this email:

> *DEAR MADAM*
> *I HAVE 2 PATIENTS WHO REQUEST FOR SEX CHSNGE SURGERY (MALE TO FEMALE)*
> *ONE ON WEDNESDAY 9.00 A.M. (VIETNAMESE)*
> *ONE ON THURSDAY 9.00 A.M. (PHILLIPINO)*
> *BOTH WILL BE DONE UNDER LOCAL ANASTHESIA*
> *PATIENT CAN TALK AND BE INTERVIEWED DURING OPERATION*
> *IF YOU WANT TO SEE/INTERVIEW, YOU CAN COME*
> *YOURS SINCERELY*
> *DOCTOR S*

We had already heard of this clinic; it is known as the 'Abattoir' by the Australian Embassy workers in Bangkok. When I first arrived in Thailand I had emailed Dr S to ask for an interview, but hadn't heard back in three weeks. Given that Dr S has been de-registered at least twice over his long career as a 'bargain basement' cosmetic surgeon I expected him to be suspicious of researchers and hadn't anticipated a response to the request for interview. His email suggested otherwise.

It was an offer I couldn't refuse, so instead of strolling around drinking mandarin juice, buying Thai silk, eating som tum and marvelling at the Reclining Buddha, I made my way to the clinic where Dr S offers male to female gender reassignment surgery for 65,000 baht (that's about US$1,600, a tenth of what the operation would cost in a more developed country). While many of his patients were tourists, they were not from developed countries but were mostly border crossers from Vietnam, the Philippines, Laos and Cambodia, and their surgeries cost them months', if not years', worth of salary.

The Abattoir has exposed fluorescent bulbs on the ceiling. The waiting room has rising damp. People are talking in Thai, English, French, Vietnamese, Laotian, German. The Bangkok traffic is hardly muffled behind the shopfront – a warm layered mix of engines and throbbing music surrounds us. There is nothing glamorous about this place. Ordinary-looking Thais sit waiting on mismatched plastic chairs and I find out later that Dr S works as a general practitioner as well as a cosmetic surgeon. Throughout the day, between the cosmetic surgery and gender reassignment operations that I watch, he rushes downstairs to write antibiotic prescriptions and to freeze warts off elbows. He tells me:

> Some clinics in Bangkok charge low prices like me. Because Thai people can't charge higher. It's difficult to charge higher than me because I am quite famous and my service good and quick. So, you charge them too much, they come here. You can have a sex change with that amount of money, with a couple of months' salary.

I ask him, 'The people who come for sex changes, do you talk to them about why they want to have it done? Or are you happy to just do the operation?'

Landlines and mobiles ring constantly, a teenaged boy comes in with a bleeding foot, the staff bustle around smiling and laughing, nothing fazes them. Dr S is able to ignore all the activity, he swings around on his chair, tells me earnestly:

> Yeah, they have been thinking about this for years. And we just don't want to insult them again – why you do it? – we know this kind of people. They are

psychologically very sensitive. And when you ask them a question sometimes it is like an insult. We sometimes, we sometimes say 'no, we cannot do it for you', for some people. But we have to select people case by case. We say no when someone comes in dressed like a man and they say they are only a woman when they're in the house, and they're not taking any hormones. And if they don't have sex with a man, if they have sex with a woman ... we don't let them in. I never do a sex change operation on a transsexual who has sex with a wife or who has sex with a woman. These kinds of people are not fully transsexual. [To get the operation] they must have a boyfriend and everything.

So, at this clinic there is very little questioning of people who want what Dr S calls sex change operations. It's weirdly assumed that trans women must be heterosexual and it seems there's some sort of discussion about personal circumstances, but none of the psychological interrogations, lengthy justifications, the having to 'prove' that one is indeed gender dysmorphic that happen in the West (Latham 2018) happen here. Dr S says that if people have been taking hormones for years, living as women for years, they don't need him to question them about their reasons. Significantly, there is no enquiring here about trans people's reasons for surgery. Dr S doesn't, in his words, insult them any further – they've been insulted enough in their lives. This philosophy is in line with what many people in trans communities are demanding – to be recognised not as suffering a psychological disorder but rather as people who simply need something to be done to their body in order to make it feel right for them, in order to make it liveable.

I'm distracted by two tailors delivering a bunch of Thai silk outfits in purple, lilac, yellow and gold: trousers, tops, jackets, they are new uniforms for the staff and there are black and grey pinstriped trousers for the doctor. Now he is telling me about orchiectomy, or cosmetic castration. He says angrily that it's an extremely straightforward operation – he thinks it's outrageous that the big hospitals here in Bangkok charge thousands of dollars for it, he only charges US$125 and insists that it's a quick and uncomplicated procedure (as he talks he makes snipping motions with his fingers) – in fact, he tells me, nose jobs and anything to do with the face are far more complex.

This clinic's nickname, the Abattoir, evokes perhaps the most closed and silent of all body-transforming venues, the most black-boxed kind of space. But the modest converted retail space that Meredith found herself in, with its public waiting room open to the street and people wandering in and out, was decidedly less heterotopic – less removed from the everyday world – than the hospitals we spent the bulk of our research in, which were very clearly places in which to cleanly hide away disturbing, painful parts of our culture. In contrast to them, the clinic was messy, seemingly unhygienic and of dubious legal standing. But it was connected to its local and regional surroundings in ways that the hospitals were not – and the surgeon was known and respected in the South East Asian transgender community. Meredith continues:

A woman from Vietnam had undergone gender reassignment surgery, including breast implants, the day before. She was recovering upstairs on a rusty bed with a thin mattress, one sheet, one blanket. Her friend had travelled with her and was feeding her instant noodles because the patient couldn't move her own arms. The patient told me: 'Dr S is very good. I heard many good things about him. My friend had breast enlargement with him. In my home we know him, we love him.'

Dr S is middle aged, barefoot, small and fast. His office walls are covered in posters of 'ladyboy' beauty pageants. I sit for a while as he juggles phone calls and emails and delves into overflowing filing cabinets to find pictures of his work to show off to me. He tells me about all his enemies – it seems that all cosmetic surgeons have enemies, mainly other surgeons as well as medical regulatory bodies – and rants about how journalists are against him, and how he believes that most of them are paid by the big hospitals in Bangkok to speak out against him. We talk about Michael Jackson, his cosmetic surgery and his death, and he tells me that the only way Jackson could have had Diprivan in his home would have been due to a corrupt doctor.

He whizzes me into a side room where a 60-year-old Thai woman is sitting waiting for him on an examination table. She must be wealthy: I'm pretty sure her Louis Vuitton handbag is not a fake. 'This a patient who had tummy tuck. She come back for arm lift. Her husband my friend.' There are enormous staples studding the underside of her arm from armpit to elbow. I watch as Dr S flicks them out and pulls out many stitches. The woman's mouth is turned down, her eyes tightly shut. She's in pain. I whisper into my recording device 'the scars are brutal-looking, crude', as one of the assistants sweeps up the staples with a small grass broom.

Then Dr S announces: 'Okay, we have one sex change, we start going to do it. Follow me.' We travel out the back, past the toilets. He calls over his shoulder: 'I have people here twenty-four hours a day.'

Up the stairs, flight after flight, past storage areas and more toilets. Concrete steps, my clogs clacking. Dr S is moving fast, and is out of sight.

On the fourth floor I follow him through a partitioned office decorated in that terracotta pink that was popular in the 1980s, and then another, and suddenly I'm in the operating area, which, it seems, is simply the largest partitioned office space.

I'm a little puffed from the climb. It is quiet in here. Standing at the entrance to the operating area I see three nurses and Dr S, who is, astonishingly, already robed up and standing between the patient's legs, which are held spread in stirrups. I can't see her face – it's behind a small green fabric screen. Dr S calls me over, and now I am there too, in there, suddenly between the patient's legs and I am struck that her testes and penis, although unwanted, look large and healthy ... they're painted with mustard-coloured antiseptic. A nurse comes and gives me a surgical mask as Dr S pulls on his gloves. I wonder where to put my bag and eventually squeeze it behind a trolley.

By the time I look back Dr S has made two vertical incisions on the scrotum, beginning the labour of tracing, scoring and cutting that opens the inside to the outside, that reshapes and remoulds and tucks the outside in, a process that goes on for the next two hours.

A nurse brings in a pair of paper flip-flops for me to put on and takes my shoes away. I murmur into my recording device: 'I'm in the theatre already, there was no scrub up.' Now Dr S is cutting away the testicles using scissors, he is working very quickly, snip-snip. Snipping tendons, snipping little bits of muscle. The patient lets out a faint cry, and I realise with a jolt that she is not under general anaesthetic (I hadn't really believed that from the email) – I find out later that Dr S prefers to use a mix of local anaesthetic and twilight sedation – he tells me it's 'safer'.

Weeks later I listen to my tape and my own whispered, inarticulate description of what I was watching:

> Now the penis is completely revealed: all the skin has been taken off it. There's not really any blood, very, very little. Now I think he's actually removing the penis, using a laser, something with sparks, anyway, a laser instead of a scalpel. The testicles are just hanging down between the legs.

> The testicles, free of the scrotum, are hanging down between the patient's legs and they're quickly cut away, freed from the body, and one slips out of the surgeon's hand and plops onto the floor, where it remains.

> He's injecting something in, all around the base of what is still a penis, just half-attached. The woman having the surgery is just chatting quietly away to the nurse. It's all looking like a fatty bloody mess at the moment. He's pulled a flap up and he's cleaning it of all its attached fat and stuff. More work with the laser, making two sort of 2.5-inch-long incisions along the length of the base of the penis – oh no, much longer than that – to this still half-attached penis.

> Smell of burning, but it doesn't smell like burning flesh ... He's slitting the very tip of the penis and clamping it. The nurses know exactly what they're doing, it's definitely a team effort, with six hands working in unison.

The patient has small elegant hands with manicured nails. Legs spread, up in the air, arms out and strapped down, I can't see her face. For much of the time there is silence as the doctor clamps. The heart monitor is beeping, one gentle beep for every three or four of my own heartbeats.

For a long time I'm silent, unable to even speak into my own recording device. For a whole hour I say nothing – later, listening to the tape, I can hear Dr S and his nurses talking in Thai, and some clicking and crimping sounds from his surgical tools, and the heart monitor. But I, the ethnographer, the person whose job it is to lace together practice and language, to suture doing and saying, have lost my words. I have come undone. Eventually, I say into the tape:

> He's just cut off the last part of the penis, I think. This is beginning to look like a vulva. Okay, so I think what he's done is he's manufactured one side of the vulva; this is out of the scrotum, so both the testicles have been removed now. He's stitching again. The skin on the patient's hand has suddenly gone very pale, greyish.

> It looks like, maybe he's making a clitoris now, not sure, maybe a minora. Smell of burning again … newspaper pictures of the young King up on the walls … it just can't be sterile in here. I don't think he had time to wash his hands, just time to put the gloves on.

> The shaft of the penis is still hanging there – oh, I see, he's made a hole in the base of it, and now it's completely off, and behind him. He's popped the penis into a little dish of some sort of fluid.

> Sewing again … I am finding this exhausting, just looking at it. This woman's leg is moving occasionally; she seems to be feeling something, she's chatting to the nurse again. Yep, definitely felt some pain then. Lots of sewing going on and more anaesthetic being injected into the groin. He's talking reassuringly to the patient, still putting in more local anaesthetic.

> She has now clenched her fist, very tight, letting out little cries. Dr S is putting on some magnifying glasses. Lots of burning going on, lots of clamps … I think he's making a urethra now.

My voice is becoming more faint.

> He put on another pair of gloves just before he started making the urethra. He pulls over a stool and sits down, getting very close to his work. He's putting on a third pair of gloves, getting them out of a box sitting next to the penis in its bowl. The green cover on the trolley is stained and looks like it hasn't been changed in a while.

> A very long and tiring operation … cutting through the perineum to make a vagina now, I think. Quite a lot of force needs to be exerted. He is forcing the

membrane and tissues apart. It's like a shoehorn that he's using to pull up what must be going to be the vagina and really making this cavity.

Wearing the mask is making my glasses steam up and I notice that the nurses used the masks to cover their mouths but not their noses.

He's really digging into the body. Oh gee, he's got a speculum now, really forcing that into the vagina; the patient is groaning and clenching her fists, he's really pushing that in. The patient is breathing deeply and we're back with the shoehorn mechanism, and he's stuffing the cavity with bandages – it's definitely about the depth of a vagina now, he's stuffed it completely with bandages. Lots more local anaesthetic being injected.

Sounds of motorbikes, cars, the occasional siren, outside. I'm trying not to take up too much room. The penis just lies there, its foreskin intact but the rest of it flayed. I am taking deep breaths. The nurses are talking, the doctor is telling me he's now putting in adrenaline injections – I must look those up and see what they're for.

He says, 'My personal best is one hour fifteen minutes.'

'Why is it better to go fast?' I ask.

'You know, they don't like to lie down like this, it really annoys, plus second time, longer time you have bleeding. So, do surgery quickly is better. When I start doing this kind of operation it takes me three hours. Now is less than two hours. So, when you are more skilful you get better results,' he explains.

There is cutting, stapling, sewing, knotting, folding, inverting, shoving. Dr S completes the operation in just under two hours, he's disappointed it wasn't done faster. We leave the patient with the nurses, she seems to be sleeping now.

We rush back downstairs and Dr S, still always darting ahead of me, disappears into the small kitchen. He comes out with a cup of instant coffee made with Carnation milk and puts it into my hands. He's probably realised I'm in mild shock. As I grip the hot cup I think, 'I shouldn't drink this, he made it after doing that operation and I'm sure he didn't have time to wash his hands.' But it is so warm, so comforting.

And then, then, something in me softens, and I make a visceral decision, nothing conscious, to just accept what this day is giving to me. I lean against the doorjamb and sip at the sweet coffee, taking this liquid, this place, into myself.

In what seems to me at that moment an astonishing act of kindness, Dr S has ordered lunch for me: pizza, garlic bread, spaghetti marinara … these Western foodstuffs are set before me at the Formica table in the kitchen, next to a pile of bandages. I ask him won't he join me but he has no time. He grabs a piece of pizza and jogs off. After eating I go to the toilet and pass the nurses and receptionists sitting on the spotless floor in a back room, sharing rice, grilled salted fish, pad thai, fried chicken. They add white sugar, vinegar, fish sauce, dried chilli. My mouth is greasy from the Western food.

And the day continues in this vein – I watch breast implants, a liposuction, a brachioplasty. All done at super speed under local and/or twilight anaesthetic, Dr S in bare feet, sometimes pulling on gloves for the sake of grip rather than hygiene, never washing his hands, and always, between operations, he or his assistants offer me small kindnesses that I accept: Coca-Cola, KitKat bars, more sweet coffee.

Ruth and Meredith experienced interactions in the field that were physical, psychic, social, corporeal, emotional and nutritional (Ruth was treated to food chosen for her by her South Korean cosmetic surgeon hosts at restaurants in Seoul, just as Meredith was fed at the Abattoir). Clearly, these were emotional journeys for the researchers as well as for the respondents. We finish this discussion with Meredith's emotions recollected in tranquillity, before moving finally to sketch the contents of the rest of this book.

I spent the next few months in a kind of shock. I couldn't stop thinking and talking about the day at the clinic – if people asked me how my fieldwork had gone I'd launch into a description like the one I've given above – whether I was at a bus stop or in an academic meeting. The experience left me raw, vulnerable, perhaps compromised – it was a day like no other and it changed me. My words, my techniques of analysis, were not enough to deal with what my sensorium had encountered. For a long time I tried, unsuccessfully, to make sense of the day using academic tools. Transgender and queer theories were helpful in situating some of the patients. Feminist theories of the body, my old familiar friends, were helpful in understanding the gender dynamics going on in the surgery between me, Dr S and the patients. But somehow none of this was enough.

The starkest difference, I think, between my day at the clinic and the previous weeks of research that I'd done with my interviewees in the hospitals, was created by one door. Being allowed into the space of the surgery itself made me suddenly aware of a significant barrier that I'd never questioned before. Relying only on the narratives of patients, surgeons and other practitioners meant that my analyses of surgical practices had always been merely discursive. But seeing breast implants squeezed in and forced up under the chest wall, hearing patients groaning with pain or murmuring nonsense through their sedations, smelling the bile-coloured fat globules in the liposuction machine, this was suddenly experiential, heuristic – and utterly confronting. What had been carefully hidden behind doors, softened with drugs and translated through narratives in the five-star hospitals was, in the clinic, on full and unapologetic display.

I had a lot in common with the Australian women I'd been with. We were more or less subject to the same cultural pressures and desires, and I'd had quite intimate conversations with some of them, about divorce, childbirth, the death of a parent. Despite this I was always able to conceal part of myself behind my recording device, able to use my notebook as a separating screen, able to go back to my hotel room and analyse things from a distance. But at the clinic, exposed to Dr S's physicality, his unexpected kindnesses, his unhygienic practices, and mostly by the opened and in-pain bodies of his patients, I had no choice but to become part of the environment, to enact immanence, to find myself opened, unlaced.

Alphonso Lingis (1983: 34) writes that painful body modification practices like cutting and scarification may extend the skin's sensory capabilities, creating new energies. Similarly, Elizabeth Grosz (1995: 199) notes: 'We cannot readily differentiate the processes by which pleasurable intensities are engendered from those by which painful intensity is produced.' Perhaps this is what happened to me at the clinic – in a sense, it was me who was being operated upon. Of course, I 'knew' from phenomenology that embodiment can never be reduced to discreet mental and physical components – and like all good feminists I knew that emotions, intellect and the corporeal are always woven together in the texture of lived experience. We live not just in or through our bodies as if our selves were already there: we are our bodies because our corporeal realities reconfigure our selves continually. This was a truth I held to be self-evident, but it wasn't until my day at the clinic that I really knew it, or, more accurately, felt it.

I now saw cosmetic surgery, and indeed all surgeries, as a wilful, trusting opening of the body and the self to the ministrations of an other, as a metaphoric joining with other humans, as a sign of being anything but a modern, bounded subject neatly contained. Surgery speaks of lacing between subjects, wounding and suturing, joining and intertwining. It is acknowledgement of the other, a recognition of alterity performed in its most quintessentially contemporary and discursive mode while also being utterly, utterly primitive, a hole without language.

Reading *Beautyscapes*

In this chapter we have tried to convey a flavour of our methods and approaches as well as a hint of the data which is analysed in subsequent chapters. We see our approach as fundamentally materialist, exploring the experiences, practices and understandings of our participants as they travel abroad for cosmetic surgery, facilitate journeys, provide care or operate to change the ways that bodies look. At the same time, we are acutely aware that our actors' narratives are shaped in part by powerful discourses that critique their practices. To close this introduction, we provide summaries of the chapters that make up the rest of this book, and that bring our data and analyses together.

Chapter two, 'Cosmetic investments', presents our theoretical approach to cosmetic surgery and its discourses in more detail, comparing these with the aspirations and practices of patient-consumers who travel abroad for cosmetic surgery. While in chapter one we note some of our own emotional investments in and costs of the research process, in chapter two we outline a starting point from which to view this highly divisive topic which does not begin from one side or the other. Instead of beginning by foregrounding our connection with participants on the grounds of gender and other shared similarities – what might be called 'identity knowledges', according to Wiegman (2012) – we acknowledge our difference, our academic privilege, while still attempting to convey a logic for cosmetic surgery tourism that does not betray our participants and that remains 'nearby'. We argue that cosmetic surgery tourists are seeking value, and that for many of those we spoke with, their bodies were the only asset it was possible for them to invest in. We argue that existing theories of cosmetic surgery fail to account for material, fleshy bodies that change (and, significantly, deteriorate/depreciate) over time. While most cosmetic surgery theories point to an external ('perfect') body of popular culture to which the cultural dopes of cosmetic surgery are subject, we point to instances of melancholy for a lost body, when comparisons are more often with one's own body as it used to be than with 'image culture'. On the other hand, of course, images do provide guides and possible styles. When one wants to change one's body, one has to illustrate how. So, while we do not see cosmetic surgery as totally outside any regime of images, we argue that images have a more complex and nuanced role than cosmetic surgery discourse allows.

Chapter three, 'Locating cosmetic surgery tourism', outlines the theoretical framing of medical tourism that emerged through the research process and that we deploy in the analysis presented in *Beautyscapes*. It draws on Arjun Appadurai's (1990) notion of disjunctive global flows and 'scapes', combining this with insights from work on networks and from assemblage thinking, in order to theorise how cosmetic surgery tourism is assembled by heterogeneous actors, and to show how this coming together is contingent and emergent. As Appadurai explored in his discussion of ethnoscapes, technoscapes, finanscapes, mediascapes and ideoscapes, global flows come together in particular places at particular times, and we show how this notion helps us understand the comings-together that characterise cosmetic surgery tourism. And while diverse actors have a hand in shaping and directing these global flows, not all of them have the same kinds of agency. Empirical detail drawn from our fieldwork enables us to develop a nuanced analysis of how networks are assembled and how cosmetic surgery tourism takes place and makes place. Our analysis is guided by a further conceptual framing that we also introduce in this chapter: Annemarie Mol's (2008) discussion of the logic of care and the logic of choice. Rather than simply counterposing these two logics, we see them as intricately entangled in the ways in which cosmetic surgery tourism is understood by the many actors with a stake in it.

Chapters four and five detail the many and varied forms of work or labour that are brought together to make cosmetic surgery tourism happen. The chapters are framed by discussions in the sociology of work that have explored 'new' forms of labour that workers are increasingly asked to perform: care work, body work, emotional labour and aesthetic labour in particular. Chapter four opens with an overview of the cosmetic surgery tourism industry to provide context for the analysis of forms of work that we then move into across these two chapters. The remainder of this chapter focuses on forms of work undertaken by those who travel with cosmetic surgery tourists and the various intermediaries who work to facilitate surgical journeys. In the former category we show how informal caregiving by travelling companions performs a vital function in enabling and supporting those travelling for surgery. And in the case of intermediaries, facilitators and coordinators, we explore how this novel set of roles has emerged as a new business sector with increasing heterogeneity and complexity. We provide a typology of MTFs, drawing on our ethnographic material to show who these workers are and the forms of work they perform. We show that MTFs occupy a central but contested position in the cosmetic surgery tourism assemblage.

In chapter five we stay with the work of cosmetic surgery tourism, and begin with a discussion of the work of nursing staff and surgeons. For the latter category, our research uncovered ambiguities surrounding professional standing and identity among the surgeons we spoke with. We also spend time exploring how surgeons narrate their career trajectories and the pride they have for their work, as well as how they attempt to head off criticisms of their specialism. We explore how surgeons negotiate an increasingly entrepreneurial role, showing in particular how tensions emerge in their necessary but sometimes fraught interactions with MTFs. And we show how key moments such as the clinical consultation frame both doctors' and patients' understandings of the transformation that surgery promises. We see how the consultation is not simply about surgeons asserting their professional authority over 'duped' patients; instead, it is a toing and froing of power and expertise, a negotiation towards a desired outcome for both parties. This crucial moment leads us into a discussion of the forms of work that patients themselves undertake in cosmetic surgery tourism. Rather than being merely passive recipients of others' labours, patient-travellers work hard to accomplish their surgical journeys – and some later capitalise on this work by themselves becoming MTFs and guiding others through the same journeys.

Chapter six examines the ways that cosmetic surgery tourists make community in both real and mediated worlds. We look at how patient-travellers deploy social media and websites in order to conduct research into procedures, destinations and surgeons/clinics, but also to share experiences with each other before, during and after their trips. We argue in this chapter that social media communities provide crucial emotional, practical and informational support for cosmetic surgery tourists. In this way we demonstrate that cosmetic surgery tourism is both a deeply personal but also a networked, performative experience made up of multifarious online and offline communities. Finally, the chapter argues that bodily self-transformation is in some senses actually brought about by and through social media and other communicative technologies.

Our aim in chapter seven is to challenge some of the dominant framings of IMT through a discussion of the shifting geographies that have reshaped patient flows, redefined centres of excellence and expertise, and redrawn the world map of medical tourism. We show first how cosmetic surgery tourism has 'decentred' the previous North-goes-South or West-goes-East models of medical travel, drawing on previous discussions of South–South, cross-border and regional patient movements. We then move on to think about how our empirical work and its theorising helps us in decolonising and disorienting understandings of how cosmetic surgery tourism is assembled geographically – where geography is as much imagined as it is a material reality. Using insights from fieldwork in South Korea, Thailand and Tunisia, we counter the dominant view of footloose global elites gliding seamlessly around the world in search of transformation. Our patient journeys were very different, often leading to disorientation. Our overall aim in this chapter is to present a more nuanced and complicated cartography of cosmetic surgery tourism, zooming in to different spatial scales and exploring different sites that have emerged as destinations for patient-travellers.

Chapter eight continues with some of the threads introduced in chapter seven, exploring how some of the patients we spoke with experienced the places they found themselves in as they travelled for surgery. We provide a detailed account of a trip we took to Tunisia with a group of British women, and then work to unpack this encounter by drawing on work discussing cosmopolitanism and conviviality. The ways the women worked on site to understand both their own journeys and those of the other people they met in Tunisia can be usefully interrogated by thinking about conviviality – defined as 'the practices and capacities which people develop for living with difference' (Noble 2013: 163). In their meetings with each other, with medical staff and, crucially, with patients being treated for injuries sustained in the Libyan

Civil War, these patients experienced both a global geopolitical reality that they were unaware of, and moments of empathy, vulnerability and generosity that were as transformative as the surgeries they came to Tunisia to access. We suggest that such encounters can be read as producing cosmopolitan beginnings – shifts in worldview that emerge as unintended effects of the surgical journeys this group of women embarked upon.

In our final chapter we draw this book to its conclusion through the story of Leigh, a cosmetic surgery tourist from Australia who travelled to Malaysia for surgery and who sadly died shortly after his return home. Through this story we discuss some of the issues raised by cosmetic surgery tourism and set out some of the implications of a growing global medical tourism industry, including consideration of the conditions that give rise to it.

Notes

1 The term 'patient-consumers' began to be used in discussions of privatised healthcare in the 2000s, signalling how the role and identity of 'patient' as used in public healthcare no longer fully reflected the way that patients were positioned and (partly) 'consumerised' in the new 'logic of choice' (Mol 2008).

2 Jordan, aka Katie Price, is a well-known (in the UK) British glamour model. Originally appearing topless in the *Sun* newspaper, she is perhaps most famous for her highly surgical look, with large breast implants and obvious facial surgeries.

3 Throughout the book, names and other identifying details of participants have been changed. For patients, their departure and destination countries are given.

4 Throughout the book, surgeons are identified by a pseudonymised surname initial only.

5 Many Australians, for example, have minor procedures like teeth whitening, tattooing of semi-permanent make-up and dermatological treatments such as broken capillary and polyp removal while on vacation in Thailand. It is common to have these procedures, especially in Bangkok, as a walk-in patient without an appointment.

6 Note that this meant that they were subjectively satisfied; we do not put this statistic forward as a clinical measure.

7 While gender reassignment surgery was outside of our project's definition of cosmetic surgery, we found that in some field sites there was a blurred distinction between the two. In Thailand, as Aizura (2009) and Enteen (2014) both show, clinics sometimes offer both 'full' gender reassignment surgery as well as its component procedures, the latter sometimes billed as cosmetic. We find lots of common ground in the broader histories of these two medical specialisms.

2

Cosmetic investments

Cosmetic surgery tourism is part IMT and part cosmetic surgery, and each of these elements evokes considerable anxiety and debate in both the media and in some academic accounts. In this chapter we elaborate our position on cosmetic surgery as well as introducing our patient-consumers and their motives for travelling abroad for treatment. Our intention is to frame cosmetic surgery through attention to the narratives our participants shared with us, drawing together their discussions and experiences to challenge existing conceptualisations. This chapter thus engages fully and directly with the research literature on cosmetic surgery more broadly rather than that specifically on cosmetic surgery tourism.

Cosmetic surgery is defined as surgical treatment for the purposes of 'enhancing' a person's appearance – treatment that is not considered medically necessary. In its infancy as a modern surgical practice, cosmetic surgery was popularly constructed in relation to vanity. As a new technology, cosmetic surgery was associated largely with the rich and famous, those who made a living from their bodies and those who used their bodies to demonstrate their own or their partner's (as in the case of 'trophy wives') wealth and success. Cosmetic surgery was an exclusive business. Secret tunnels were rumoured to run between high-end clinics and elite hotels in Switzerland and Los Angeles, ensuring the bandages and scars of movie stars would never be exposed by a predatory paparazzi. Cosmetic surgery had to be secret because without the aura of natural, superior beauty, these stars would be just like the rest of us (or we could be like them).

In reality, cosmetic surgery has a long and complex history beyond its association with glamour and luxury. Its technologies and practices have developed and expanded often as the result of disease (Gilman 1999) or the work of surgeons to reconstruct the bodies and faces of war-wounded soldiers hoping to reintegrate into society after injury and disfigurement (e.g. the work of Harold Gillies in the First World War). Developments in this field of so-called 'reconstructive' surgery (defined as medically or socially necessary, and therefore often free in nationalised healthcare) have frequently spilled over into 'cosmetic' surgery, where the same technologies provide 'enhancements' in a market more lucrative than the repair of damaged bodies (see Haiken 1997). The tension between reconstructive and cosmetic surgery continues to shape discourses around these treatments today (Naugler 2009). As we will show later, this distinction is key to understanding why more and more people travel abroad for surgery – as procedures previously available at no cost in public healthcare become redefined as elective and pushed into the medical marketplace.

Statistics on cosmetic surgery today, largely collated in the West by surgeons' organisations like the American Society for Aesthetic Plastic Surgery (ASAPS) and the British Association of Aesthetic Plastic Surgeons (BAAPS), tend to place the proportion of people having cosmetic surgery at 10 per cent men and 90 per cent women. However, there is considerable debate about these figures. Despite strict controls for women undergoing breast reduction surgeries – prospective patients must often be over a set cup size and under a set body mass index to qualify for treatment as well as experiencing negative physical and psychological symptoms – for men, breast surgery is often granted for a chest that appears 'feminine' (Singleton *et al.* 2009). Men's breast surgeries are also often subsumed in the category of breast reduction, which is then assumed to be female (Miller 2005). Figures on other common surgeries for men, such as hair transplants or cosmetic dentistry, are simply not recorded (Holliday & Cairnie 2007). And, while rising rates of genital cosmetic surgery for women are viewed with alarm in both the media and surgeons' organisations (Holliday 2019), male circumcision rarely warrants a mention – even when performed on adolescents for aesthetic reasons (Fox & Thomson 2017). Nevertheless, the available figures have led to cosmetic surgery being associated largely with women's bodies and theorised from a feminist perspective.

Feminism and cosmetic surgery

For feminists, vanity is not a natural preoccupation of women; rather, it is a regime of evaluation imposed on women's bodies by a male or patriarchal gaze. Women, the argument goes, are judged superficially on their looks (and propriety), while men are judged on important factors like intellect and character. This is a vicious circle, where preoccupation with their looks distracts women from more worthy pursuits, leaving them in the trivial world of surfaces while men attend to the deep and the serious. Consequently, many feminists have called on women to reject the world of beauty, constructed as it is by men, and to return to the natural body to find women's true essence. This kind of argument underlies many anti-cosmetic surgery tracts, such as Sheila Jeffries's (2005) *Beauty and Misogyny*, in which she constructs any alteration to the body – even tattoos or piercings – as patriarchal violence, often carried out by women themselves on behalf of men.

Marginally more nuanced positions juxtapose cosmetic surgery with body modification where, (selectively) following Foucault, the former is rejected as normative and the latter celebrated as 'transgressive' (MacKendrick 1998) – although, of course, framings of body modification as 'modern primitivism' are subject to their own postcolonial critique (Pitts 2003). While writers like Spitzack (1990) and Wegenstein and Ruck (2011) evoke a disciplinary gaze – used by surgeons and readers of popular culture, respectively, to fragment and redefine women's bodies as objects for improvement or technological reconstruction (see also Wegenstein 2012) – Kathryn Pauly Morgan (1991) argues women should seize these means of beauty production and use them instead to resist patriarchy through the 'uglification' of women's bodies, using cosmetic surgery to create breasts that droop, faces that sag and so on. Acclaimed body artist Orlan appears to have taken this invocation literally, performing non-normative cosmetic surgery as art on her own body (Davis 2003; O'Bryan 2005). While these accounts attempt to challenge what their authors see as a patriarchal culture imposed on women's bodies, in the process they confirm beauty as a trivial and misguided pre-occupation with women as its victims and cultural dopes, and only feminists and artists as able to see beyond the normalising and disciplining gaze of cosmetic surgery: if only ordinary women would listen, feminists could eradicate cosmetic surgery by making visible the gendered power between women and surgeons, or women and the creators of media images.

The relationship between media images and women's bodies is given prolonged and serious attention by feminist cultural theorist Susan Bordo (1993). Beauty, she argues, is a discourse – a 'beauty system' that presents perfect bodies as normal ones. In this discourse real women are made to feel their bodies are lacking and inadequate because they can never achieve the constructed images of physical perfection that flood the media around them. So powerful has this position become that we argue it is now *the* position on cosmetic surgery, invoked by feminist activists, media commentators, politicians and cosmetic surgeons alike. Many of the surgeons we spoke to in this project invoked 'pressures on women from the media to look perfect' as a rationale for cosmetic surgery, even as they insisted on 'realistic expectations' from surgery in patient consultations (we will return to this later).

In juxtaposition to Bordo's media analysis, Kathy Davis (1995) spent considerable time and attention talking to women having cosmetic surgery for free in state healthcare in the Netherlands. Davis argues that far from wanting to achieve physical perfection, the women in her study simply wanted to be 'normal'. She argues that feminist writers on cosmetic surgery should refrain from being overly judgemental and should take women's narratives seriously. Unlike Bordo, who focused on women only as subjects of a discourse that could be read from media images, Davis emphasises women's choice and agency in their attempts to secure cosmetic surgery and improve their lives. She rejects Bordo's portrayal of conformity with a beauty system next to which women find their own bodies wanting, and instead stresses that cosmetic surgery patients just want to be 'normal' (not beautiful) and that improving their bodies means individually taking control of their lives. Women, she argues, want bodies that express their inner identities externally. Drawing on a more sociological approach based on theories of structure and agency, Davis does not dismiss the limitations that culture places on women's bodies, but argues that women are active in navigating these limits. Her participants did not want to become the images of beauty they saw in magazines, they wanted modest changes to avoid anxieties that were localised to one or two body parts and procedures – they were well aware that changes to their bodies were not going to make them 'beautiful'. However, despite giving careful consideration to women's agency, Davis locates their choices in pain – the psychic pain of having the 'wrong body' and the physical pain of surgery.

In many ways this analysis expressed the mood of feminism at the time, as feminist writers struggled to think through the surgeries of trans people who both wanted to have gender reassignment surgery and wanted to be feminists. This was not an easy reconciliation. Feminists largely saw gender as inessential culture that used cosmetic surgery to produce women's material bodies from medically constructed norms of the feminine via the surgeon's scalpel (Balsamo 1992), while trans people often saw gender as essential and the surgeon's knife as setting free the trans person's real gender identity. While cis-gendered women only had to ask and pay for cosmetic surgery, trans women were made to 'prove' their gender, sometimes for years before surgery was granted. Sandy Stone (1991) shows how trans women learned the medical definition of gender dysphoria as outlined in the *Diagnostic and Statistical Manual* – the key guidebook for psychiatry – and recited it to the psychologist gatekeepers of their surgeries, since simply wanting to have surgery to become the 'opposite sex' was not considered indication enough for surgical referral. Some critics of Davis have similarly implied that since her women patients were having free surgery (paid for by the state), they needed to invoke the discourse of psychic pain to qualify for surgery. In both settings, cosmetic surgery gets psychologised. Bordo is highly critical of Davis' approach, claiming that:

> The rhetoric of choice and self-determination and the breezy analogies comparing cosmetic surgery to fashion accessorizing ... efface not only the inequalities

of privilege, money, and time that prohibit most people from indulging in these practices, but also the *desperation* that characterizes the lives of those who do. (Bordo 1997: 337, our emphasis)

In dismissing Davis's approach to agency and choice – empowerment, we would now call it – Bordo retains the discourse of cosmetic surgery as located in pain and desperation. This discourse is shared by surgeons. In his work on Brazilian cosmetic surgery, for instance, Edmonds (2010) explores the mind/body split in Western biomedicine and the strange anomaly of cosmetic surgery as the (embodied) surgical 'cure' for the (mental) problem of self-esteem. He terms the bringing together of these apparently incompatible branches of medicine in cosmetic surgery 'aesthetic medicine', and quotes one Brazilian surgeon, who joked: 'What is the difference between a psychoanalyst and a plastic surgeon? The psychoanalyst knows everything and changes nothing. The plastic surgeon knows nothing but changes everything' (76). Self-esteem is a notion that continues to puzzle psychologists, in terms of why some people with fairly significant disfigurements seem relatively unaffected while others with very minor complaints seem troubled. The history of self-esteem is explored by Alexander Edmonds in some depth, demonstrating how it is often deployed to mask social problems like poverty or racism. Yet connecting self-esteem and beauty seems to provide a more holistic vision of the self than the Cartesian model of medicine can allow.

Despite a fairly universal appeal to self-esteem in cosmetic surgery discourse, Debra Gimlin (2007a) reminds us how important different national healthcare systems can be in structuring health discourses and patient accounts. This is the focus of her cross-national comparison of cosmetic surgery narratives in the UK and US, in which she argues that justifications for surgery are produced in specific national healthcare contexts, so that UK discourses centre on negative comments from partners or friends and are justified (guiltily) in relation both to spending money on oneself and taking up public health resources that properly sick people might need. On the other hand, women in the US spoke about 'deserving' cosmetic surgery and justified it by having saved for it and positioning it as a reward for taking care of their health and bodies (see also Adams 2013). So, there is plenty of scope for a robust critique of Davis, since in the Netherlands a discourse of psychic pain (low self-esteem) produces the entitlement to free surgery. Yet Bordo – perhaps to defend her feminist empathy in the face of charges of judgementalism – also embraces pain as a motive for cosmetic surgery, even in the US. So, while Davis rejects Bordo's theory of normalisation to the 'system of beauty' and reinstates the body as a site of expression and identity, both critics locate the cause of cosmetic surgery in the pain experienced by women who resort to surgery to alleviate their own suffering.

Cressida Heyes (2007) claims it is precisely the turn to identity which is at the heart of techniques of corporeal normalisation. Adopting a more complex and distributed model than a simplistic 'beautiful images cause cosmetic surgery' formulation, she argues that cosmetic surgery is a site where

> transformed technological possibilities, consumer capitalism, the ideology of a medical subspeciality, television culture, the body-as-self, and diverse forms of resistance to the surgically constructed body all converge. (Heyes 2007: 91)

Yet she too is keen to foreground pain. Davis, she argues, justifies cosmetic surgery as an acceptable treatment for 'unbearable suffering', despite claiming that her participants' bodies were not significantly different from other women who live more happily with their 'flaws':

> I did not necessarily share these women's conviction that they were physically abnormal or different. Their dissatisfaction had, in fact, little to do with intersubjective standards for acceptable or 'normal' feminine appearance. For example, when I spoke with women who were contemplating having cosmetic surgery, I rarely noticed the 'offending' body part, let alone understood why it required surgical alteration. (Davis 2003: 77, quoted in Heyes 2007: 106)

Drawing on Davis's evidence, Heyes proposes that psychological pain is attached through medical discourses, after the fact, to body parts that fail to live up to ever-rising external standards. Heyes (2007: 109) argues that the cosmetic surgery recipient is 'encouraged through the discourse of identity, to displace her unhappiness onto her failed body', and she develops this theory through an examination of the US reality TV show *Extreme Makeover*. Since failed body parts are not, for Heyes, the real source of pain, then cosmetic surgery can never eradicate that pain. Instead, when happiness does not result from the first surgery, another body part becomes problematic and the process is repeated.

While there is much of merit in Heyes's critique of Davis, and, we would argue, in Davis's critique of Bordo, there are limitations in using TV as evidence, and in tackling cosmetic surgery through the lens of feminist theory. Most TV shows on cosmetic surgery follow a 'makeover' format with the aim of producing visual pleasure for audiences. Visual pleasure is produced by choosing subjects who are already beautiful in many ways, but whose bodies have the exact characteristic that the technologies of cosmetic surgery can successfully 'enhance'. This is not the same thing as real patients who want a specific problematic body part made better with whatever technology is currently available. As the technology is comparatively straightforward, the results are instantaneous and because sexualisation adds interest, representations on TV have been over-preoccupied with breast surgery. A number of feminist writers on cosmetic surgery take these shows as the empirical truth of cosmetic surgery rather than a piece of entertainment constructed for viewers' enjoyment.

In chapter one we outlined our methodological approach, drawing on Hollway and Jefferson (2009) to critique the idea that interview data is 'truth', and that interview participants are fully present or transparent to themselves. We demonstrated that our participants are both 'defended' and 'defensive' subjects, protecting themselves from anxieties about risks and culturally imposed narratives about cosmetic surgery being irresponsible and vain or the result of being duped by the media into wanting to look like beautiful celebrities. We also used Robyn Wiegman's (2012) work to show that participants are not the only ones with investments at work here, and that feminist researchers have tended to deploy identity knowledges: but looking for women's pain in order to uncover injustice inevitably results in finding it. Wiegman talks about the problem of the academic speaking *about* and *for* a particular group as one of its members. Feminists speak about women's experiences, and speak for women to effect political change – and they speak as women, representing all women. While Judith Butler (1990) has alerted us to the problems of representation – given that the women doing the representing are often much more privileged than the women they claim to represent, 'women' are often what middle-class, white feminists imagine them to be – Wiegman alerts us to the difficulties of attaching the self to uncovering injustice. Drawing on Wendy Brown's (1993) work, Wiegman explores feminist subjectivity as one that seeks out and identifies with the 'victim of patriarchy' – a subject position located in Brown's notion of wounded attachments.

Explorations of cosmetic surgery by feminists, then, are often designed to explore women's experiences of and motivations for having surgery, to politicise this through feminist theory, and to identify, as a woman, with these 'other' women's exploitation by surgeons and clinics. In other words, women with wounded attachments interview women with defended subjectivities. Women who write on cosmetic surgery are invited to speak at conferences and submit papers as women who share victimisation by a beauty system with the women they write about, turning subjugation into capital – albeit in a way that white men cannot even imagine. We are all women, we are all made to think about our bodies and beauty, the only difference between us (feminists) and them (victims of cosmetic surgery) is that 'we' see the operations of power that produce cosmetic surgery and resist them while 'they' do not. Yet academic feminists and feminist activists have many sources of value other than their bodies, and their bodies are not key to their success or failure in the labour market or financial security through marriage. For us to claim to be wounded by a beauty system in the same way as our participants would be disingenuous.

As we discussed in chapter one, we certainly align our research with those who argue that explanations for cosmetic surgery are not to be found in the psyches of individuals or in the plotlines of reality TV, but rather in the complex medical, social, cultural and economic networks in which cosmetic surgery unfolds – a nexus between materialities (of bodies and spaces) and communications, technologies, media, patients, discourses, surgeons – and in narratives (Jones 2008a), especially national ones (Gimlin 2012). Before we move on to explore this empirically, we also want to pry open some of the unacknowledged attachments of previous writers on cosmetic surgery, which, we argue, are often unacknowledged classed attachments.

Class and cosmetic surgery

To explore the issue of social class in relation to cosmetic surgery, we now turn to the work of sociologist Pierre Bourdieu (1984), who argues that different class fractions deploy their knowledge of and access to culture as 'capital' in the process of effecting 'distinction' from other class fractions lower down the class hierarchy. Cultural capital is learned early in life in family settings and is accrued and deployed by learning and making judgements of taste. While cultural capital can have many different forms, only one form – the cultural capital belonging to the middle classes – becomes the legitimate 'symbolic' capital that comes to hold value. The wealthiest do not need cultural capital, Bourdieu argues, since they have enough financial capital. The middle classes need to effect distinction from the working classes (and from each other), but this is tricky when their incomes are not always much bigger, so the accumulation and display of cultural capital becomes vital in asserting class status.

Cultural capital is acquired through educational qualifications, knowledge of art and literature, 'tasteful' consumer goods and 'embodied capital'. Most middle-class people who make these classed judgements – usually by comparing the taste or consumption habits of someone lower down the class hierarchy unfavourably with their own – are unaware that they are making a class distinction based on habits learned early in life without ever being obviously taught. While working-class taste might seek to emulate the more obvious and graspable elements of upper-class taste, albeit through cheap replicas, the middle classes prefer to counter the trappings of the established elite with their own style.

Beverley Skeggs (2013) expands on Bourdieu's work to develop a fuller theory of value. She argues that middle-class selves have developed a sense of entitlement, that they are 'self-possessive individuals'. These individuals organise themselves to accrue value to the self which they can 'rent' in the labour market, where not only being good at one's job is important but so are excellent social skills and, vitally, being well networked – or having 'social capital', as Bourdieu puts it. These middle-class selves are also cosmopolitan. They have travelled and have knowledge of the world, most readily expressed through knowledge of different cuisines (Bell & Valentine 1997). Savage *et al.* (1992) claim that the professional middle class consolidates its position through 'body capital' – cultural practices such as taking care of the body (running, going to the gym, eating healthily) and therefore staying more productive – in addition to increasing education, gaining promotion and so on. These practices accrue value to the self. Skeggs (2013) talks about the middle-class appropriation of working-class practices such as tattooing, and we might add that it is no coincidence that muscles on white-collar middle-class men became fashionable at precisely the moment when hard manual labour (which produced muscles) disappeared from the post-industrial labour market. Working-class muscles were simply brawn, matching working-class men's natural bodies to manual labour, while middle-class muscles communicate a care of and attention to the self – the self as a 'project' (Featherstone 2000) marking (white) middle-class men out as valuable subjects.

While Skeggs makes class central to her analysis, Lisa Adkins (1995) argues that women in particular occupations are employed for their 'feminine characteristics', but that these are not seen as skills, only as 'natural' attributes. Women, she argues, are not 'optimising subjects' because they have already been optimised and exploited by employers who make value from these feminine cultural performances (being sexy or caring, for instance) and to which they are already subjected. As Skeggs summarises:

> A central difference then appears. On the one hand there are those who are depicted as rational and accruing individuals, who can secure the necessary properties in order to either exploit themselves or avoid exploitation, and who, as a result, become subjects of value. On the other hand, there are those who are depicted as not having the potential to be a subject of value, without access to the resources required to produce themselves as such. This latter group are born into positions where resources may be given different values. It thus becomes a matter of how different forms of culture and labour are given value and how these can be exchanged or not. (Skeggs 2013: 71)

Or as Bourdieu (1984: 192) succinctly puts it, the body is a 'sign-bearing, sign-wearing … producer of signs which physically mark the relationship to the body'.

Returning to Alexander Edmonds's critique of self-esteem discussed earlier in this chapter, we might reframe cosmetic surgery as 'beauty capital' – which is one source of capital among others that individuals can accrue to the self. And beauty capital is particularly important to those whose body is part of what they offer to the labour market – celebrities and stars, of course, and those who work in the interactive service industries. Middle-class subjects whose jobs do not rely on how they look, or those with many other sources of capital such as financial, educational or cosmopolitan capitals or those embedded in 'reverse discourses' (like feminism) which celebrate the natural body (Murphy 2012), can easily withstand small embodied divergences from the norm. However, others, especially working- and lower-middle-class women, may be more reliant on beauty capital. This would explain why, outside of a minority of clinical cases, psychological concepts like self-esteem largely correlate with relative wealth (Davies 2016). And this is why investing in one's body may logically represent the best source of value for some subjects.

Neoliberal bodies and biopower

A final point worth mentioning in this discussion is the economic system of neoliberalism and how this impacts on the classed cosmetic body. Neoliberalism is a political economy that transfers responsibility (and cost) from the state to the individual, transforming what Foucault (2010) calls the power of the 'sovereign state' into the self-governing 'technology of biopower', whereby individuals manage their own lives in the interests of the state. For Rabinow and Rose (2006), biopower involves three things: truth discourses about the character of living human beings; strategies for intervention on the collective in the name of human health; and modes of subjectification by which individuals work on themselves under certain forms of authority in relation to truth discourses. Neoliberalism becomes manifest in what Meredith Jones (2008a) calls 'makeover culture', wherein people are rewarded for working on their bodies in line with discourses that circulate in the media, particularly in relation to reality or makeover TV. Makeover TV exposes not just idealised results but also the mechanisms and technologies necessary for improvement. As Ouellette and Hay (2008: 12) put it, citizens are increasingly obliged 'to actualize and "maximize" themselves not through "society" or collectively, but through their choices in the privatized spheres of lifestyle, domesticity, and consumption'.

According to Brenda Weber (2009), cosmetic surgery makeover TV aims to produce a 'new you' who is at the same time the 'real you': 'To communicate an "authentic self" one must overwrite and replace the "false" signifiers enunciated by the natural body' (4). Image, body and self are collapsed so that all the failings of the self can be resolved by 'correcting' the body – creating an image with which the self can identify. Unlike previous genres of reality TV that concentrated on competitions between contestants in studio settings, the makeover genre draws on the rules of society (of attractiveness), imposing a normative gaze through cultural intermediaries in the show who invite viewers at home to accept their judgements as experts about how contestants can be 'improved'. In the makeover show, the rules are generalised and the setting is naturalised, while the authenticity of the subject/participant is foregrounded, focusing on who the contestant is, not what they can do. To be empowered is to be yourself while at the same time being just like everyone else (255). This discourse is most particularly at work in weight-loss shows like *The Biggest Loser*, which educate viewers in techniques of self-governance for the good of a healthier self and a healthier society.[1] However, the social context of obesity is rarely addressed; rather, obesity is positioned as an individual failing.

Assembling these approaches, then, we might understand cosmetic surgery not as a something reached for from a position of pain, caused by a failure of real women to live up to an unachievable ideal, but rather as an attempt to achieve self-actualisation by 'taking control' of one's own life and possibilities for the good of society (here beauty is inextricably linked to health and vitality rather than vanity). Cosmetic surgery is a private response but it is also an ethic – a taking care of oneself, a form of 'self-optimisation'. For its consumers, cosmetic surgery also retains something of its origins as elite practice engaged in by the rich and famous, so it also marks the body/self as valuable – as the tag line goes, 'Because you're worth it'. Many of our participants claimed the moment at which they felt best about themselves was the moment at which they *decided* to have surgery, as opposed to their post-surgery 'reveal'. This was the moment at which they took back control of their lives, recognising their own value as a self worthy of investment.

However, the value that one might accrue from cosmetic surgery is precarious because feminism has already marked it as failure of individual resilience in being able to resist patriarchal beauty norms, and patriarchs have marked it as feminine superficiality and vanity. And for middle-class commentators it circumvents the 'work' that people ought to invest in their bodies through diet and exercise, offering instead an undeserved quick fix (for instance, see Throsby [2008] on weight-loss surgery), or it is associated with 'vacuous celebrities' who are only 'famous for being famous', who 'invite' classist insults by virtue of being at once working class (tasteless) and successful and in the public eye (Tyler & Bennett 2010).

So, while cosmetic surgery is an attempt to accrue value for the self in the form of embodied capital, the discourse of cosmetic surgery as a quick fix attempt to meet a feminine ideal imposed through an unquestioning acceptance of popular culture – or 'false consciousness' – makes it difficult for cosmetic surgery to be transformed into symbolic capital. Attempts to use cosmetic surgery to seek 'value' for selves, then, often fail, because the cosmetic body is classed – marked by excess and fakery and associated with (talentless) celebrity, lack of effort and the non-self of false consciousness in feminism. Even worse, it may transgress accepted aesthetic standards, for example by implanting large breasts that go against middle-class ideals of natural, restrained and desexualised beauty (Gimlin 2013; Holliday & Sanchez

Taylor 2006). Or, cosmetic surgery may be appropriated by employers as necessary for service work, rather than appreciated as an investment in or asset of a self-possessive individual.

The framings of cosmetic surgery that circulate in media and academic accounts and in the broader 'public conversation' are very important for our understanding of how patients themselves talk about their surgeries and how medical professionals and other workers talk about patients. We also need to be mindful of what happens when the troubled term 'cosmetic surgery' is joined by an equally troubled term – 'tourism' (Bell *et al.* 2011). As we discuss below, an intention in our research design and recruitment strategy was to be open to finding out who was travelling abroad for treatment, and to listen to their accounts, rather than deciding at the outset what (and who) we would find.

Accounting for cosmetic surgery

Given that we were already alerted to the possibility that women were not the only consumers of cosmetic surgery, we began this project with an openness to different patient groups. We selected two departure countries – the UK and Australia – and what seemed (based on our online searches) to be the most popular destination countries for patient-consumers travelling from them. We also selected South Korea, as the destination with the third-highest number of cosmetic surgeries per head of population (after the US and Brazil) and on account of its reputation for a developed medical tourism industry, to see who travelled there and why. We advertised for participants on portals, in gyms and beauticians and with agents, and we hung around in clinics, hospitals, hotels and hostels, speaking to patient-consumers who used them. We circulated postcards asking: 'Thinking of travelling abroad for a procedure to change your appearance?' – deliberately sidestepping language that might appeal to specific groups. By the end of the project we had recruited and interviewed 105 patient-consumers, 25 per cent of whom were men. This was all the more surprising because forums on which we posted often had names like 'Sofeminine', which on the face of it appealed only to women – and certainly many men we spoke to expressed discomfort about using these sites. We also encountered a number of men who declined to participate in our study, fearing reputational damage if their secret surgery was revealed.

Two explanations might account for the high numbers of men in this study compared with many others and with 'official' statistics: either many more men travel abroad for cosmetic surgery than stay at home, or statistics in the UK, US and Australia are simply wrong. As we noted earlier, this is partly a problem of definition and counting. It is also a problem of disclosure – of who self-reports to having travelled for surgery. The widely acknowledged problems of data for IMT (Horsfall & Lunt 2015a; Lunt & Carrera 2010) are perhaps exacerbated precisely by the discourses surrounding cosmetic surgery that we outlined above. Interestingly, South Korean statistics include men at about 30 per cent of cosmetic surgery recipients, and in our fieldwork there we found a much greater acceptance of men's cosmetic surgery than in Western countries.

A second characteristic of our participants from the UK and Australia was that they were largely (though not exclusively) white and predominantly working class or lower middle class. The average annual income of the British sample, for instance, was around £22,000, and only 9 per cent of our UK sample had a higher education qualification, compared with about 42 per cent of 25–65-year-olds in the general population. However, Chinese patient-consumers travelling to South Korea for surgery were wealthier than their UK and Australian counterparts, suggesting a different demographic engaging in cosmetic surgery in China (Holliday et al. 2017).

While the kinds of cosmetic surgery consumer varied from destination to destination, so too did the types of surgery involved. Some surgeries seemed fairly universal (such as breast augmentation) while others were more specific – so-called Asian blepharoplasty, for example. In addition, certain destinations appeared to specialise in particular surgeries – three of our UK patient-consumers went to the Czech Republic for bariatric (weight-loss) surgery, followed by body contouring surgery (abdominoplasty, or tummy tuck) in Poland. Participants broadly agreed that Budapest was the place to go in Europe for dental work, and women travelled from Australia to Thailand and from the UK to Belgium for breast augmentations. So, a complex picture emerged of different places offering different surgeries and patient-consumers giving diverse reasons for having surgery or for choosing one destination over another.

Some of these surgeries were highly gendered – breast augmentation for women, breast reduction for men, for example – and others less so, such as facelift, blepharoplasty (eyelid surgery) or nose tip augmentation. In one Belgian clinic we visited, problems arose when a patient from the UK whose appearance read as masculine requested a breast augmentation – an illegal procedure in Belgium. It transpired that the patient was intersex and that despite having been brought up male was feeling increasingly uncomfortable in that gender and now wanted to explore being female. The clinic was able, after some negotiation, to provide pectoral implants that appeared very similar to breasts. Gendering – whether normative or non-normative – is a common part of life in the cosmetic surgery clinic. In reality, different procedures on different parts of the body have very diverse meanings. Our findings are at odds, then, with the vast majority of the literature, which theorises cosmetic surgery with a single frame, whether that is beauty, normalisation, gender, identity, fashion or pain. Some patterns or tendencies, however, did emerge, and we have characterised surgeries into themed groupings where the first two correspond more closely to 'reconstructive' surgery and the latter to 'cosmetic' surgery. Neat taxonomies were not possible, however.

Correction was predominantly represented as the framework for understanding young people seeking ear pinning, nose reshaping, blepharoplasty (eye-widening/enlarging), breast surgery for symmetry, breast reduction for very large breasts (women) or gynecomastia (men), and a very small number having surgery to reduce large labia minora. We might also argue that those undergoing sex reassignment surgery fall under this category. Respondents saw these surgeries as a correction for 'abnormalities' that they were born with or that developed during puberty. Such surgeries were largely taken as justified and as reconstructive.

The *repair* category included people whose bodies had undergone trauma or sudden change. Most common were post-pregnancy surgeries such as breast uplift and abdominoplasty, and repair to vaginal injury or prolapse, often called 'vaginal rejuvenation'. Also included were repairs to other sudden bodily traumas, for example scar removal or sporting (or fighting) injuries to ears and noses, and body contouring after weight loss (removal of excess skin), especially after gastric bands or bypasses.

Anti-ageing as a category shared similarities with correction and repair, except that its procedures tended to be viewed as a more elective intervention into a natural process. However, 'premature ageing' was used to justify surgery in some cases. Procedures included face, neck and brow lifts, eyelid lifts, breast uplifts and hair transplants. Anti-ageing was sometimes justified differently by men and women: staying youthful or taking care of one's body was explanation enough for some women, while men more often used staying competitive in the labour market as a reason for their surgery. However, these gendered accounts were also only differences in tendencies rather than discrete accounts.

Enhancement largely referred to young people having 'fashionable surgeries' (see Balsamo 1992) such as breast augmentations in the UK and Australian context, and jawbone 'shaving', nose tip augmentation and blepharoplasty (to enlarge eyes) in South Korea – a surgical package known as the Korean Look. This is the category most frequently represented in the media and is tied to celebrity and glamour cultures in the UK and Australia and to *Hallyu* (the Korean Wave) and K-pop in South Korea. Young people in the enhancement category rarely related their surgeries to deficiencies in their own bodies, but rather wanted breast augmentation or the Korean Look (or to look 'cute' or 'independent') to add to and mark their body's value. The exact nature of these surgeries changes over time, with larger or smaller, round or teardrop-shaped breasts, or more or less fat removed from around the eye, becoming desirable at different times, such that these enhancement surgeries conform to current fashions in a similar vein to tattoos or hairstyles. While the specific style of surgery changes, however, having cosmetic surgery here performs a function much like other kinds of fashion. As Elizabeth Wilson (2009) argues, fashion is about 'integration and differentiation': the point is to stand out from the crowd while fitting in with one's peer group, but not to look 'like a clone'. In relation to 'enhancement' cosmetic surgery, the importance of peer groups was evidenced by some young people's practice of travelling together with friends for similar surgeries (see chapter six).

While enhancement surgeries, then, were largely acknowledged by our participants as surgeries performed on already normal or healthy bodies, correction, repair and, to some extent, anti-ageing surgeries were conceptualised as reconstructive, whether or not this aligned with formal definitions in health insurance or nationalised healthcare (especially given that these definitions become more restrictive in times of austerity or appear to prioritise one group of patients over another). The label 'reconstructive surgery' is therefore highly contested since it grants not only legitimacy but also free access to the surgeries sought. So, for instance, when weight-loss patients had undertaken gruelling regimes or surgeries to achieve socially sanctioned 'healthy bodies', they were hugely dispirited to be told that the excess skin obscuring their achievements could not be legitimately removed for free. Similarly, some women complained that injuries to their vaginas were dismissed by doctors as the natural result of childbirth and repair as unnecessary and 'only cosmetic'. These women complained they were not being taken seriously as sexual subjects once they had fulfilled their reproductive roles. Both of these groups felt that they had acted as good citizens; being denied 'reconstructive surgery', however, made them feel they were not recognised as valuable subjects, and this is what led them into cosmetic surgery tourism.

Cosmetic surgery as body capital, then, has the double function of both adding value to the body and also of marking a body of value – a body worth investing in. Thus, very different surgeries on different parts of the body and in different geographic and cultural contexts had the same meaning for our participants in terms of creating a fashionable body. However, notions of fashion were not always straightforwardly mapped onto the cosmetic body and there was some disagreement between Korean surgeons and Chinese patient-consumers over the precise meaning of the surgeries they sought (see also Holliday et al. 2017). While Korean surgeons often understood Chinese patients as desiring a Korean Look, inspired by Korean beauty standards exported regionally through Korean TV and music videos (on the so-called Korean Wave), Chinese patient-consumers often rejected this interpretation and labelled their surgeries a Western Look. Yet Korean surgeons distance themselves from the idea that the surgeries they perform constitute a Western

Look, emphasising small differences in technique. As one surgeon told us, this would involve the removal of too much fat from the eye area which 'would look ridiculous on an Asian patient'.

Figure 2.1 shows Hwang's progress through a typical set of procedures associated with the Korean Look. While Hwang was delighted with his new look, another participant we spoke with in Seoul, called Domino, was not happy with the outcome of her surgery. As she explained: 'I like Michele Reis's style, not Angelababy's. I prefer faces with strong features.'[2] When asked whether she felt the surgery had made her face too cute, she responded:

> Yes. I just wanted my face symmetrical and to look better. But according to Korea's aesthetic standard, beauty is the kind of boring faces I have seen in the street … it's Korean style. It's not like Western style, which has strong features … I like faces that look cool, but can also fit in diverse styles. It doesn't necessarily have to be cute … I don't like being the same as others, or having a similar face with other girls in the street.

Unlike the UK and Australian patient-consumers, our Chinese participants were middle-class and relatively wealthy. They were well travelled and many went to university in the UK or US. They characterised the Korean Look as a 'cute' or 'girl-next-door' style. Chinese patients expressed a desire to look more (but certainly not entirely) Western, which they felt connoted independence and cosmopolitanism. Sharon Kinsella (1995) has written extensively on *Kawaii* (cuteness) in Japan, demonstrating its connection in that culture to independence. Looking very young and cute enables Japanese women to postpone marriage, which in Japan brings with it significant social burdens and family duties for women (changes to employment legislation since the mid-1980s, including measures seeking to equalise pay for young Japanese people, have made staying single a more viable option). Forty per cent of Japanese men now remain single and a similar pattern of extended youth and low marriage rates is at work in South Korea. However, China has a different cultural history of gender, under communism, in which men and women were given more formal equality earlier. For the Chinese women we spoke to, looking mature and elegant was more valuable than looking young and cute, even while the surgeries they undertook were largely the same and connoted independence in both cultures (see Holliday *et al.* 2017 for a fuller discussion). Breast augmentation in the UK and Australia similarly signals maturity for women, but also connotes sexuality – a sexuality which women control, and in which they are desirable but also desiring, choosing and not simply chosen. So enhancement surgeries can also be seen as a neoliberal investment in becoming empowered as an 'independent woman' in a way not altogether unconnected from feminist aims (see Holliday & Sanchez Taylor 2006).

It is important to note that there was no clear and definitive separation between the category of enhancement and the other categories listed above. For instance, one young Australian woman, Cindy, who seemed to fit the enhancement category (having breast augmentation surgery in Thailand along with a small group of women all travelling together for the same procedure), told us about a boat trip she took on the body-conscious Gold Coast. A rival boat full of young men rowed past and pulled down their underwear to 'moon' their naked bottoms at Cindy's boat (which was full of women). In response the women in her own boat pulled down their bikini tops to 'flash' back at the men, but Cindy did not join in because her 'boobs just weren't good enough', by which she meant they were small and obviously asymmetrical. It was this incident that led Cindy to investigate and then purchase a breast augmentation in Thailand. Similarly, some patient-consumers talked about getting a 'designer vagina', which on elaboration meant repair to prolapse or untidy stitching post-partum. Correction and enhancement are clearly tangled in these narratives. In contrast, older and more middle-class women were more likely to use the language of repair and reconstruction and to strongly justify their procedures in terms of personal pride and identity:

> A lot of people have said [it's just vanity] but I say so what if it's vain, there's nothing wrong with wanting to look your best and feel good about yourself, it doesn't matter what everyone else might think – 'oh yeah, it looks fine' – but if you're not happy with it and you want it done, then go for it, I'd say. (Viv, UK to Poland)

> I mean, it is your face and body that frame you at the end of the day, so you have got to take it seriously. (Mary, UK to Poland)

The discourse of investment was often used in referring to breasts, which are sometimes colloquially referred to in the UK as 'assets'. Breasts have a long history of being 'sold', in sex work, of course, but also as part of the 'interactive service encounter' (e.g. Adkins 1995) especially in bars, clubs, betting shops and so on, where flirtatious banter is considered to be part of the package for male customers. But 'making the best of yourself' – the time and money required to look good – was considered important by our patient-consumers in both work and non-work settings, and looking good was considered vital to securing employment (irrespective of the work sector).

In South Korea, where competition between young people for jobs is very strong and popular discourses of cosmetic surgery are less critical than in the UK and Australia, people talk openly about *kyo˘rhon so˘n-ghyo˘ng* (marriage cosmetic surgery) and *chig'o˘pso˘nghyo˘ng* (employment cosmetic surgery), both of which are seen as investments in the body that are likely to reap tangible rewards through social mobility in the job or marriage markets. While in the past these surgeries have been highly gendered, it is now accepted that a man might also undertake either surgery. Cosmetic surgery in South Korea is also socially important because an untidy appearance is considered rude (Holliday & Elfving-Hwang 2012). We argue that marriage and employment cosmetics extend beyond the local context of Korea; however, 'marriage cosmetics' is disparaged in Western countries as the tactic of gold-diggers or passive women who are unduly reliant on men. Many women in the West deny they have cosmetic surgery for men, with more acceptably claiming they have it for themselves. However, one recently divorced man we interviewed who was having a hair transplant claimed he needed to look good because he was 'back on the market', meaning he was looking for a partner.

Yvonne from Australia, who was travelling to Thailand for a facelift, told us: 'I'm a prison officer. You can't look like someone's granny and work in a prison.' A facelift for Yvonne was thus a way of restoring her authority and staying in work longer – an investment in her future earnings, but also in being taken seriously in an ageist culture. Sharon, a mental health nurse, travelled from the UK to India for a facelift. She chose India because she had some family there and had visited a few times before. She talked openly of cosmetic surgery as an investment:

> It's self-improvement. I mean, a lot of people say to me, 'Why do you do this? You should grow old gracefully.' And I say, 'No. When you go to your house … if the paint is flaking off the walls, are you going to leave it? Or if you've got cracks in the tiles on your roof, are you going to leave it? No! … If there's rendering coming off your bricks, will you leave it to grow old gracefully?' I say, if there's the technology and the means for self-improvement, then you should embrace it.

Houses make good analogies for cosmetic surgery, and all the more so since participants in our study had lower-than-average rates of home ownership. Sharon was one of the minority of participants who did own her own home, which had been left to her after her parents' (early) deaths. Consequently, she lived in the same small-town cul-de-sac where she had grown up. She had maintained the garden in her parents' style but she had added a huge stained-glass window featuring Cleopatra to the house, and had imported a colossal hand-carved chair from Thailand for the living room – her throne, as she called it.

Writing about home decor styles in Australia, Ian Woodward (2003) demonstrates the classed nature of domestic interior styles, concentrating on the difference between the old and new middle class. He shows that while the new middle-class homeowners he researched preferred fashionable styles and were vigilant in their consumption of interiors magazines to stay up to date on changing fashions, by contrast the old middle class cared little for style and instead prioritised comfort. Other work demonstrates that cleanliness is key for working-class dwellers as a largely defensive strategy against associations with (moral) dirt (McClintock 1995). Thus, while growing old gracefully is a strategy mirroring comfort (being comfortable in your skin) that is made possible from the position of enduring lineage and inherited wealth – demonstrated through patina – this cannot work for those who lack sources of capital other than how their body looks or what it can do. For the wealthy, selfhood is distributed across their assets. For the less well off, the body might be the best asset they have, so maintaining it is vital. But this is not about prolonging life and health as in middle-class health and beauty regimes: health is often already compromised by bad diets brought on by overwork or shift work, or by the toxic environments in which many working-class people are employed (the cause of Sharon's parents' early deaths, for instance), and long life often means an old age living with poverty and illness.

This investment ethic is astutely summarised by Suzie, who lived in expensive southern England:

> I've had my nose done in the UK, because I broke my nose when I was a teenager and wanted it straightened to get my confidence back. I've had my boobs done in Belgium. When the kids are older, I want to go back to college and get some qualifications because at the end of the day, living down here, it's all about the money, isn't it?

Suzie needs her nose 'corrected' and her breasts 'enhanced', but crucially she equates these procedures with education and both as 'about the money'. Suzie's statement also shows us what we in universities use multiple strategies to try and forget – that education is capital for the job market, organised around a set of values and knowledges that celebrate and benefit a middle-class habitus. Cosmetic surgery and education are capitals to deploy in the job market, but only education is formally valued. Confidence is a kind of capital too, rooted as it is in the accumulation of other types of capital. Class is, as Bourdieu (1984: 170) claims, a 'structuring structure'.

So, a neoliberal discourse of investment can be seen in participants' accounts of accessing procedures like breast augmentation and those to achieve the Korean Look. These accounts also carry with them the cultural prohibitions that sometimes inspire their journeys – gaining credibility at work in later life through anti-ageing surgery, for instance. But cosmetic surgery is not only about discourses: it is also about bodies. Bodies vary: they are genetically discrete and come in different shades, shapes and sizes into a context where some bodies are valued more than others.

We have already recounted Jason's story and our travels to meet him in chapter one, but it is worth returning to his narrative here. Jason was, in his own description, a very fat man. While he was, of course, aware that obese people are socially sanctioned (though his wife preferred 'big men'), and he was also aware of the critique of that position, it was his increasing lack of physical mobility that prompted him to travel to the Czech Republic for weight-loss surgery. As Karen Throsby (2008) notes, weight-loss surgery is not simply a transition from illness to health. In many ways Jason, who was immediately sick if he ate too much, was 'ill' by most standards. He also had many underlying health problems: while his prediabetes was cured by the surgery, he had also recovered from liver cancer and other medical issues. What he recovered through surgery was his mobility, especially important to him as a former sportsman. He talked happily about being able now to run around with his grandchildren. As time progressed, however, his satisfaction at losing weight was curtailed by his once filled-out skin now hanging loose about him. Jason's disgust with this somatic excess was most keenly experienced during sex, when the loose skin on his abdomen hung down, covering his partner's body and obstructing his view of their intercourse and making sex clumsy and difficult. Similarly, Jenny talked about being 'flat chested', having no breast tissue at all. During pregnancy and breastfeeding her breasts had filled out and she said that for the first time in her life she felt like a woman. But her breasts shrank away once her babies were weaned and, as she explained, 'I really felt that when I was having sex with my husband, it must've felt to him like he was like he was having sex with a man'. In these accounts there is no mention of external frames of reference. No desire to be like celebrities or film stars was expressed. Instead, these participants, and many others, refer only to their own bodies, then and now, talking about playing with grandchildren and having satisfying sex. Cosmetic surgery for these recipients is about getting back a body that once embodied value, and clinic websites are where these material bodies can be found (see also Holliday et al., 'Beautiful face, beautiful place', 2015).

Next to the glossy media bodies used to evoke the high quality of the clinic, before-and-after pictures of actual patients can be something of a shock. Depicting small breasts, sagging breasts, asymmetrical breasts, breasts on men, crinkled faces, angry-looking faces, loose and sagging stomachs, fatty deposits and loose skin hanging below the triceps,[3] bent and broken noses, hooded eyes, receding hair, patchy hair and skin, broken and missing teeth – features that many people would find difficult to live with – in many ways clinic websites epitomise the critique of media bodies as unrealistic. Clinic websites use Photoshopped 'media bodies' to evoke quality and beauty, while juxtaposing them with the material, fleshy, before-and-after bodies of actual patients that very obviously could never achieve the perfection represented in the advertising images. Yet, as we highlighted earlier in the chapter, for Bordo, Davis and Heyes, bodies are not important. Davis could not tell what part of the body the women in her study wanted to change; Bordo sees cosmetic surgery as the pursuit of an ideal; Heyes sees pain attaching to a body part 'after the fact'. Or perhaps for these feminists it is not possible to agree 'Yes, you would really benefit from cosmetic surgery' – perhaps 'No, you look fine as you are' is the only polite/feminist/compassionate response possible.

The majority of the patients we travelled with had body parts that were difficult for them to live with – that we would have found it difficult to live with – not because these features cause them deep emotional pain, but because they knew they could be improved through surgery. The patient-consumers we spoke with talked about dissatisfactions with certain parts of their bodies that were mostly significantly and materially divergent from socially valued bodies; importantly, however, they talked not in terms of psychological pain, but from a practical orientation of being able to do something about it. And while most had thought about living with their problematic body part for many years, it seemed to them obvious that they should take action to overcome this problem that was holding them back. Having surgery meant moving on and taking control of their lives, by accessing a readily available technology for improvement (abroad, where surgery is financially possible). As Heyes (2007) explains, just saying no is not an option – it is the passive voice against the valued, active 'I will act to turn my life around'. Why, our participants wondered, would someone not have surgery to a body part that needed it? Why would they try to keep living unhappily with something that could be easily fixed if they had the money? Would we live with a damp ceiling when we could get it repaired? For these patients, surgery was not rooted in pain but in hope, and their hopes were justified: as noted in chapter one, 97 per cent of the patient-consumers we surveyed were happy with the result of their surgery and would recommend their surgeon to a friend.

In chapter one, we also met Janet, whose face had become lined through ageing in a way that made her look permanently angry. She had always been a happy, sociable person – and she wanted her face to express that – yet people seemed wary of her, expecting her to be difficult and cross. Of course, social interactions are intersubjective. They rest as much on what we think others think of us as on what they actually think. Yet we could also certainly see a 'harshness' in Janet's face (though it disappeared when she became animated). Many participants receiving anti-ageing cosmetic surgery talked about ageing as a loss of identity – hair that could no longer be styled, eyes that could no longer be shadowed or lined with make-up in a personal style, lips that had become thin, crumpled or pale. Their stories referred less to an external cultural referent or youthful ideal and more to a loss of a previous body/self, a nostalgia for a lost body and identity. Cathy, a participant in her sixties said: 'Inside I still feel 27, but when I look in the mirror I don't even recognise myself. There is only an old lady looking back.' Similarly, patient-consumers whose bodies had changed suddenly through pregnancy or childbirth talked about the shock of seeing themselves in the mirror and how much their bodies had changed since before pregnancy. They experienced this new embodied state as a shocking loss of self, not a failure to live up to media images.

Cosmetic surgery enabled these participants to take back their identities, to find a face or body that more closely resembled who they felt they were. And this was a difficult battle for people in certain overdetermined social categories like 'old' or 'fat' by which they felt subsumed into the (undervalued) classification. Cosmetic surgery offered these participants a means of recreating themselves as valued individuals – at least to a degree that was manageable. As Charlotte Cooper (2016) reminds us, when overweight people are spat at or called names while walking down the street, this is not a problem of self-esteem, or, we might argue, of media images of perfection. Material, fleshy bodies matter. Paul, who travelled from the UK to Spain recounted:

> My first surgery, to be honest, was a big risk [due to not knowing the clinic]. I was so tired of having boobs. I went on a big holiday and being on the beach made me more body conscious. It was abnormal, it was [*he points at his chest*] more like breasts than a chest. It was the first time I went for a big holiday and I knew that I would like to go to many more places, I would like to have more holidays and I don't really want to feel bad every time so I decided to come here. I just wanted to feel more masculine, more flat. I didn't like my feminine appearance, I didn't want to have breasts any more. So, I think the result is good.

Cosmetic surgery is thus about restoring (gender) identity – but it is also about desire, pleasure and fun. For Jenny, getting breasts meant she was able to imagine herself as a sexy, desired and desiring woman during sex. For Paul, having his breasts removed opened up a whole new world of travel and holidays.

It is important to note that many participants wanted to frame cosmetic surgery as a serious business in order to evade accusations of frivolousness, especially in a context when they have been blamed in popular discourse for additional costs to public healthcare providers (the NHS in the UK or Australian Medicare) when things go wrong, or as taking up valuable medical resources for reasons of vanity. However, some participants felt able to talk about their experiences in a more playful way:

> Linda: Despite having surgery and having a little bit of discomfort I had a whale of a time actually.
> Olive: You had fun?
> Linda: Yes. Not so much laughing and that, it was just nothing I had ever done before. I mean some people want to climb Mount Everest don't they, and get a kick out of it? I mean, you go on all these excursions in the sea just to see dolphins that are never there and then all you see is a bit of sea – how boring is that, you know? Or pyramids – what are they all about?

Olive: Whereas, this, it was interesting, because it was …?

Linda: Yes, it was interesting, and talking to the others that were having it done. And there was a rather cute receptionist guy that spoke really good English. He was quite yummy and I took my bandages off and I asked if he fancied me yet and I had a bit of a giggle with him. I made him blush quite a few times.

Viv, a police officer from the UK, had a blepharoplasty in Tunisia. Her narrative speaks for many other participants in this study when she talks about fun:

Viv: I got too excited; I told everyone. I have got to go in about forty or fifty shops when I start work next week just so they can see the difference … Although I love to put make-up on and I love going out I am not particularly a vain person [but] I thought I am at the right age to do it. I don't think you should do this too young, but I think at 55 I have still got six years before they kick me out of the force. I am in a pretty young environment work wise, because I am still on the streets. I still go out socially.

Kate: So, it might be hard to explain, but what did you think would be different after having it done? How did you imagine it would look?

Viv: Well, I didn't think my life would be that much different because I tend to quite enjoy life anyway. I do a lot of talking as you can tell! I thought my eye make-up might look a bit better. It won't change my life, but it might just make me feel a little bit better. I like to try to keep myself fit and I like to try to keep myself in order. I don't want to go into the life of old age, I am all for enjoying life and I think you can do that at any age.

Of course, it would be easy to read this narrative as a woman trying painfully to cling on to youth in an ageist culture. But to read along with Viv's intended meaning we would have to say something more like: Viv works in a youthful environment. She is very active both at work and in her social life. Having a blepharoplasty makes her feel younger and like she still fits in. She is not ashamed of having surgery; on the contrary, she is proud of it and cannot wait to show everyone. She is excited. She wants to enjoy herself now and express a youthful and active self, not wait until she is old and inactive ('in a wheelchair'). She is a self worthy of investment. While some would read Viv's narrative as normalisation to a beauty ideal, we read it more like an identity/body modification narrative, of fitting into a youthful and playful culture while differentiating herself from other older women who might want to lead quieter, more sedate lives.

Another participant, Debbie, travelled from the UK to Spain to get her breast implants replaced and reduced. When she was younger she had acquired very large implants, but having achieved a degree of social mobility she now saw these implants as inappropriate to her current work environment. She wonders whether, looking back, she should not have had breast implants at all, and concedes that had she been the more educated and more financially secure person she is today, she probably would not have had the procedure:

> I was really young when I had them, and now I'm older, you know, and more confident, I probably wouldn't have them now … but then again, I have enjoyed them! [*laughs*]

So, while Debbie no longer 'needs' breast implants, they have provided her with a source of confidence and value as well as pleasure and fun throughout her young adulthood. Fun, pleasure and desire are all elements that have received little academic attention and yet need to be taken seriously in studies of cosmetic surgery.

Investing in cosmetic surgery tourism

Investment was also used in a more literal context in the UK and Australia too. Many people paid for their surgeries with unexpected windfalls such as small inheritances or compensation (for example, from the payment protection insurance miss-selling scandal in the UK that revealed banks had sold unnecessary insurance products to customers taking out credit facilities). They saw spending this money on their bodies as creating an asset that paid dividends (see also Adams 2013), as opposed to a car or holiday whose benefits seemed ephemeral by comparison:

> I had a dear old aunt that was as poor as a mouse die in January, but she had a little bit of life insurance, which me and my sister got about three or four thousand pound each from. So, I thought, 'what should I do with this?' And I had thought about my eyes before, but I totally would never take it out of my savings for [the children], but there was something totally selfish that I wanted and that was my eyelids. (Julia, UK to Poland)

Other sources of finance included bank loans or credit cards, but patient-consumers were always careful to affirm their surgery would never impact negatively on other family members and that most of the time they put the financial needs of their children before their own need for surgery, which was paid for by 'leftover' or 'spare' money. In his book on shopping, Daniel Miller (1998) argues that 'treats' for the self are a valuable method of restoring self-hood, especially for women who are often subsumed to the family. Depression too is a kind of loss of self, so treats perform the function of separating a woman from her household and restoring her self/individuality. Cosmetic surgery could also be viewed in this way – as an investment in a self that is often sacrificed for others.

In fact, the most obvious reason for travelling abroad for surgery was cost. An abdominoplasty in Poland, including flights and accommodation, was

£3,000 compared to £7,000 or £8,000 in the UK for the procedure alone. A breast augmentation in Australia in 2018 cost AU$12,000 but AU$4,000 in Thailand. For some younger patient-consumers undergoing simple surgeries, the destination was part of the package, but most said the destination was unimportant and the quality of the surgeon was the most important factor in choosing where to have surgery. Patients were also very aware of the narrative of bad cosmetic surgery abroad shown in TV programmes like *Cosmetic Surgery Nightmares* or *Botched Up Bodies Abroad* and were keen to show how carefully they had researched their clinic before they travelled (we deal with this more fully in chapters five and six). However, they were also angry about the image of surgery abroad compared with their home country and vocally criticised this discourse:

> I think we are quite snobby in Britain to be honest. We tend to think, 'oh, the National Health'. Although it is good in its way, it isn't the best, it truly isn't, and I have worked in hospitals as well. (Jean, UK to Tunisia)

> It [the hospital in Poland] was a very modern building. People have such a blinkered view. My other half used to say, you know – you think Poland, and you still think of horse and carts. I said, 'For heaven's sake!' It's like Americans in Scotland: they think it's just a big puddle here and everybody knows everybody. No, it isn't. (Julie, UK to Poland)

> It is three times more expensive [in Ireland compared to in Poland]. The surgeons are equally good and qualified as Irish surgeons. (Siobhan, Ireland to Poland)

Some of the greatest contempt was reserved for surgeons back home, who were often constructed as 'only in it for the money', in a way that surgeons abroad were not. In contrast to some of the cosmetic surgery literature, the latter were seen as offering genuine care, as we will show in chapter five.

It seems likely that part of the dissatisfaction with surgeons at home arises from the prohibitive cost, being priced out and excluded and so needing to travel to access surgery. This exclusion was keenly felt. For instance, Suzie spoke for many when she described her experience in the UK:

> I went to a clinic in London and the surgeon came out of scrubbing up and he said, 'Right, I can have a quick consultation with you.' And I said, 'Can I just ask – you said you were scrubbing up – is there a patient waiting for you to operate?' And he went, 'Yeah, yeah, but I have got ten or fifteen minutes that I can spend with you now.' And I said, 'I am sorry but I don't want you to do the same to me when there is a paying client in there. Sorry, I won't come to you, so I won't waste your time.' So, I just walked out … I was just seen as a walking chequebook really. I felt like I was a number in a sales process.

Yet while our participants were in some senses forced to travel because of their lower incomes, they sometimes imagined themselves as intrepid explorers accessing surgeons who others were too nervous to seek out. They were adventurers in search of a better life:

> I think you do your research yourself and what you don't know, you ask. It's not a whim, it's a big step. You're facing people – some of my friends were like, 'Oh my God, your face. Oh, no, I couldn't get that done abroad!' And then I got it done and they went 'Okay, maybe I could'. Somebody has to be a guinea pig in your party. (Jenny, Australia to Malaysia)

But such adventures, as we shall see, are never without their risks.

Cosmetic surgery, scandal and regulation: the case of Poly Implant Prosthèse

Having shown the ways in which both academic and popular discourses of cosmetic surgery and cosmetic surgery tourism fail to address the material body, the class of cosmetic surgery patient-consumers and the neoliberal culture which invokes people to take control of their own lives in order to improve their chances as individuals, we would like to end by demonstrating what cosmetic surgery discourse does.

While we were conducting the empirical research for this project, a scandal broke in which it was claimed that breast implants were being made from mattress filler. On 23 December 2011 the French government announced a link between breast implants made by the company Poly Implant Prosthèse (PIP) and a rare form of breast cancer. As the scandal unfolded it emerged that the US Food and Drug Agency (FDA) had inspected the PIP factory in 2000 and had banned PIP implants from sale in the US. In the UK, however, the safety of medical implants is overseen by the Medicines and Healthcare products Regulatory Authority (MHRA). Classed as medical devices, breast implants (unlike medicines) do not require a clinical trial, instead needing only to obtain a CE mark, indicating they have been quality-approved by a notified body in Europe. To secure the CE mark PIP would have to have produced a dossier of evidence supporting the quality of its products and consented to have its factory inspected. Breast implants also fall within the EU's Medical Devices Directive (93/42/EEC), which states that '"particular attention" must be paid to the potential toxicity of materials used and to reducing "to a minimum" the risks posed by substances leaking from them' (Hertzell & Moore 2012: 115). While in the UK the MHRA monitors CE marks, the marks are assessed and granted by a notified body which does not have to be in the same country as the manufacturer. In addition, the company chooses the notified body it uses. PIP, based in France, chose a notified body in Germany called TÜV Rheinland. The company had a good reputation but due to its remote location routinely notified PIP ten days in advance of an inspection – allowing PIP staff to hide their fraudulent activities.

In 2010, following an anonymous letter about practices at PIP and the company's declaration of bankruptcy, a medical device alert was issued by the MHRA. UK surgeons were asked to report concerns over ruptures and tumours after scanning a number of patients. However, the rupture of an implant is not in itself reportable, since even good breast implants have a rupture rate of around 1 per cent. In a normal silicone implant, rupture is not necessarily a serious medical problem because the silicone filling remains in the outer shell, even under pressure. In a saline implant, on the other hand, the filling quickly escapes and dissipates, but since the saline is sterilised there is no harm caused to surrounding tissues. The silicone filling in the PIP implants was liquid, however, allowing an untested and potentially toxic substance to seep into and travel around the patient's body. One member of our project team was able to see this design fault first hand with an implant given to her by a surgeon (figure 2.2).

Because the MHRA licenses drugs but has no licensing responsibility for approving medical devices, the only course of action available to the MHRA when concerns are raised about a product by clinical staff is to send out letters to doctors warning them of potential risks, which it did in 2010. In the same year, rupture rates for PIP implants were still being widely reported as 1 per cent in the UK, but privately, as the scandal began to unfold, some companies alerted government ministers on the Health Select Committee to rupture rates of nearer 8 per cent. On 9 January 2012 the British government told the three thousand women who had received PIP breast implants on the NHS, mostly for reconstruction after surgery for breast cancer, that they could have them removed and replaced for free. It said it expected the same service for the estimated fifty thousand women who had received the implants from private clinics, though the government could not require private companies to do this without a change in the law.

Initially, BAAPS told the UK media that many British women had been given PIP implants in clinics in central and Eastern Europe. So, a British surgeons' association clearly deployed the discourse of dangerous and irresponsible cosmetic surgery tourism as a way to deflect blame from UK surgeons. However, it soon became clear that almost all of the UK patients had their PIP implants fitted by private clinics in the UK and that most countries in Eastern Europe are subject to the same EU regulations that regulate medical devices in the UK. It emerged that four companies – the Harley Medical Group (HMG), Transform, The Hospital Group (THG) and Linia – had fitted the vast majority of the implants, and they refused to foot the bill for replacing them. HMG's chairman, Mel Braham, told the BBC in January 2011 that the firm did not have the surgeons or operating theatres necessary to re-do the surgeries. Transform quickly announced a removal and replacement price of £2,800, while THG (who claimed to have provided implants to 13,900 patients) agreed only to remove PIP implants that had already ruptured (Bloxham 2012).

As we now know, once PIP implants have ruptured the silicone inside them begins to seep into the body's tissues, making it almost impossible to remove. In fact, there is some evidence of silicone seeping through the implant's outer shell even while the implant is intact, and this cannot be detected through a scan. Where the silicone has come into contact with tissue, surgeons have noticed a white milky substance secreted that is indicative of irritation. While the MHRA and NHS claim the silicone filling used by PIP is not toxic, it has since come to light that different mixes of silicone were used by PIP at different times. Campaigners claim that the presence of octamethylcyclotetrasiloxane (D4), identified in the MHRA's report, is toxic, particularly to reproductive functions, and therefore demand further tests. They cite in letters to MPs that 'French Authorities brought concerns over D4 toxicity to international Regulators attention' and have written to the UK Department of Health and the MHRA to make them aware that France, Belgium, Germany and the Czech Republic have now recognised D4 as toxic.

The forty-five thousand women who had purchased their implants from private UK clinics were told by the then Health Secretary Andrew Lansley to contact their clinic for a replacement, and on Sunday, 8 January 2011 he told the BBC that private clinics refusing to remove and replace PIP implants were 'not stepping up to their responsibilities'. Despite pressure from ministers, HMG, Transform, THG and Linia all maintained they would not routinely remove and replace implants and that the fault lay with British medical regulators who had allowed PIP implants to be marketed in the UK for over a decade (Donnelly 2012). Lansley said the NHS would remove but not replace PIP implants for women who were refused help by their clinics, and that the government would pursue payment from these clinics to cover costs to the NHS. However, most lawyers agreed that the government would be unlikely to recover these costs as there was no contract between the state and the clinics, despite clear legal culpability on their part (see Hertzell & Moore 2012).

On 9 November 2012 HMG went into administration, transferring their debts to a holding company which could not be sued. Although HMG continued to trade under the same name, with the same directors, the liabilities for the legal claims made by PIP patients were not transferred, meaning that no legal claims could be made against them (Zuckerman *et al.* 2012). HMG blamed 'sophisticated fraud' by manufacturers and the failure of regulators to identify a problem. The private clinics, in other words, abdicated responsibility for replacing faulty PIP implants.

When Lansley announced that the NHS would remove and replace implants that had been fitted by the NHS but not those implanted by private companies, he contributed to a discourse that separated 'deserving' (reconstructive surgery) victims from 'undeserving' (cosmetic surgery) consumers of implants. Public anxieties about the potential costs to the NHS of replacing faulty implants were reflected in misogynistic vitriol broadcast on radio phone-ins and newspaper comments forums, and this came to a head in what can only be described as an angry mob confronting and spitting at women with PIP implants who were demonstrating outside Parliament (according to a Parliament employee we spoke with).

In the furore that followed the scandal, many 'expert' commentators offered up their own explanations. Rather than focusing on the companies who profited from the sale of PIP implants yet failed to replace them once their health consequences were discovered, or the clearly substandard system for approving medical devices for sale, or indeed the almost totally unregulated private cosmetic surgery industry, some simply pathologised consumers of cosmetic surgery as desperate cultural dopes. Dan Poulter, MP for Central Suffolk and North Ipswich and member of the Health Select Committee – an important stakeholder making policy around the PIP scandal, and part of the Keogh Review of the regulation of cosmetic surgery that followed – espoused the following opinions on cosmetic surgery:

> In other parts of the world … there is a much greater emphasis on ensuring psychological support and counselling before surgery, to ensure that women are not suffering from some kind of dysmorphic disorder. … Programmes like [reality TV show] *The Only Way is Essex* and celebrity culture and glossy magazines have glamorised cosmetic procedures and the body beautiful … they are also linked with psychological problems, and obsession about appearance and body dysmorphia. (Cited in Donnelly 2012)

Questions about the PIP scandal that should have been focused on profit motives and regulation instead constantly sought to blame and pathologise the women whose health was put at risk. Even their aesthetic choices were subject to harsh criticism. Why do they do it? the newspapers asked. Why do they put themselves through it? Why would anyone have their breasts made bigger? And these media reports, in a kind of circular handwringing which nevertheless emphasised their own importance, drew on psychological studies of the media and self-esteem conducted by academics to show that looking at images of beauty causes low self-esteem, which in turn creates the demand for cosmetic surgery.

A vital point to make here is that despite the voluminous literature from psychology on studies testing self-esteem before and after looking at images of feminine beauty it has been well established in the media studies literature since the 1970s that readers and viewers actively negotiate with media texts on the basis of prior knowledge (Hall 1973). Yet it is worth remembering that just as these cosmetic surgery patient-consumers are pathologised as cultural dopes with body dysmorphia or low self-esteem, they are still made subjects of risk and choice and left unprotected by the law (see Latham 2014). All of these issues are compounded, as patient-consumers cross national borders, by problems of jurisdiction such that transnational compensation claims are virtually non-existent (Smith *et al.* 2012).

From research that we conducted as a side project to the current study, the majority of women who received PIP breast implants were on low annual incomes, averaging around £17,500 (the average salary for women in the UK in 2012 was £24,273). Many had acquired their implants in the UK using bank loans or finance deals from clinics. A very large proportion were experiencing health problems. In this context we interviewed an industry representative, who told us:

> At the moment there's no evidence that they should have them all removed. They should all go and be checked and that check should be free ... If they have really got very anxious, then obviously they should be removed free of charge. I don't think the replacements should be free of charge because it was their choice in the beginning ... This is not due to a provider buying a cheap implant, it is due to a certain extent to the CE mark not being checked and it's due to a fraudulent manufacturer.

When it was pointed out that the women we had spoken to could not afford the replacements because they were still paying off the finance on their original implants, the industry representative replied: 'Well, they shouldn't buy things they can't afford.' At that point the representative had to leave for a meeting with 'her civil servant'.

One of the recommendations from the UK (post-PIP) Review of the Regulation of Cosmetic Interventions was that other procedures such as Botox or fillers, for safety reasons, should be reclassified as prescription drugs (Department of Health 2013). In other words, their administration should be placed back into the hands of doctors – the very doctors that implanted fifty thousand women with PIP breast implants. In this account of the PIP scandal, we can see how different interests are protected and how women recipients of cosmetic surgery are repositioned from victims to cultural dopes and made responsible for the scandal by wanting breast implants in the first place.

Conclusion

In this chapter we have argued that cosmetic surgery cannot be explained using a single conceptual lens. Different surgeries involve more or less serious procedures and technologies, different levels of risk, and have different meanings and connotations. Instead of rooting motives for surgery in pain, pathology (problems of self-esteem) and media images, we have emphasised the material body, fun, desire and pleasure, and identity – albeit within a neo-liberal culture that invokes individuals to 'take control' and 'do something' to improve their lives and 'be themselves' – to be the best that they can be (because they are worth it). We have tried to show that existing discourses of cosmetic surgery, which focus on psychological understandings of body image, neglect actual bodies and the ways they change over time, sometimes quite suddenly, to produce a longing for a lost body rather than an idealised media image. Although we have separated bodies into four categories of surgical transformation – enhancement, correction, repair and anti-ageing – all of these are in certain ways about investing in a self of value, for example in the markets for labour or relationships – a self that is classed and often denied other sources of value such as incomes, qualifications and home ownership.

We found that cosmetic surgery tourists are active and responsible consumers who attend to the financial needs of their families before attending to their own surgeries, using windfalls such as inheritances and compensations:

> I thought about it for about a year. A year, seriously. I had a consultation here, in the UK, but it would have worked out really expensive and they wanted to give me a loan, so it would have put me in debt. This way I could save for six months and get it done and not be in any debt. (Jess, UK to Poland)

We have also shown how conventional explanations for and discourses of cosmetic surgery, rooted in psychological studies that pathologise patient-consumers, are used in two ways. Firstly, they disguise the classed relationship between patient-consumers and those who 'represent' them – through either misogynistic or 'wounded' attachments. Secondly, they are used to deflect and circumvent calls for regulation of cosmetic surgery by its industrial represent-atives both at home and across national borders. Moreover, cosmetic surgery tourism is scapegoated by surgeons' associations and industry representatives when things go wrong in sending countries. Patient-consumers are aware of all of the criticisms levelled against them for having surgery and for travelling abroad. They are 'defended' and 'defensive' subjects, not only unconsciously, as Hollway and Jefferson (2009) imagine, but politically, as they create narra-tives to explain and justify their cosmetic surgery tourism against the power-ful weight of cosmetic surgery discourse.

Notes

1 *The Biggest Loser* began in the US in 2004 and the format has since been exported to more than thirty countries worldwide.
2 Angelababy is a Chinese-born Hong Kong actress and model who is strongly asso-ciated with the 'cute' look of Korean stars like Jun ji-hyun. Michele Reis is a Hong

Kong actress and winner of the Miss Chinese International Pageant and Miss Hong Kong who cultivates a more sophisticated and mature aesthetic.

3 These under-arm fatty deposits are known colloquially in the UK as 'bingo wings' and in Australia as 'tuck shop lady arms', both highly classed and gendered euphemisms.

3

Locating cosmetic surgery tourism

It's been quite helpful to see other girls who are going and who are there and seeing photos of them over there, seeing photos of them post-op. You see the whole journey and it's really personal ... Some have been having a bad time, they've been in more pain than they expected, whereas some of them are out on the back of elephants, so it's good to see how everybody is different ... and one girl got, like, an infection, you know. So, it's not showing only the good side of the story. I hope none of this happens. I'm very excited. (Lisa, Australia to Thailand)

In this chapter, we introduce the theoretical framing of cosmetic surgery that emerged through our research process and that informs the analysis we present in this book. Researching cosmetic surgery tourism brings us into contact with broader debates – including but also extending well beyond those around cosmetic surgery and around IMT – as well as reminding us of the importance of attending to the specificity of the places, people, things, practices and ideas that come together when someone travels abroad to access a procedure to enhance their appearance, and when someone is on hand to enable that access, whether directly (a doctor, a clinic) or indirectly (a website, an MTF). This encounter is not only about people, of course: technologies, practices, ideas, places and all manner of things are all mixed together in this moment (Whittaker 2008). Our aim in this chapter is to elaborate these mixings, and to build a conceptual framework for understanding cosmetic surgery tourism. We want to provide a framework that works much as the social media posts that Lisa, one of the participants in our study, accessed: to helpfully show all sides of cosmetic surgery tourism. And, like Lisa, we are excited by that prospect.

Two key elements of the definition of cosmetic surgery tourism are significant for the account we provide in *Beautyscapes*. The first is the electiveness of cosmetic surgery. A procedure is classed as elective if it is a scheduled, non-emergency treatment. This classification means a number of things for how cosmetic surgery (tourism) is understood and positioned in the broader contexts of contemporary healthcare: in the context of cosmetic procedures in particular it conveys choice – the patient elects to have the treatment rather than it being deemed medically necessary or an emergency. This attaches to arguments about the consumerisation of health practices, potentially querying whether 'health' is a useful notion for considering these forms of elective bodily transformation at all. In practice, this means that even in situations where public health systems provide for many elements of medical care, some of those deemed elective fall outside its reach and so must be accessed via private healthcare. Similarly, in situations where health insurance underwrites patients' medical bills, elective procedures may be excluded from insurance cover. In most cases, this means that cosmetic surgery patients pay out of pocket for their chosen procedures. This shapes accounts of and accounting for the purchase of cosmetic procedures, at home or abroad. We explored this issue in more detail in relation to academic and popular accounts of cosmetic surgery in chapter two.

The second definitional element is the 'tourismness' of cosmetic surgery tourism (see also Bell *et al.* 2011). As has been discussed in the broader context of medical tourism, there is heated debate about whether the term 'tourism' is appropriate to use for travel for healthcare (e.g. Roberts & Scheper-Hughes 2011). This issue hangs over professional, lay, media and academic discussion of cosmetic surgery tourism, with one prominent framing being the drawing of a distinction between patients and consumers – the former deserving, with 'real' medical and care needs, the latter turning healthcare into shopping, mobilising a market logic and deploying consumer practices framed by the idea of choice (Mol 2008). As our own research made clear, however, the reality is far more complicated. Nevertheless, the patient/consumer dichotomy or antinomy retains a level of explanatory power in many accounts, whether those of academics, industry commentators or patients themselves (we ourselves sometimes deploy the hybridised term 'patient-consumer' to signal this tension). In the next section we want to briefly discuss this and some other paired antinomies that routinely appear in discussions of cosmetic surgery tourism (and IMT more generally).[1] Our purpose is to acknowledge their rhetorical force while simultaneously complicating them as we move into our subsequent analysis.

Antinomies in cosmetic surgery tourism

Patient/consumer

As we have already sketched the patient/consumer pairing above, we will begin again here: the patient/consumer antinomy holds a central position in

many contemporary debates about changing healthcare systems, with privatisation in its various forms and across many national contexts converting
healthcare at least in part from a public good to a private commodity (Mol
2008). As such, the patient/consumer distinction prefigures debates about
both cosmetic surgery and medical tourism, but it is reshaped by the addition
of travel/tourism, which has tended to be seen as heightening the consumer-
ist aspects of an already marketised practice. As noted earlier, in terms of
discussions of cosmetic surgery, the electiveness (and 'cosmeticness') of such
procedures has similarly led to their positioning firmly within a consumer
system (Adams 2013).

While many aspects of medicine have been marketised, those that involve
paid-for procedures (and paid-for journeys) seem to speak most clearly of the
transformation of patients into consumers. However, the paid-for nature of
aspects of cosmetic surgery tourism does not always completely consumerise
the experience, particularly for travellers who are more used to being positioned as patients at home. And while they might benefit from some forms of
consumerisation – feeling a sense of entitlement because they are footing the
bill, so taking up the mantle of the sovereign consumer – they are still engaging with medical professionals, and there are ingrained habits on both sides of
this encounter (Mol 2008).

Furthermore, the status of patient is not necessarily one that cosmetic
surgery recipients long to escape from, or even can escape from. While a
trip abroad might offer a holiday from some sedimented social locations and
relations, for many there is no magical transformation here – no miraculous
emergence as, to use Charis Thompson's (2011: 207) phrase, 'empowered,
neoliberal, biosocial citizens', not least because, as Thompson adds, medical
tourists 'are a much more diverse group than they are commonly portrayed
as being' (207). To be sure, patients who pay to travel for treatment are also
travelling along this line, from patient to consumer, but it is perhaps better
to think of this as a mutable continuum, to replace the slash with a hyphen
and to talk of patient-consumers. It is also worth adding, as we will return to
later, that patient-consumers are not the only group on the move in cosmetic
surgery tourism.

Home/away

Perhaps it might seem less contentious to explore the antinomy between home
and away: if anything marks the tourismness of tourism, it is the experience
of being somewhere other than at home. But these terms are both more complicated than they first seem, and more polysemic. Where is 'home', and what
does it mean to be 'at home'? As geographers (and others) have reminded us,
there is often no simple answer to these questions (Blunt & Dowling 2006).
This conundrum has been explored in tourism studies too, leading some to

argue for the jettisoning of fixed terms or dichotomies like tourist/local or host/guest, which become harder to delineate and differentiate in an increasingly mobile world (Aramberri 2001; Sheller & Urry 2004).

When it comes to medical tourism, researchers have begun to unpack the data and to explore who is travelling, from and to where, and who should therefore count as a tourist (Buzinde & Yarnal 2012). Lee *et al.* (2010), for example, interviewed Korean immigrants now resident in New Zealand who return to South Korea for medical services. While they clearly argue that a brief return trip 'home' (from New Zealand to Korea) solely or principally for healthcare reasons cannot be simply classified as tourism, the question of where home is becomes more complicated. This is especially the case when, as for Lee *et al.*'s (2010) respondents, a key motivation for travel was to access healthcare that offered greater 'cultural comfort' – another way for expressing a sense of 'at-homeness'.

Even for those patient-consumers who do travel from a clearly defined home to an equally clearly defined destination 'away', this notion of at-homeness applies. Laurent Pordié (2013) talks about this in terms of insulation versus immersion – do tourists want to fully experience another place and culture (to immerse themselves) or do they want to retain some home comforts such as familiar food (and thereby partly insulate themselves)? For our respondents, the home/away antinomy was also more like a sliding scale, with some relishing (some aspects) of 'awayness' – as might be expected of a tourist – and others keen to retain elements of at-homeness. Indeed, hospitals attracting tourists, and the various intermediaries who assist in their journeys, have a key role to play is modulating home/away experiences, providing the right balance (Ormond 2013a; Whittaker & Chee 2015).

Global/local

Connected to the home/away dichotomy is a second spatial pairing: global/local. This carries connotations of home (local) and away (global), but adds in issues to do with globalisation. Indeed, in many accounts the rise of IMT is seen as inextricably bound up with globalisation, either as a symptom or as a stimulus. Yet critics such as Eliza Sobo (2009) call for research which refuses to oversimplify medical tourism as globalisation, at least by unpacking exactly what is meant by globalisation. To complicate things further, the literatures on medical tourism (including those on cosmetic surgery) also use assorted collateral concepts, such as Global North/Global South or core/periphery to describe dominant geographical relations and related flows. Put simply, the dominant assumption is that patient-consumers are from the core/Global North and are beneficiaries of globalisation, able to exploit flows that carry them to peripheral/Global South destinations, where 'locals' both provide medical services (local medical professionals) and are also either exploited/

harmed by medical tourism (local healthcare systems and local patients) or economically enriched by it (through medical and tourism revenues, for example). Yet the findings of the growing number of empirical studies (including our own) simply do not bear this out.

Another version of the equation sees global healthcare corporations similarly exploiting (or possibly 'developing') the local. In many such discussions, there is a sense of globalisation being both problem and solution (Toyota et al. 2013), with an implicit sorting out of 'good' and 'bad' globalisations. In such formulations, 'local' often really means 'national' – the opposition is between the 'footloose' global and the 'rooted' nation. Indeed, as Ara Wilson (2011) persuasively argues, it is at the scale of the nation that much of medical tourism takes place – the very notion of medical tourism, she writes, presumes national territorial location (i.e. home). But accounts of medical tourism cannot presume the North's exploitation of the Global South, not least because 'because people don't stay in their "proper" place' (Roberts & Scheper-Hughes 2011: 7). Expatriates, diasporas and migrants complicate the distinctions here. But, we would argue, it is not only because of movement and resettlement that the North-exploits-South version of the global/local narrative does not hold; the geography of medical tourism is much more variegated than this, with other spatial scales, such as the regional, also being of profound importance (A. Wilson 2011). And within regions, the effects of medical tourism are uneven (Ramirez de Arellano 2011). These issues are explored further in chapter seven.

The problem in some accounts seems to be a rather oversimplified version of globalisation, one that assumes it is coterminous with westernisation and that its primary effect is homogenisation. Critical globalisation scholars have dismantled this lazy equation, either pluralising their discussions of various globalisations, or entangling the global with the local, as in the term 'glocalisation' (e.g. Robertson 1995; Swyngedouw 2004). In the case of cosmetic surgery tourism, one problematically assumed homogenising effect is the production of global beauty norms reflecting Western ideals; assumptions about globalised beauty too often overlook (or ignore) local specificities which might give different perspectives on apparently westernising bodily transformation (Aizura 2009; Atkinson 2011; Holliday & Elfving-Hwang 2012). As we will discuss below, insights from critical globalisation studies continue to be important for theorising the flows of medical tourism; it is important, nonetheless, to blur any sense of fixed distinction between global and local – and to remember that, as Toyota et al. (2013: 31) put it, 'the globality of medical tourism is a project that is constantly in the making by local actors'. This is not to deny any notion of core and periphery or of power-geometry at work in how medical/cosmetic tourism maps out. This is not a level playing field; but neither is it a one-sided game.

Choice/care

Our final antinomy and a further major theoretical guide for our analysis comes from Annemarie Mol's (2008) ethnographic study of patients living with and being treated for diabetes in a Dutch hospital. In her discussion Mol describes two underpinning logics that frame healthcare in particular ways, which she names the logic of choice and the logic of care. The former is associated with changes in the understanding and positioning of the patient, who is remade as a consumer of healthcare and given the (apparent) freedom of choice when it comes to deciding about treatment. This figure has become increasingly prominent in discourses and practices of healthcare (and elsewhere), and is positively framed as freeing the patient from a position of subservience or submissiveness to the doctor, who is conversely repositioned from an all-powerful expert to a provider of information to help the patient choose. So, here the patient is empowered to become an expert – an expert in their own disease and in its treatment. Choice also turns a person into a subject, Mol adds. And who would not want to be free to choose? Choice has become a central aim of contemporary life, offered as an unquestioned good. How could anyone want less choice? As Mol writes, choice today is 'turned into a fact of life. Making choices is what people do' (67).

But Mol (2008) reminds us that becoming a 'chooser' brings with it burdens of choice, too: especially the burden of responsibility. If patients are free to choose how they engage with healthcare, they are also held responsible for any choices they make. Doctors and other health professionals make options available, but do not steer the patient towards a particular choice. The final decision is entirely down to the patient, and is essentially, as Mol writes, a private matter: 'It's your choice.' She adds, however, that patients can help each other choose, working together as organised consumers. This idea has been used in IMT contexts to think about the politics of choosing, and how patients might use their choices to voice their political concerns about healthcare at home (Ormond 2015a).

Running alongside choice, Mol (2008) describes a second logic – the logic of care. To be clear, she does not see these two logics as always antithetical or in opposition, nor does she simply see care as good and choice as bad. As she writes, '"patient choice" and "good care" may sometimes complement each other', though she adds that 'more often they clash' (1). She concludes that 'the "good" relevant to each [logic] is different in kind – and so too is the "bad"' (85). Moreover, each logic has its own way of enacting that 'good'. In choice, autonomy is good and the patient should be empowered to make free choices; in care, attentiveness is good, and 'doctoring patiently' becomes a shared activity for the entire care team, which involves both formal and informal caregivers (108).

Mol's aim is to explore how these two logics work (and complement and clash) in the case of people living with type-1 diabetes, and to ask what is at stake (for patients, their family, friends and colleagues, and for health professionals) when either logic is used to guide treatment. As Maria Puig de la Bellacasa (2017: 10) summarises, 'a logic of care and a logic of choice are in constant friction in medical practices' – sometimes this is a productive friction, other times not. In 'real life', Mol (2008: 96) reminds us, 'these two modes of thinking and acting get mixed together'. But all too often, 'mobilising the logic of choice can lead to poor care' (xii).

So, where choice has been heralded as a way to free and empower patients, Mol (2008) turns attention instead to practices of care, and her enquiry turns to encounters in consulting rooms. For Mol, attending to these practices is important, as care is an open-ended process, not a tidily boxed product. In addition, care involves many actors, including patients themselves, who are not consumer-choosers, but active, embodied members of the care team. All these actors share the task that Mol labels 'doctoring'. And here, in the consulting room, she is able to outline some of those frictions between the two logics. Firstly:

> According to the logic of choice ... professionals should provide good information, and properly implement the interventions for which their patients opt. They should be knowledgeable, accurate and skilful ... but it is the patients who determine the direction to be taken. (Mol 2008: 63)

At first glance, this may seem like a productive way for doctor and patient to encounter each other, better certainly than the passive patient being simply told by the doctor what treatment is best for them. Here, the patient 'opts' and the doctor 'implements'. But Mol (2008: 64) counterposes this to the work of doctoring that she argues is at the heart of the logic of care, where as well as being knowledgeable, accurate and skilful, those engaged in care are also 'attentive, inventive, persistent and forgiving'. This, she writes, opens up a new way of thinking about the democratisation of expertise, more complicated than the apparent role-switching of the logic of choice, in which 'patients are called upon to manage their doctors' (65).

In the logic of care, doctoring is shared throughout the care team. Care is about relationships, not positions of expertise. It is about practices, not values. It can still be about choosing, but how choices are framed is very different, and choices are left open, subject to change. Care is ongoing, whereas in the logic of choice, once you have chosen, the matter is closed, other than carrying the responsibility if the choice turns out to be poor: 'The logic of choice comes with guilt. Everything that follows after a choice has to be accepted as following from it. ... In the logic of choice, having a choice implies that one is responsible for what follows' (Mol 2008: 91). In the logic of care, contrastingly, guilt has no place; instead, tenacity is called for, and practical action. That action can include making choices, certainly, but here choosing is one practice among many. Mol reminds us that 'the requirements for good care are exceedingly difficult to meet' (97) – perhaps helping to explain why it has been substituted for choice.

Mol (2008) is keen, finally, to remind us that her research offers a situated case study, looking at one disease and its treatment at a particular place and time: how people live with and are treated for type-1 diabetes in a hospital in a Dutch city in the early 2000s. The interactions of choice and care, she speculates, are likely to be 'highly variable' in different healthcare contexts (96), and she argues that it is important to attend to their specificity through detailed empirical study. Our work on cosmetic surgery presents one such empirical study, and in the contexts that we focus on we can see both similarities and differences in how cosmetic surgery tourism is framed by the logics of choice and care. First, while Mol focuses on a particular disease, our study is based around patients seeking various interventions, not all of them framed as treatment for disease (see chapter two for our typology of motives for seeking treatment). Second, and related, cosmetic surgery is by definition elective, and is an intervention that patients pay for. This brings the logic of choice centre stage, framing patients as consumers working within a market logic based around freedom to choose.

In media and academic accounts, and in the broader public conversation that surrounds cosmetic surgery, choice and responsibility are key concepts (and key judgements). Patients are blamed for poor choices, while their demand is blamed for making those poor choices possible in the first place: if people did not want surgery, or did not want it at bargain prices, they would not end up with 'botched up bodies', to use the name of a popular UK reality TV show. Surgeons and clinics are only meeting demand; it is the patient's choice. As we outline in the case of the so-called PIP scandal in chapter two, the logic of choice can be used to shift liability and responsibility onto patients. And the tourism aspect of cosmetic surgery tourism further emphasises this issue, by turning patients into tourists and by framing the decision to travel abroad for treatment as trivial, consumeristic and hedonistic.

But through our empirical research we found many examples of the logic of care at work, powerfully countering the discourse of poor choice. As we explore in chapters four, five, six and eight, practices of care are shared across the cosmetic surgery tourism assemblage, undertaken by many different actors. Caring and being cared for are at the heart of cosmetic surgery tourism, sometimes in surprising ways. Moreover, the logic of choice itself needs rethinking here, as patients do undertake the work of choosing. Unlike diabetes care, cosmetic surgery begins with choice – the decision to have surgery (Mol [2008] notes that a diabetes patient can opt to refuse treatment, but we would argue that the stakes are very different here). The cosmetic surgery tourist is immediately positioned as a patient-chooser, or even simply as a chooser, since the 'patientness' of the cosmetic surgery recipient can be called into question by the elective nature of the intervention. But through our research we found out *how* patients choose, and found choice to be active, informed and often shared. Patients sometimes celebrated their role as active chooser, as savvy consumer, as adventurer; they decided that they wanted treatment, and they sought it out and accessed it. But they did so in care-full ways, right from the inception of their therapeutic journey. In many cases the caring-ness or care-full-ness of their surgeon was the primary factor in patients' choice of clinic or destination. Along the way, they participated in practices of care in consulting rooms and airport lounges, in hotels and hospitals, at home and abroad. They also cared about the workers, patients and other inhabitants they encountered in their destinations. So, the logics of choice and care are entangled in cosmetic surgery tourism in distinctive ways, and part of our task in this book is to trace these entanglements in practice. The beautyscapes we trace in our research are in turn refracted by and refract the logic of choice and the logic of care.

In briefly discussing these antinomies, we have sought to address what have threatened to become truths in the discourse around medical tourism. There are other antinomies also at play here (see Perfetto & Dholakia 2010 for examples), but in highlighting and critiquing the patient/consumer, home/away, global/local and choice/care binaries, we hope to have cleared the ground for a more nuanced or complicated analysis. One thing that should be clear from much of the previous discussion is the importance of notions of place, scale and geography. That is hardly surprising, but it is worth reiterating in light of what is to follow: issues such as place, territory and scale are at the heart of our conceptual toolkit, as are ideas about relations, encounters and entanglements. Drawing on our own fieldwork and related studies, the discussion that follows explores these themes through three interlinked concepts: flow, network, assemblage.

Flows, networks and assemblages

It is partly to provide a more nuanced account of globalising processes that the notion of assemblage has been popularised (Collier & Ong 2005). Beyond the small body of literature using assemblage thinking in the specific context of IMT (Chee *et al.* 2017; Inhorn & Gurtin 2011; Whittaker 2008), in our account we draw on three disciplinary contexts where assemblage thinking has proved helpful, and draw together some of the insights from these sites of assemblage thinking for the discussion of our empirical findings.

First, in science and technology studies, assemblage thinking has been productively utilised – sometimes as an extension of the 'network' thinking in actor-network theory (ANT) – to theorise the coming together of heterogeneous people and things and to bring our attention to the agency of nonhumans. Warwick Anderson (2002), for example, deploys assemblage to rethink technoscience in relation to globalisation, rewriting the globalisation narrative away from a straightforward westernisation/modernisation model. This allows us to see more clearly, as Anderson puts it, 'the mutual reorganization of the global and the local [and the] the increasing transnational traffic of people, practices, technologies' (643).

Second is the related work in anthropology. Ong and Collier's (2005) *Global Assemblages* maps out an agenda for anthropology in the 'problem-space' of globalisation; hence their titular pairing of 'global' and 'assemblage', which they argue 'suggests inherent tensions: global implies broadly encompassing, seamless, and mobile; assemblage implies heterogeneous, contingent, unstable, partial, and situated' (Collier & Ong 2005: 12). This tension, they add, is characteristic of what they call 'the *actual* global' – the global as it is encountered, experienced and lived. The list of assemblage terms that Collier and Ong introduce is repeated in variants across the literature; summarising anthropological assemblage thinking, Marcus and Saka (2006: 101) name its concerns as 'the ephemeral, the emergent, the evanescent, the decentered and the heterogeneous'.

The third disciplinary context we draw on, critical human geography and urban studies, has welcomed assemblage for its emphasis on contingency and emergence, and for thereby allowing researchers to

> foreground ongoing processes of composition across and through different human and non-human actants; rethink social formations as complex wholes composed through a variety of parts that do not necessarily cohere into seamless organic wholes; and attend to the expressive powers of entities. (Anderson *et al.* 2012: 172)

In this formulation, assemblage opens up the possibility of rethinking what globalisation means: not seamless abstract processes, but messy, contingent comings-together that can (and do) dissolve away, or might disintegrate and then reform in different ways. This is not to imply some sort of amorphous liquidity, however; assemblages can be durable, ordered and predictable. Geographers in particular have been keen to stress that assemblages can be grounded or placed, that the term implies both territory and relations (McCann & Ward 2011). But what is assembled can also be disassembled and reassembled – hence the calls to think in verbs rather than nouns, to stress the processes and practices of *assembling*. However, as a description of things in the world, assemblage as noun is also useful, though it is important not to 'fix' assemblages but to see them as always in a state of flux. It is also important, as Anderson *et al.* (2012: 172) write, to see how 'spatial forms and processes are held together, often with degrees of internal tension, and might have been assembled otherwise'. Finally, like the anthropological stress on the 'actual global', McCann and Ward (2011: xvi) talk of the 'local globalness' of assemblages, reiterating the need to look closely at how assembling takes place and makes place.[2]

In the research literature on IMT, assemblage thinking has been used in work on cross-border reproductive tourism, to explore 'the reconfigurations of society that arise from globalisation and the use of new biomedical technologies' (Chee *et al.* 2017: 246; see also Inhorn & Gurtin 2011) and to theorise the role of particular actors in the work of assembling. In this regard, Chee *et al.* (2017) have described how MTFs participate in the IMT assemblage, noting their role in articulating and stabilising (but also destabilising) the assemblage. Their nuanced account of MTFs working in and around Malaysian hospitals highlights how 'MTFs as assemblage components are simultaneously independent and connected with other components [including hospitals, doctors, patients, airlines and others], to differing extents and depths of interaction, and may have arisen from or continue to be part of other assemblages' (243). In their view – one remarkably consonant with our own – 'international medical travel comes to consist of, and is maintained by, interactions and relationships of elements drawn together at particular conjunctures' (243–244). The particularity of the conjuncture is especially significant: assembling happens in particular times and places, and is contingent and emergent. In the discussion that follows, we draw on the insights of assemblage thinking sketched here in order to explore forms of assembling and of assemblage that make up the local globalness of cosmetic surgery tourism. To do so, we begin by exploring two collateral concepts: flows and networks.

Assembling cosmetic surgery tourism

Cosmetic surgery tourism flows

Collier and Ong (2005) open their discussion of global assemblage via reference to Arjun Appadurai's (1990) well-known discussion of globalisation as a set of disjunctive global flows and 'scapes'. Appadurai identifies five nonisomorphic global flows: ethnoscapes (flows of people, both temporary and permanent), mediascapes (flows of images), technoscapes (flows of technology – high and low, mechanical and informational), finanscapes (flows of money) and ideoscapes (ideological flows). This remains a very productive analytical device for exploring particular global assemblages, though it is important to remember that assemblages are not reducible to flows. It is clear from our fieldwork, however, that cosmetic surgery tourism is strongly related to flows, and here we outline some of these relations.

In terms of ethnoscapes, the most obvious movements are of tourists themselves: medical and cosmetic tourism depends definitionally on their movement from one place to another (notwithstanding the complexities discussed earlier in denominating these as 'home' and 'away'). Appadurai's discussion of people flows reminds us that some routes are relatively enduring – pilgrimages might be an obvious example – while others ebb and flow, for a variety of reasons. In our research, we found a similar mixture of well-worn routes, often mapping onto existing tourist itineraries (Australians travelling to Thailand, for example), alongside newer pathways that have emerged specifically to tap into the cosmetic surgery market (some of the European destinations, such as those in Poland, to which British patient-consumers travel). In some cases these map onto flows in the opposite direction (Polish migrant workers coming to the UK, opening up new routes for low-cost airlines). It is also important to note that even well-worn routes are reinscribed, reinvented and subverted by surgical journeys (Thompson 2011) – a previous tourist destination might become, over time, primarily associated with medical tourism, changing the meaning of a trip there. The construction of Gangnam in Seoul, South Korea, as a world-renowned destination for particular surgeries can overdetermine understandings of who might go there, and why (Holliday *et al.* 2017).

Patient-travellers are not the only people on the move in cosmetic surgery tourism: we encountered doctors and other health workers travelling to clinics, and the industry involves various other intermediaries, notably medical travel agents/brokers/facilitators, some of whom are also frequent travellers (whether to meet surgeons and scope possible new clinics, or travelling with patients). Medical staff sometimes trade on past movement, in particular overseas education, training and experience (often in Western countries – a form of credentialising to reassure prospective patients; see also Casanova & Sutton 2013). Health workers also migrate as a result of medical tourism, for example from rural to urban locations, and from public to private healthcare (Connell 2011a). Medical tourists also often travel with companions, if they can afford to – usually a family member or close friend. These companions take on informal caring roles (Casey *et al.* 2013a, 2013b), but might also be the ones doing touristic activities (particularly if patient recuperation takes longer than planned). We explore the forms of work undertaken by travelling companions in chapter four.

A focus on ethnoscapes also reminds us to pay attention to the actual practices of travel: flows are not abstract processes, but real events with embodied participants, which produce real effects for those travelling. Meghann Ormond (2015b) has discussed the travel practices of medical tourists, exploring embodied experiences on planes, buses and taxis. In our research, we encountered sometimes epic journeys – not least when low-cost travel options were also decidedly more long-haul, or when the vagaries of the weather combined with low-cost carriers' customer services to shunt travellers around from one regional airport to another, as we recounted in chapter one. And while aggregate level studies tend towards depersonalisation by talking about 'patient flows', we remain mindful that these flows are peopled: these are 'affective journeys' (Solomon 2011) undertaken by socially located subjects, moving from one place to another, compelled by complicated imperatives. Ethnographic studies and autobiographical accounts have helpfully revealed the subjective and intersubjective experiences of medical tourists, mapping an emotional geography alongside the patterning of global patient flows (e.g. Kangas 2002; Kingsbury *et al.* 2012; McDonald 2011; Solomon 2011). This work on the emotional geography of affective journeys has productively explored the experiences of international medical tourists and of others drawn into their travels, highlighting the particular ways in which travelling abroad for medical treatment can produce both 'emotional amplification' and 'emotional extensivity' – heightening feelings and a greater range of emotions (Kingsbury *et al.* 2012).

The technoscapes we encountered included flows of medical devices such as implants, which travelled sometimes considerable distances along circuitous routes to land on a surgeon's desk before moving into a patient's body (figure 3.3). The migrations of defective PIP breast implants around Europe offer a particularly tragic example that took place during our study (see chapter two). Flows of technique and medical knowledge also traverse the globe, though their direction of travel can be unpredictable (see chapter seven). Here again, the credentialising role of 'Western' training is worth noting, as forms of skill (embodied in surgeons) travel. Given the emergence of global centres of expertise in particular cosmetic techniques, technoscapes do not always flow from the West: in East Asia, for example, a regional network has developed, with pioneering procedures flowing around and beyond the region (such as so-called Asian blepharoplasty; see Holliday *et al.* 2017). Meanwhile, the reputation of Brazil as a centre of expertise in cosmetic surgery makes it the origin point for some related technoscapes (Edmonds 2010). Sometimes, of course, there are blockages to particular flows; new techniques developed in one location might be prevented from travelling (or from acting as attractors to other flows, such as of medical tourists), as Cook *et al.* (2011) show in their work on xenotransplantation tourism. Here, institutional and regulatory blocks prevented techniques developed in Mexico from diffusing outwards.

Attending to flows of money (finanscapes) in cosmetic surgery tourism means following both the direct transactions as patients pay for treatment and the interrelated impacts of global financial markets on changing the geography of affordability for prospective patient-travellers. The impact of financial crises has produced wide-reaching effects on the map of medical tourism, in some cases leading to the opening up of new tourism markets where economic problems have shrunk domestic demand for private medicine (for example in South East Asia; Bochaton 2013; Ormond 2011). Favourable exchange rates and financial incentives and inducements (such as package deals or subsidies) mean that while cosmetic surgery tourists are enabled by finanscapes, at the same time they are constrained by their effects in other contexts (the instability of global finance can switch particular destinations 'on' and 'off'). And given that in most cases cosmetic surgery tourists are paying out of pocket for procedures, there is an especial sensitivity to financial gradients among cosmetic surgery tourists who are not high-flying and high-spending elites (even though, in some cases, they are able to experience 'luxury' and private healthcare for the first time when they travel abroad). It is no surprise, then, that cost is frequently cited as a primary factor affecting tourists' decision-making: both the decision to travel, and the decision about where to travel. Finanscapes both enable and demarcate the flows of cosmetic surgery tourism.

The mediascapes that play central roles in cosmetic surgery tourism include the news media and reality TV, with their often-sensationalised accounts of surgery gone wrong (Casanova & Sutton 2013), and the media that emanate from within the phenomenon itself. The latter category, which we focus on here, includes professional and trade publications, travel guides and assorted highly important online resources – websites, online forums and social media. It is a truism that without the Internet, medical tourism would probably not exist in its current form (Horsfall & Lunt 2015b) – online information is a vital resource for travellers, and those offering services have developed sophisticated online information and guidance (and advertising – often these boundaries are indistinct). We have previously analysed cosmetic surgery tourism websites, unpacking the imagery and messages they project to potential clients: images of exoticness, of beautifully transformed bodies, of surgical excellence, messages favourably comparing the standards offered with those at home, reassurances about outcomes and testimonies from satisfied customers (Holliday et al., 'Beautiful face, beautiful place', 2015).

Guidebooks are a particularly interesting media form in IMT; often written by former tourists, they offer insider accounts and travelogues as well as narratives centred on choice and possibility and on the 'doability' of medical tourism (Ormond & Sothern 2012). Undoubtedly, these media have a vested interest in promoting certain images and discourses of medical travel. As Appadurai (1990: 299) notes, mediascapes and ideoscapes can have greater isomorphism than some other global flows – both are 'concatenations of images' – but it is important not to simplify this as Western ideologies assuming global hegemony. In discussions of cosmetic surgery (tourism), this has tended to focus on the notion of a global beauty norm, noted above. However, more nuanced studies have shown that 'the complexities of the interfaces between global processes and local cultural diversity apply equally to the flows of images of beauty' (Atkinson 2011: 628), so while there are undoubtedly global flows of beauty ideas (and related products, technologies, styles, practices) that is not the same as saying that one ideal of beauty is globally dominant – the global and the local mix together, each reworking the other, producing new hybrids (Faria 2014). And global flows emanate from many different locales: the Korean Wave and the rise and dissemination of K-pop in East Asia (and beyond) is producing new regional images and ideas of beauty which then themselves circulate globally along mediascapes and ethnoscapes (Holliday et al. 2017; Ryoo 2009).

Other ideoscapes traced in studies of IMT include the widely circulating ideas around patient choice and the understanding of healthcare as (at least in part) marketised/commoditised while also still seen as a right – as we discuss below. Ideas about what 'health' means, and how an individual might think of themselves as someone who *could* travel to access healthcare obviously exert a powerful pull on medical tourists, while the same notions about choice and consumerism are also deployed in critical accounts to demonise international medical tourists either as cynical exploiters of global flows or as unwitting dupes propelled by discourses they unthinkingly swallow. Such unhelpful stereotypes prevent more nuanced understandings of how medical tourism works (Kangas 2011), even as they are felt and experienced by medical tourists who undertake their own explanatory work in order to distance themselves with such stereotypes, albeit while wrestling with affective responses such as guilt (Solomon 2011), as we shall see in chapter seven. As we discuss in this chapter, cosmetic surgery tourism sits at the intersection of two prominent ideoscapes or logics: those of choice and of care.

One final ideoscape should be mentioned here: the flow of hope. To understand how hope works in this context, we turn here to the notion of the political economy of hope, most associated with the work of Rose (2007) and Novas (2006; see also Rose & Novas 2004). In their account, the political economy of hope relates to ideas of 'biological citizenship'. It is about how particular (hoped-for and hopeful) futures are brought into being, through interactions between patients (assembled into organisations through biosociality – new communities based around shared biological categories, into which category we would include the Facebook groups we discuss in chapter six) and biomedicine (both state and private), where all actors are also interested in 'biovalue' – the different forms of value that biological objects (for example genes) have commercially and therapeutically. In the field of biomedicine then, hope is brought into contact with both health and wealth (Novas 2006). Biosocial groups lobby for treatment, and commercial and state healthcare providers take decisions about whether to meet these needs. Here we see intersecting 'regimes' of hope: 'governments look to the national economic potential of new treatments in the longer term, [while] patients and their carers often hope for at least some improvement in the not-too-distant future. On the other hand, private providers hope to profit from the provision of treatments' that are in some cases as yet clinically unproven (Petersen 2015: 65). Hope is thus multi-layered and ambiguous; even so, it is certain that in international medical travel, hope *flows*.

In the case studies Rose and Novas work with, patient organisations (biosocialities) grouped around particular (usually genetic) conditions interact with biomedical organisations (public and private) around both shared and distinct hopes, which we could oversimplify as hope of a cure and hope of profit, though such an oversimplification obscures some of the complexities at work when hope is mobilised. Given the uneven geography of 'hopeful technologies', accessing hope today often means moving, either because biomedical treatments have a cost gradient or because particular treatments are not available everywhere – often the case with emerging, experimental and 'unproven' treatments. As Beth Kangas (2007: 304) writes, hope often propels medical travel: 'advances in medicine can make treatment options seem almost endless, suggesting there is always one more thing to try. Medical care "abroad" can seem limitless as well: if the desired results are not found in one treatment destination, there is another country to try' (see also Brophy 2017).

Alan Petersen and colleagues (2013, 2017) read stem cell tourism through the lens of hope: here patients travel to countries which offer particular procedures, often 'rapidly modernising' countries who have enthusiastically embraced a future based around 'the market driven pursuit of high-tech interventions' (Petersen *et al.* 2013: 671). So, the promise of biomedicine is at once individual and collective, personal and institutional, economic and political, and this promise is unevenly distributed globally, prompting travel by some people hoping for a cure or for a more liveable life with their condition. Hope is managed by various actors, and there are attempts to sort 'hope' from 'hype'.

Hope is in fact a powerful mobilising emotion in many forms of IMT, not just for patients but for many elements in the assemblage, from doctors and scientists to national governments. And, as already noted, hope flows – for example, as patients scan the world for potential sites to travel to for treatment (Petersen *et al.* 2017). At times, however, such hope is dashed when global (which often in practice means Western) regulation tightens its grip on experimental treatments and the places that seek to offer them – as in the case of stem cell tourism in South Korea, stalled by a high-profile scandal (Kitzinger 2008), and xenotransplantation tourism in Mexico, shut down by the actions of an international regulatory body (Cook *et al.* 2011).

As noted above, it is important that global flows are not seen as seamless and frictionless: they do not circle the earth in smooth, regular orbits; they warp and bend, stop and start, come and go. Yet flows do produce their own momentum, carrying people and things along, sometimes passively bobbing in their currents, other times aligning their own movement to that of the flow, and still other times trying to fight the tide. Different actors are differently able to play a role in shaping and directing global flows, to be sure, but this is not simply a powerful 'core' and weak 'periphery' model (Cook *et al.* 2011). Two key ideas can be productively used to think about IMT here. The first is the notion of momentum. Emily McDonald's ethnography of medical tourists in Buenos Aires shows how momentum is a force generated by medical tourists, but also one that carries them along their journey: 'patients did not simply enact movement, but simultaneously moved – and were moved by – forces in excess of themselves' (McDonald 2011: 499). Tourists generate momentum by making arrangements and building social obligations even before their journey begins, and this momentum carries them along even in moments when they doubt their decision to travel or seek treatment. As Kangas (2007) notes, in the context of hope, medical travel by definition stirs movement – to begin to think of oneself as someone who might travel abroad for treatment is already building momentum, already producing a particular orientation towards health and movement.

The idea of friction counters the seamlessness of globalisation, reminding us that movement depends on 'grip' – what Anna Tsing (2005: 5) refers to as 'the grip of encounter'. While Tsing's ethnography of global connection has a focus very different from ours, her discussion of friction resonates with our conception of forces at work in global flows. To be clear, she does not see friction as a brake on momentum: 'friction is not just about slowing things down. Friction is required to keep global power in motion' (6). Yet, as she concludes, 'global connections are made, and muddled, in friction' (272). We like that last phrase, that friction both makes and muddles global connections, as it seems to concur with the image of global flows we are using here to think cosmetic surgery tourism with. Momentum and friction can be thought of, to borrow a term from Cook *et al.* (2011), as 'textures' of the global (and of IMT), a term they use to remind us of the unevenness of globalisation and its rhetorical or performative dimension. Certainly, the texture of cosmetic surgery tourism is marked by both momentum and friction, as global flows both carry and are carried by people, technologies, money, media and ideologies.

This discussion of flows and 'scapes' takes us part way towards assemblage thinking. Flows are important elements in assemblages – an assemblage like a city or an IMT destination is the point at which various flows 'land' or come to ground (Briassoulis 2017). In landing, flows mix and mutate, meaning that the assemblage is emergent, and always open to possible change. For instance, in one clinic, located above a carpet shop in Marbella, we met a German surgeon who claimed to have introduced 'Botox parties' to the UK but after the 2008 financial crisis began mostly catering to Russian cosmetic surgery tourists (especially, he boasted, personal friends of President Putin) in Spain. Things that travel as flows come together in places, therefore, even if the terms of that coming-together are uncertain. Appadurai prefigured that with his stress on disjuncture and nonisomorphism: even seemingly orderly and ordered flows can change, sometimes rapidly and dramatically, other times subtly, almost imperceptibly. In thinking cosmetic surgery tourism through the notion of flow, then, we are beginning our own act of assemblage: assembling the diverse cartographies of people, things, practices, ideas and so on that criss-cross the world (or parts of it – it is important not to lose sight of spatial scales other than the global; A. Wilson 2011). Now we want to add one more element to this assemblage: the network.

Cosmetic surgery tourism networks

As noted earlier, assemblage thinking bears close relation to ANT, at least in some accounts. While we do not intend to provide an outline of ANT here, the stress on networks is important for us (see Latour 2005). Adding networks to flows gives a sense of those nodal points that flows travel between, a sense of connectivity (Pordié 2013). Again, some connections are intermittent or ephemeral; others are enduring and consistent. While flows have the capacity to switch and bend, places have varying capacities to attract some and repel other flows – though this capacity does not simply map onto core/periphery or global/local distinctions. Networks of connectivity provide an important focus, therefore, and, setting ANT aside, there have been two prominent ways of thinking networks in relation to medical and cosmetic tourism. The first relates to the Internet. As previously noted, the Internet is a vital enabler for medical tourism and a site for various experiences of connectivity, as well as a stimulus for the engagement with travel itself. The Internet also enables forms of imaginative travel (to new places and to a 'new me') and provides opportunities to engage with our second form of networking: social networks. Here we need to consider both online social networking – through the use of platforms such as Facebook – alongside (and increasingly inseparable from) forms of 'offline' social networking (face-to-face contact with family, friends or fellow tourists, for example; see chapter six).

Social networks are drawn upon throughout the surgical journey, from discussions with family and friends in the decision-making stage to consulting past recipients of procedures via online forums, and then on through the journey itself, keeping in touch online with family and friends and sharing experiences with others recuperating on-site. The use of Facebook before, during and after surgical tourism is particularly ubiquitous. Accessing social media via mobile devices means that patients frequently document their entire journey, sharing their experiences and building a strong sense of community with others. Shared social media narratives and images become a collective resource for patients and would-be patients, enabling forms of biosociality to emerge.

While online social networks were of vital importance to patients in our study, they also overlapped with face-to-face networks, particularly for groups of patients who travelled together and then stayed in touch. Meeting online before travel, they had already developed friendships by the time they met either in transit or at the destination, and they stayed close throughout their trip. Once back home, they kept in touch via Facebook and, in some cases, continued to meet up. Social networks allow prospective patient-travellers to access forms of warm expertise and peer knowledge which has higher value than marketing messages from clinics; they also enable patients to be producers of that expertise and knowledge, making cosmetic surgery tourism an interesting site in which to examine user-generated content and new forms of expertise. However, it is not just online that the use of social networks as trusted sources of information blurs with marketing – Audrey Bochaton (2013) discusses the recruiting of Laotian shopkeepers and other key social actors by Thai hospitals keen to encourage cross-border medical travel. These advocates then encourage others to consider making the trip to Thailand. In a relatively new market, friendly advice from trusted figures is positioned as more reliable that marketing messages – hence the desire of at least some MTFs/agents to position themselves more like the former, by trading on their own past experience as capital (see chapter four).

We should note, lastly, that it is not only patients that form networks in the context of cosmetic surgery tourism. Professional bodies and trade associations still tend to be nationally based, but their reach extends well beyond national borders. Tourism agencies have their own networks and outposts, while individual hospitals might have overseas consulting rooms and representatives (Chee *et al.* 2017). Networks are in fact a prominent feature of the organisation of cosmetic surgery tourism at all scales. One of the MTFs in our study leased a consulting room in London's Harley Street, for instance, where surgeons from a range of international destinations offered consultations to UK patient-consumers who subsequently met their surgeon in a destination abroad to undergo their procedure. Forms of accreditation, such as those provided by Joint Commission International (JCI), arguably function like networks, connecting those facilities that meet the required standard (see Ormond 2013a). Meanwhile, on the ground, MTFs and other intermediaries are densely involved in forms of networking, especially in bringing together the diverse flows that allow a cosmetic surgery journey to take place (Chee *et al.* 2017). MTFs arrange trips, consult with surgeons, recommend destinations, handle logistics, sometimes travel with patients and build networked businesses (often with very modest foundations). They are the quintessential networkers, in both senses of the word: they network relentlessly with all the other players, and they work to build a network with the MTF at the centre – becoming, perhaps, to use the words of ANT, an obligatory point of passage, a node in the network through which all flows must pass. This self-centring in the cosmetic surgery tourism network can be a source of tension, especially in MTFs' relationships with surgeons, who can feel somewhat displaced and overly dependent on the entrepreneurship embodied by MTFs – a challenge to surgeons' professional status (Skountridaki 2015; see also chapter five).

Assembling cosmetic surgery tourism

The preceding discussions of flows and networks open the door to thinking cosmetic surgery tourism as assemblage: a contingent, mutable coming-together of heterogeneous people and things that might coalesce into a more-or-less stable network, but might be evanescent and transitory, shaped by internal and external forces, shaping and being shaped by global flows and by interactions and relations at other spatial scales (Kangas 2007).

It is important to acknowledge that cosmetic surgery itself is also an assemblage. We see cosmetic surgery as a practice formed through interwoven actors – technologies, media, patients, discourses, surgeons and narratives (Gimlin 2013; Jones 2008a). As we discussed in chapter two, we have been dissatisfied by dominant feminist readings of cosmetic surgery. Yet we found that certain feminist conceptualisations of cosmetic surgery as a discursive and intersubjective set of processes fitted many of the complex intertwinings of patients, stories, medics and places that we encountered (Jones 2008b; Pitts-Taylor 2007, 2009), offering a more useful analytical lens than other feminist writing could. Thus, we tried always to situate explanations for cosmetic surgery not in the psyches of individuals but rather in the complex medical, cultural and economic networks in which it unfolds locally, nationally and globally.

In her review of feminist writing on cosmetic surgery, Victoria Pitts-Taylor (2007) argues that cosmetic surgery is most often understood – via psychological, medical and feminist discourses – as located in the individual. Thus, the identities and psyches of patients have been foregrounded by researchers as they attempt to find out why something like cosmetic surgery or cosmetic surgery tourism even exists. This focus not only risks leaving out key sociocultural aspects but has also actually *produced* cosmetic surgery subjects. Writing about her own rhinoplasty, Pitts-Taylor (2009: 120) suggested that feminist interpretations of cosmetic surgery that focus on individuals, especially those that situate them in terms of their mental health, are themselves a form of oppression, pathologising and thereby stripping agency from cosmetic surgery patients. Jones (2008b) meanwhile argues for feminist theories of aesthetic surgery that do not centralise the interiority of aesthetic surgery *within* the patient-consumer. Instead, aesthetic surgery is viewed as an interactive, intersubjective set of processes enacted by human and nonhuman actors – as an assemblage.

Jones (2008a) uses ANT to position cosmetic surgery patient-consumers as just one of a multitude of actors in a relationship where agency is not an immutable position rooted in either self-hatred or empowered rationality. Rather, agency flows, mediated through networked relationships. Fraser (2003) and Pitts-Taylor (2009), moreover, argue for a shift from viewing subjects as either oppressed or liberated, arguing that the subject should be seen as an actor in and among ideological and political contexts that shape perceptions and understanding of cosmetic surgery processes. These important insights frame our analytical approach, placing the patient-consumer within a dense network of people, practices and ideas that together constitute cosmetic surgery. Adding tourism to this assemblage further complicates it, bringing in yet more actors, as we now move on to discuss.

In chapter eight we provide a lengthy vignette from our fieldwork in Tunisia, where we travelled with a handful of British cosmetic surgery tourists and found ourselves sharing spaces and experiences with victims of the conflict in neighbouring Libya (see also Holliday et al., 'Brief encounters', 2015). This encounter in Tunisia had its unique elements, as we explore later, but it was in many ways also typical of the emerging cosmetic surgery tourism beautyscape. Like many other places around the world, Tunisia is being assembled as a medical tourism destination – while also being plugged into other assemblages. In our encounter with the field site, this did not only mean opening up to patient-travellers; it also meant opening up to medical professionals and, as Marc Lautier (2008) shows, to transnational flows of images and ideas: Tunisia has become constructed as an IMT destination – it has marked its place on the map. This situation is emergent: the decision to shift healthcare policy – in part a response to changing global financial conditions – has an outcome that is still uncertain. Tunisia was not on our map of key destinations for European cosmetic surgery tourists prior to beginning our project: it was through conversations with MTFs that we learnt of its nascent medical tourism industry. While the cosmetic tourism assemblage is becoming 'loosely institutionalized' and ordered (A. Wilson 2011: 127), it is at the same time always in motion.

Moreover, the patients we met in Tunisia were archetypal cosmetic surgery tourists, by which we mean they were ordinary people, not jet-setting elites. They were shocked by the conditions that surrounded their stay and by the situation they had landed in the midst of. Some were unaware of the geopolitical context, or even of basic geography. Tunisia was made accessible to them because of cost and ease – a short hop on a low-cost carrier – but its reality was obscured by the mediascapes they chose to access in planning their trip. For the patients we met, this was definitely an 'affective journey' (Solomon 2011), for both expected and unexpected reasons. The Tunisian example is typical in that there is a beautyscape in formation here, too: our patient-travellers were motivated to travel there in part with an idea of how they wanted to transform their bodies, as well with an expectation as to what that transformation would achieve for them; the clinic is a site of hope and of promise – and the networks of information that brought the patients there carried along with them particular messages, constructing Tunisia and the clinic as hopeful.

Our Tunisian example clearly represents cosmetic surgery tourism as assemblage; indeed, one of the features of assemblages concerns how 'new and unpredictable directions develop when assemblages encounter novel perturbations' (Anderson *et al.* 2012: 182) and how parts of one assemblage 'can be disconnected or plugged into a different assemblage in which their interactions are different' (181) – in Tunisia both of these shifts are clearly observable, as the cosmetic surgery tourism assemblage meets with the Libyan conflict, itself another kind of assemblage. The clinic is plugged in to both assemblages at once, and becomes a site of concentrated connectivity (Pordié 2013). These observations also remind us of the emergent temporality of assemblages; what we found in Tunisia was a very particular time as well as place. And that place is both territorial – located nationally, regionally and locally – and relational, formed out of particular entanglements. Such assemblages are emergent wherever cosmetic surgery tourism takes place and makes place.

Conclusion: mapping beautyscapes

> Mapping is the primary method for assemblage thinking. … [M]apping is not a mimetic tracing of a territory; rather, it is a production of ideas. (Wood & Dovey 2015: 56)

While we are wary of simply adding another 'scape' to Appadurai's (1990) typology, we introduce the term 'beautyscape' as a way of capturing the complexities and contingencies of cosmetic surgery tourism as assemblage. To be clear, we do not mean to imply some sort of homogenising global beauty norm that is sweeping the world and turning everyone into identikit versions of some imagined gold standard – though this is sometimes implied in literature that critiques the westernisation of beauty ideas worldwide (Atkinson 2011) This notion has been challenged by accounts that stress local, regional and national discourses and practices of beauty, even as these interact with assorted global flows (e.g. Faria 2014). Nor are we using the term 'beauty' in a gendered way, assuming that cosmetic surgery tourism is only about women's beautification. This too has been a dominant narrative in academic and media accounts, positioning cosmetic surgery patient-consumers within gendered frames. But as our research makes clear, the question of who cosmetic surgery tourists actually are is partly an issue of definition and accounting: if we include 'male' practices (such as hair transplants) or gender-neutral practices (dental work, body contouring, etc.) then we get a different map of cosmetic surgery tourism. This point notwithstanding, we find the term 'beautyscape' a useful way to bring together our conceptual framing.

Our notion of beautyscapes wraps together the flows and 'scapes' that Appadurai lists, stabilising them (albeit loosely and contingently) to form an assemblage. As we showed in the preceding discussion, this beautyscape has nested within it ethnoscapes, finanscapes, technoscapes, mediascapes and ideoscapes. Each of these can in itself be thought of as an assemblage, or plu-ralised assemblages. In their work on MTFs, Chee *et al.* (2017) recount how particular ethnoscapes (flows of migrants and refugees) have brought particu-lar actors into the IMT assemblage to work as MTFs; we can note too how the work of MTFs draws in and contributes to flows of money, technology, people, images and ideas. These flows are both produced by and produce both momentum and friction, meaning that globalisation is manifest in 'textures', not in a smooth globe. Every component of the assemblage can be produc-tively read this way. To be sure, the world is contoured by ideas and practices of beauty, as it is by ideas of choice and care, but often in unexpected ways, as flows interact on the ground to produce particular comings-together. Our field sites each revealed this patterning, this interaction of global flows and local contexts, making us ever mindful of the need to look and listen carefully, to engage in research practices that opened up the assemblage we encoun-tered, to resist easy readings. The beautyscapes that we encountered and that are presented in this book are the outcome of this research process.

Notes

1 Our use of the antinomies device is inspired by Warde (1997).
2 For a discussion in relation to tourist destinations that is resonant for our analysis, see Briassoulis (2017).

4

The work of cosmetic surgery tourism I: caregiving companions and medical travel facilitators

Our aim in the next two chapters is to outline the various forms of work or labour that are brought together to make cosmetic surgery happen.[1] Through this focus on work we aim to provide a detailed overview of the cosmetic surgery tourism industry, focusing on the key actors whose work is central to the production of cosmetic surgery tourism. In this chapter we look closely at two key groups, one providing unpaid, informal support for cosmetic surgery tourists – their caregiving companions – and the other offering paid-for services in support of parts or all of the patient's journey – MTFs. Both are vitally important groups whose labours are central to cosmetic surgery tourism, though they are very different in character. In chapter five, our attention turns to healthcare workers, focusing on nurses and surgeons in particular. We close our discussion by exploring the work that patients themselves do: rather than being passive recipients or consumers of medical tourism, we show the many ways that patients contribute to the production of cosmetic surgery tourism. We should note that we do not focus here on every key player in the cosmetic surgery tourism assemblage, though we will shortly provide an overview of the structure of the industry that gathers up everyone with a stake in it. In the two chapters presented here, we do not focus on legislators, policymakers and regulators, though they also undertake important work in shaping how cosmetic surgery tourism is assembled – they were not the focus of our research project.

The cosmetic surgery tourism industry

At its simplest, cosmetic surgery tourism is a matter of supply and demand: healthcare providers offer treatments, and patients take them up. The reasons behind the supply and demand of cosmetic surgery tourism are discussed elsewhere in this book. As a form of privatised, marketised and consumerised medicine, cosmetic surgery is often seen as emblematic of neoliberal healthcare, unconstrained by the discourses and practices of public healthcare provision such as the NHS in Britain or Australian Medicare (sometimes this is seen as a good thing, sometimes not). In classic neoliberal rhetoric, patients want treatment, they are free to choose to have it and can decide whether to purchase treatment at home or abroad. For those who choose to travel, there are many options available: where to go, how much to pay, what treatment to have. To guide those choices and enable patient journeys, the cosmetic surgery industry has developed a distinctive structure or landscape, operating at a range of spatial scales from the local neighbourhood level through to the national to the global. At different scales, different actors come to prominence. As we discussed in chapter three, cosmetic surgery tourism is assembled at different scales from flows and networks. These are peopled, and the people are doing work. That work in its various forms is the focus of this chapter and chapter five.

At the supply end of the industry are healthcare providers: hospitals and clinics and the people who work in them. These range from large, high-profile, specialised hospitals geared towards international patients flows – the most iconic being Bumrungrad International Hospital in Bangkok. These high-end hybrid hospital-hotels (Whittaker & Chee 2015) sharply contrast with the very small-scale clinics we found scattered across destination countries, often nestled into high streets or shopping malls or, as we found in Gangnam in Seoul, arranged in tower blocks with a different clinic on each floor (Holliday *et al.* 2017). Some of these providers, large or small, target international patients solely, but others mix domestic and foreign patients. Some mix public and private patients, too, and some are also general practitioners/physicians, dermatologists or dentists. The largest hospitals employ countless staff and offer a full range of treatment options, while the smallest are often sole-trading clinicians specialising in one particular treatment – maxillofacial procedures, breast surgeries, dental implants. Many of the surgeons and other medical staff we spoke with were very positive about specialising in cosmetic surgery and about working with international patients, though some voiced concerns about the image and reputation of their chosen field, and others expressed concerns about particular patient groups (see chapter five).

The supply side of the landscape is increasingly cluttered, with new entrants jockeying for position among established players. Advertising and marketing – especially online via websites, portals and social media – have therefore become vital tools for providers seeking to secure and maintain a foothold. And intermediaries such as travel writers and online portal managers have made roles for themselves in guiding prospective medical travellers through the sometimes bewildering choices on offer. Clinic websites trade on particular attributes, ranging from surgical skill to the beauty or glamour of their location, as well as outlining the treatments on offer, often coupled with 'before and after' photos of patients (Holliday *et al.*, 'Beautiful face, beautiful place', 2015). The Internet, along with mobile telephones and apps, also enables medical travel by keeping patients constantly in touch – with friends and family, with facilitators and medical staff, and with each other (see chapter six).

Patient journeys are also enabled by many intermediaries who position themselves in between providers and patients. These include the facilitators, brokers and agents who we focus on later in this chapter – but they also include countless other service providers, such as those who actually enable travel. These providers range from low-cost airlines, whose itineraries have often opened up new routes for medical travel, to taxi drivers and others carrying patients along their journeys (Ormond 2015b). Other intermediaries are on hand to guide travellers in particular directions, either face to face – meeting them at airports, for example, to suggest/advertise particular clinics – or virtually, via online media designed to channel patients towards particular destinations or clinics. At destinations, meanwhile, there are providers of many other services that IMT requires – accommodation, medical supplies, food and drink, company, entertainment and touristic pursuits. IMT assembles hotspots of entrepreneurial activity in destinations, as both formal and informal work is carried out in support of patients choosing places for treatment.

Of course, cosmetic surgery is only one form of IMT. And while the shape of the IMT industry as a whole bears strong resemblance to that of cosmetic surgery tourism, there are some important distinctions – distinctions often based around the specific character of cosmetic surgery within the healthcare landscape.[2] This means that certain key players shaping the IMT industry as a whole, such as health insurance companies, have less at stake in our study, since most cosmetic procedures are by definition outside the remit of health insurance and are paid for out of pocket by patients. The need to pay directly for treatment arguably brings to greater prominence here other players, such as loan providers. While some clinics offer financial products to patients, in our research we found patients more commonly using savings and small windfalls, or securing loans from family, friends or mainstream financial providers, such as high-street banks. Raising the funds to travel and access treatment is, in fact, a key form of work undertaken by patients, as we discuss in chapter five. These flows of money constitute one key finanscape of cosmetic surgery tourism.

While cosmetic surgery tourism might be characterised as fully marketised and thus only shaped by the market's invisible hand, it is important to flag the regulatory and legislative interests that also contribute to the emerging beautyscape. And here the national scale becomes important, despite all the rhetoric about globalisation: national governments maintain a key role, even in heavily marketised private healthcare, as both regulators and promoters (with the emphasis often on the latter). Many nations have actively courted IMT as an engine of economic development, and their governments have steered both marketing efforts and regulatory frameworks (such as visa provision for medical travellers or controlling which treatments are legally available; see Holliday *et al.* [2017] on these issues in South Korea). Beyond the nation, important accreditors such as JCI have established themselves as highly visible global quality benchmarkers (see Cohen 2015; Ormond 2013a), providing another way for patients (and health insurance providers) to navigate the global market. Industry associations, professional bodies and trade bodies, conventions and shows have also developed to both regulate and promote the industry from within (see Crooks *et al.* 2017; Labonté 2013), producing and shaping an ideoscape extolling the virtues of the industry for patients, health providers and nations.

This sketched outline of the structure of the cosmetic surgery tourism industry begins to hint at the work that underpins the production of beauty-scapes. Each of the activities discussed, from national regulation to taxi driving – some more visibly than others – is peopled by workers whose labours come together in the cosmetic surgery tourism assemblage. As Anthony Elliott writes:

> From flight attendants to hospital cleaners, from hotel staff to nurses, there are very large numbers of workers involved in assisting, checking, monitoring, providing hospitality, customer service, ground transportation and so on. Such workers, and the economic and social processes in which they are implicated, are not incidental to the phenomenon of surgical holidays; they in part help to constitute it (Elliott 2008: 102–103).

In order to focus on the work that gets done in the cosmetic surgery tourism assemblage – the work that in part constitutes the phenomenon – we now move to consider in more detail some of the forms of labour in cosmetic surgery tourism, drawing from our extensive ethnographic fieldwork and setting this in the context of existing accounts and broader academic debates.

Forms of work in cosmetic surgery tourism

Our discussion of the different kinds of work or labour that are brought together in cosmetic surgery tourism, which makes up the remainder of this chapter and the next, is embedded in and indebted to social science research on changing forms and meanings of work. In particular, we situate our analysis in connection to four key debates that have profoundly refocused the study of work practices and meanings. Using their most common labels, we contextualise our focus here around research on care work, body work, emotional labour and aesthetic labour. To begin, we offer a brief definition of each, bearing in mind the ways these forms of work are often entangled, along with an adjunct category: tourism work.

Care work

Care work refers to practices of caring for others. Care work is often divided into formal (paid) and informal (unpaid) subcategories, with the latter associated with family members. Informal, unpaid care work located within the family is central to social reproduction, and classically this has implied both gendered and spatial divisions of labour: men go out to work, women work at home. Historically, this equation has also been classed, as richer families employed servants to supplement domestic care work otherwise undertaken by the housewife. On the other hand, either 'in service' or in the factory, working-class women have usually worked outside of their own homes. Global political-economic transformations since the second half of the twentieth century have produced a booming service economy, and Linda McDowell (2009) argues that this primarily reflects the shift of women's care work from being unpaid and in the home to paid work in the formal economy, unsettling these associations (and the realities of who works where). However, informal, unpaid care work remains gendered, classed and associated with the domestic sphere, even though such caring practices have become increasingly mobile or deterritorialised (H. Brown 2012), assembled into 'convoys of care' whereby care is provided both formally and informally by different carers in dynamic, evolving formations (Kemp *et al.* 2013).

Formal, paid care work has been a significant growth area in terms of global employment and the global movement of workers in recent decades (Ormond & Toyota 2018). This sector includes those who perform care work in the homes of other people – nannies, au pairs, domestic cleaners and home carers – and those who work in non-domestic workplaces such as nurseries and hospitals. Care workers are increasingly stitched into global care chains, migrating to find work in places where demand outstrips supply in the local labour force (Yeates 2004, 2012), producing new ethnoscapes and 'landscapes of care' along the way (Milligan & Wiles 2010). In the healthcare context, migrant workers are increasingly commonplace, making hospitals sites of 'everyday cosmopolitanism' (Yeoh & Huang 2015), as workers (and patients) of many different nationalities mix and mingle (see chapter eight).

In the research literature, this kind of formal, paid care work is often seen as intertwined with the other types of labour discussed here, especially body work and emotional labour (Dyer *et al.* 2008). As we go on to illustrate, formal and informal care work overlap and interweave, and caring is distributed in an ongoing process across various actors, whose roles can shift according to need. As discussed in chapter three, cosmetic surgery tourism provides us with a context in which to interrogate how what Annemarie Mol (2008) names the logic of care and the logic of choice intersect and interact. While from the outside, cosmetic surgery tourism might appear to be shaped by the logic of choice, we show here how the logic of care is equally important in shaping what happens when someone travels for treatment to enhance their appearance.

Body work and emotional labour

Body work has, in the sociological literature, been either broadly or narrowly defined. In the former case, it includes working on one's own body or appearance, using one's body in a work practice, bodily management at work and ways in which work shapes the worker's body (Gimlin 2007b). Narrower definitions limit the concept, for example in health and social care, to 'work that focuses directly on the bodies of others: assessing, diagnosing, handling, treating, manipulating, and monitoring bodies, that thus become the object of the worker's labour' (Twigg et al. 2011: 171). For us, both approaches have their merits and uses for our analysis: the expanded definition opens our eyes to the myriad ways that labours and bodies come together, while the tight focus of Twigg et al.'s conceptualisation focuses our attention on those who are paid to work on the bodies of others – a useful distinction in the healthcare setting, though one that is difficult to sustain at times. In medical sociology, research has explored the social meanings of body work and the status hierarchies in the medical professions that produce an effective distancing from the patient's body (or the embodied patient) as the work is elevated – healthcare assistants undertake the 'dirty work' that nurses sometimes consider below their occupational/skills remit, while doctors further avoid direct interaction with the embodied patient, dealing with symptoms, aetiology or body parts (Twigg et al. 2011). Later we will revisit and contest this formulation in the context of cosmetic surgeons.

Debra Gimlin's (2007b) expanded definition of body work, noted above, includes other important forms of labour: work on one's own body/appearance (and, of course, in the case of cosmetic surgery tourism, this form of self-work intersects with the body work of healthcare workers), the shaping of the worker's body *through* work (she discusses 'work stress' in this context) and issues of bodily and emotional management *at* work. On the last of these, and drawing on a lineage of social science research on the topic of emotional labour such as Hochschild's (1983) study of flight attendants, Gimlin shows how emotions are central to many workers' experiences and performances of work, notably in the service sector (McDowell 2009). For Hochschild and subsequent researchers following her line, emotions are commodified at work, becoming part of the package that the worker 'sells' to their employer, though Gimlin argues persuasively that it is important to acknowledge how some care/

body workers also derive emotional wellbeing and satisfaction from their work. Clearly, there is a significant overlap here between body work and emotional labour, though in some of the literature body work and care work are separated via an emotional axis: body work means attending to the fleshy materiality of the body, which can be a site of displeasure, even disgust; care work focuses on the person, and on emotional engagement (Dyer *et al.* 2008; Twigg *et al.* 2011). Care work can still be embodied, of course – for example, in the ways that care workers touch patients so as to demonstrate concern and empathy.

Aesthetic labour

Discussions of service work, including in healthcare, have explored how workers are expected to perform aesthetic labour too. This is a particular form of the body work that Gimlin includes in her definition – working on one's own body/appearance. In the workplace, how one looks can be very important, and not just in professions that centre on appearance such as hairdressing and beautification. In health settings, forms of appearance management such as uniforms can be thought of as elements of aesthetic labour as they help transmit certain ideas about health work. And in the context of the consumerisation of healthcare and the logic of patient choice, elements of aesthetic judgement extend from hospital facilities to the appearance of staff, for example in international hospital-hotels targeting overseas patients (Whittaker & Chee 2015). Rollerblading hospital assistants might be the most spectacular form of this we encountered across our field sites (figure 4.1), but in many other clinics and facilities we found issues of personal appearance and self-presentation used to embody the cosmetic services on offer, either directly (when the bodies of workers have been reshaped by the clinic surgeon, making employees into walking advertisements) or indirectly (when grooming, dress and demeanour are used to convey beauty, transformation, luxury and other 'sales' attributes).

While in public health systems, especially huge organisations such as the NHS, there is a hierarchy at work – with the appearance of doctors more or less exempt from the controls exerted on nurses and other lower-status workers – in private, consumerised healthcare everyone (up to and including surgeons) can be required to perform aesthetic labour. We routinely heard patients comment that their surgeon was handsome, and surgeons lament that young patients sought out their more youthful colleagues, prioritising assumed understanding of surgery fashions and youth culture over accumulated surgical experience (see chapter five).

Tourism work

In the bulk of this chapter and the next we read the forms of work undertaken by the numerous people assembled into cosmetic surgery tourism by thinking about these four types of work/labour. As we noted earlier, it can be difficult in practice to disentangle these from each other, and often workers are undertaking multiple forms of work at once. So far, we have based our examples in health work, but we should not lose sight of the extra dimension to the focus of our project: that this is a study of cosmetic surgery *tourism*. While, as noted in chapter three, the 'tourismness' of this assemblage is a contested terrain, we have retained the term in part to remind ourselves to look beyond the clinic. In tourism studies we find parallel discussions of distinct forms of work/labour (Gibson 2009; Veijola 2010a). The tourist industry has long been a key site of emotional and aesthetic labour, and latterly has also been thought of as a place of care work, not least the care that goes into hosting (Veijola & Jokinen 2008). This work, like other forms of care work flagged above, is often gendered, though it is argued that the gendered practice of 'hostessing' has come to be performed by both men and women in the tourism sector (Veijola 2010b).

Tourism involves care, bodies, emotions and appearances, most notably for front-line workers in the hospitality trades and for those who interact directly with tourists, such as tour guides and other hosts (Swan & Flowers 2018). But other locals may also be conscripted into performances designed to encourage tourism and to welcome tourists. In our discussion of strategic essentialism and strategic cosmopolitanism (see chapter five) we encounter the same logic at work: locals asked to perform 'naturally caring' dispositions extend beyond healthcare settings to other sites of tourist encounter, meaning that in IMT as well as in other forms of tourism, 'hostessing' is distributed across many bodies – studies have found care work provided by taxi drivers, interpreters, hotel staff and other patients (Ackerman 2010; Ormond 2015b). Of course, not everyone drawn into this performance is actually a local: healthcare and hospitality/tourism workers are increasingly mobile, and may carry with them those attributes associated with their national character which they then trade (or try to trade) in new geographical settings (Beladi *et al.* 2015; Connell & Walton-Roberts 2016; Duncan *et al.* 2013).

Soile Veijola (2010b: 110) reminds us to recognise 'the ways in which travelling and tourism are often experienced as laborious – as work in itself' for tourists, too. This comment draws attention to the work that tourists – in our case cosmetic surgery tourists – undertake themselves. While being a tourist has conventionally been framed as a leisure activity, as the antidote to work, this binary has been breached by studies that show how tourists and their hosts often work together to produce tourism experiences, and that tourists can become key performers of tourismness, called upon to embody their own touristic identity (Edensor 2001). And like the work of tourists, we also need to attend to the work that patients do. The work of patients in healthcare settings has been relatively neglected in academic research, at least until discussions of 'responsibilisation' and imperatives to take on our own healthcare under the logic of choice (Mol 2008). But, as we shall see, patients *work*: on themselves, on each other and in collaboration with (and sometimes opposition to) paid healthcare workers. They also often work to become 'expert patients' and empowered consumers before, during and after travel and treatment (Ormond & Sothern 2012). When patients travel abroad for treatment, the forms of work they undertake multiply; we attend to the work of patient-travellers in chapter five.

One key characteristic of IMT is that patient-tourists are often accompanied by family members or significant others who undertake diverse forms of informal work before, during and after the journey itself. In the promotional literature on IMT, price comparisons flag that it can be cheaper to travel abroad for treatment even if one is accompanied by friends or family. This attraction of medical travel is usually sold as making up part of the 'tourist' appeal: companions can holiday while the patient recuperates, and everyone can be together in a resort – all for less than the price of surgery alone at home. It is to these companions that our attention now turns.

Travelling companions

Informal caregiving companions in IMT are usually close family members or friends who accompany the patient as they undertake their medical journey, and who carry out various forms of work along the way. As researchers (ourselves included) have found, contrary to the promotional hype about family members enjoying a holiday, the care work undertaken by travelling companions usually outweighs any touristic activities, and these informal caregiving companions become, in some contexts and depending on patient recovery, vital to the 'care chain' or 'convoy' of the patient-traveller. In many cases they are the one element of continuity in an otherwise dispersed network. The care work of these companions should not, therefore, be underestimated. On numerous occasions in our fieldwork we witnessed the caring labours of friends and family members who had travelled with patients, and we saw firsthand the toll this could take on them. This experience certainly ran counter to the prevailing industry discourses stressing that such a trip is essentially a cheap holiday for travelling companions. Indeed, sometimes the carers seemed to be suffering more than the patients. In one example, Patrick had travelled with his partner, Maureen, from Australia to Bangkok. The night before her scheduled surgery, Maureen decided to 'go for the full package' rather than just breast augmentation: this meant she would be having liposuction too, and consequently was taken into the operating theatre two hours earlier than expected. Patrick, a little dazed, told us several times that 'it happened really quick' and although he thought it was good that Maureen had gone in earlier than expected because that meant 'she didn't have time to worry about it', he was himself very anxious all day, and had to call his sister for comfort.

Other carers included parents, fiancées, roommates met at hotels, friends and one large group (four sisters and three friends) who travelled together from Australia to Bangkok for breast reductions or augmentations. Riri's mother accompanied her, and Riri told us that it is crucial to bring somebody for support and that it had been important for her to have her mum with her: she was glad that she had not come alone. Much of her mother's emotional support included reassuring Riri that she had made a good decision, including praising what she called the surgeon's 'beautiful suture work', which she compared to her own large caesarean section scar.

People who have not met before also serve as support for one another during cosmetic surgery tourism. Annelise and Belle, middle-aged Australian women, met each other in Pattaya, Thailand. They shared delight in the efficiency of the clinic ('that's the quickest x-ray I've ever had!') and in the couple of days before their surgeries they spent time shopping and sightseeing together. On the morning of their surgeries, as they waited to make their payments and fill in forms, they asked each other periodically if they were nervous, replying adamantly 'no' each time, perhaps serving to bolster themselves at a challenging time. When a mistake was made with Annelise's payment, about which she became very upset, it was Belle who went to speak to the marketing consultant. She returned saying: 'She'll look at the price again. I told her that you're thinking of not having the surgery.' The price was subsequently dropped for Annelise. When they were due to be discharged from hospital, Annelise was feeling sore and sorry, more than she had expected. She said that she did not realise she was so sensitive to pain and was 'such a sook'. Belle said that she felt almost no pain and took on the role of reassuring her new friend that her decision had been the right one. She told us: 'Can't you see that Annelise has stopped hiding her breasts? She used to always cross her arms but now she doesn't need to.'

An agent we interviewed in Malaysia told us that she had started her business after a good friend had asked her to help research where to have a breast augmentation and to help look after her during the post-operative recovery period. It was important for her friend to have complete privacy but adequate support. The exercise was successful and led the agent to set up a business based on this model. Here then is another slippage between unpaid and paid caring models, and an example of the huge importance of emotional support in the cosmetic surgery tourism industry, whether it comes from friends, family or professionals.

Studies by Victoria Casey and colleagues (2013a, 2013b) have approached this issue, albeit in a roundabout way – they interviewed international patient coordinators (IPCs, more of whom later in this chapter) about their experiences of informal caregiving companions. Their findings identify three major (often overlapping) roles: (i) as knowledge brokers, providing and collecting information, and handling communications; (ii) as companions, providing hands-on care and emotional support; and (iii) as navigators, coordinating paperwork, liaising with medical facilities and overseeing logistics. Such workers are, they note, vital to IMT yet are 'unpaid, untrained and largely unrecognized care providers' (Casey *et al.* 2013a: 9). They shoulder a weighty 'care burden' and can be susceptible to 'care burnout'. In addition, at least from the perspective of IPCs, these companions can actually disrupt the provision of care, for example by contesting medical authority, by encouraging inappropriate post-operative activities and by adding additional stress and anxiety to already difficult situations – especially, perhaps, if the companion is very close to the patient, and finds it emotionally challenging to be with them through treatment. IPCs working with cosmetic surgery patients, Casey *et al.* (2013a) report, often advise patients to travel alone, as companions can be very distressed by the immediate post-surgical appearance of their loved one. Nevertheless, in our own research we found cosmetic surgery tourists were often accompanied by friends or family members.

In a later paper drawing on caregivers' own accounts, framed by an ethics of care approach, members of the same research team explore 'care transitions' in IMT and the hidden roles informal caregivers take up in places away from the clinic – from the plane and taxi to the hotel room and, importantly, back home – highlighting the distinctively and inherently transnational character of care in IMT (Whitmore *et al.* 2015). As they note, carers in their study also supported each other, forming loose groupings in hospital lounges, cafeterias and waiting rooms: a network of carers and of care simultaneously. Here companions carry out numerous daily forms of care, body and emotion work, supporting patient recovery and providing a sense of home. In such in-between, non-clinical spaces, others can be drawn in to care informally for patients – even academic researchers. Emily McDonald (2011) recounts her own care work, emotional labour and body work as she conducted ethnographic research with cosmetic surgery tourists in Buenos Aires: cleaning and dressing the post-surgery wounds of participants who she shared accommodation with, running errands for them, reassuring them about their recovery and surgical outcomes. We too were called upon to perform care for participants, from chatting and sharing meals with them to being asked our 'expert opinion' on their chosen procedures, to helping patients download mobile phone apps so they could keep in touch with their family back home, and sometimes translating between patients and healthcare staff.

As international medical tourists move along their itinerary, in fact, they are variously cared for informally and formally. In other health studies contexts, this has been conceptualised helpfully as a 'care convoy' (Kemp *et al.* 2013) – care is delivered (and carried along, in the case of IMT) as patients move through the various stages of their 'care career', and this both shapes and is shaped by personal and structural contexts. In the case of IMT, the care convoy can bring many and varied participants into caring relationships. And, as Ormond and Sulianti (2017: 107) summarise, 'formal and informal care economies are made possible by medical travel flows *and* make medical travel flows possible'. Helping to shape and guide the care convoy, bringing together forms of care for patients, are various intermediaries who work to facilitate medical tourism.

Facilitators, coordinators and intermediaries

We now move on from the informal, unpaid care work undertaken in support of international medical tourists' therapeutic journeys, and into the realm of formal, paid work. This means that we are engaging with a different set of experiences, orientations and ways of working – and with some unique work roles that have come into being as a result of the particular formation of medical tourism, with its mutable combination of healthcare and travel/tourism. As Meghann Ormond (2013a: 54) writes, the evolution of IMT has 'led to a proliferation of specialized intermediaries in a range of entrepreneurial forms and along a spectrum of involvement' with medical travellers themselves. These intermediaries have been the focus of significant attention by researchers seeking to understand their make-up and their role in IMT. A number of scholars have thus attempted to classify important groups such as MTFs, and to show how MTFs and other intermediaries interact with key players across the industry. Here we discuss some of these typologies before going on to detail our understanding of the emerging MTF sector in cosmetic surgery tourism, based on our fieldwork findings. Throughout the discussion, we attend to the forms of work that MTFs carry out.

Medical travel facilitation is a new business sector that has sprung up to meet the particular needs of medical tourists, and MTFs are key intermediaries connecting supply (treatment providers) with demand (patients). The MTF sector as a whole exhibits considerable heterogeneity in terms of size, structure, business model and work practices:

> Some [MTFs] deal with hundreds of patients a year and are in corporate forms; others are sole proprietors who deal with fewer than twenty patients a year. Some specialize in a certain subset of the industry, such as fertility or cosmetic, while others will handle multiple forms of procedures. Some see their role as patient advocates coordinating care for patients and also trying to be agents of change for the health care system in the patient's home country, while others

see themselves as technical middlemen handling logistics of care abroad but not much more. (Cohen 2015: 25)

Hierarchies of intermediaries

One emerging distinction in the industry (and in academic accounts) that we need to note here is between MTFs and IPCs. The latter group, who we met earlier in this chapter passing judgement on informal caregiving companions, are defined as 'professionals who work at or with medical tourism destination facilities to coordinate the on-site care of medical tourists. Among many other activities, they often create itineraries for patients and serve as a point of contact for questions of concerns' (Casey *et al.* 2013b: 2). Crucially, IPCs tend to be based in a particular hospital or clinic, usually with dedicated office space, and are often employed by that facility (hence they are sometimes referred to as 'internal' patient coordinators). They are more or less members of hospital administration. Clearly, this role has arisen specifically in response to the international patient flows that IPCs are tasked with coordinating. In large international hospitals, patient coordination staff can be numerous and there is some specialisation within the role, for example in working with particular (national) groups of patients (Whittaker & Chee 2015). IPCs do more than handle the administrative duties surrounding international medical tourists; as Harris Solomon (2011) recounts in his ethnography of a private hospital in India, staff from the hospital's international patient services unit undertook forms of care work and could be seen as 'brand ambassadors' for the facility, embodying its values and developing relationships with international patients. IPCs often have more time to provide these forms of care than nursing staff.

While the distinction between IPCs and MTFs is not always so clear-cut in the industry or in the literature, we can helpfully distinguish IPCs from MTFs in relation to their contractual status. While both roles are sometimes collapsed under labels like facilitator, intermediary or agent, for our purposes it is useful to split hospital-employed IPCs from freelance MTFs, often known as agents (see below). Perhaps the most significant distinguishing feature to note here is that in our field sites agents were usually ex- or current patients themselves, whereas the IPCs we met were largely not. Agents are self-employed entrepreneurs carving out a niche in IMT, whereas IPCs are salaried employees working for providers. Agents are therefore much more invested and emotionally connected to their clients – sometimes in potentially damaging ways, as we discuss below.

Matthew Dalstrom (2013: 13) classifies MTFs in terms of business models and practices, with a three-fold division into full service facilitators (who often bundle services together into packages), referral service facilitators (who simply connect the patient to the medical provider) and individual service providers or stand-alone specialists – 'foreign medical providers who directly market their medical services to patients' and who are 'physically present during the medical encounter' (this is contrasted in some discussions with domestic medical tourism facilitators, who work solely in the sending country and do not accompany patients abroad; see Gan & Frederick 2011). In practice, these distinctions can be hard to hold onto, as individual MTFs sometimes move across these types, flexibly fitting themselves into the IMT assemblage – an assemblage that is in itself constantly changing. At the more informal, ad hoc end of the MTF spectrum, we encountered unaffiliated facilitators touting at airports and attempting to drum up trade through leaflets and business cards. At the other end of this continuum sit the smartly uniformed MTFs trading inside medical facilities, backed by impressive marketing materials and a slick social media presence (though even these attributes can sometimes cover over the reality of very small and sometimes precarious businesses).

Further significant elements of the heterogeneity of the sector are the contractual and/or financial relationship to the patient and to the clinic: some MTFs are contractually connected to and paid referral fees, commission or retainers by hospitals (bringing their role closer to that of IPCs), while others are paid directly by patients and have more informal, sometimes insecure relationships with healthcare facilities (Chee *et al.* 2017). In some of the cases we found in our field sites, MTFs handled all of the financial aspects of the IMT transaction, in fact – keeping direct association with money away from surgeons. This aspect of money (and impression) management might be particularly significant with patients from countries with public health systems, or those unfamiliar with and uneasy about paying for healthcare. It also enabled surgeons to be seen as offering only 'necessary' surgery, or the best techniques, unsullied by financial incentives – to be seen to act according to professional judgement rather than profit. We return to this important aspect of surgeons' impression management in the next chapter.

Our research identified four levels of MTFs at work in the cosmetic surgery tourism industry. At the top of the hierarchy are IPCs paid by and located in hospitals and clinics. Second in line are MTFs with IT specialisms. These are often men, who are relatively powerful in the industry and often employ other staff. These MTFs undertake a large amount of international travel, speak at international conventions and conferences, and have connections with senior managers in international hospitals and with governments. They push forward developments in their industry and lobby for the electronic resources in which they specialise to be expanded – for example, by advocating mobile electronic medical records or internationalised medical terminology to facilitate greater ease of patient movement. These MTFs run trade magazines, conduct and collate research on the industry, act as its spokespeople and develop and manage portals on which other types of MTFs advertise. We could say that they work mainly with the technoscapes of cosmetic surgery tourism. They are heavily invested in the industry but do not undertake any care, body, emotion or aesthetic work. These first two tiers of MTFs work broadly in IMT across many specialisms – not only cosmetic surgery tourism.

On the next level down are the MTFs more usually recognised as agents. Often former patients, and frequently women, these MTFs usually directly facilitate the travels and surgeries of cosmetic surgery patients specifically. They are based in the sending countries that patients travel from, and they advertise on portals, run Facebook groups for actual and potential clients, and book surgeries, flights, accommodation, transfers and pick-ups between hospitals, apartments and hotels for patients travelling to one or more destinations (though many are linked to only one destination, even to just one clinic or surgeon). Sometimes these agents also provide aftercare in the form of peripatetic nurses who conduct post-operative checks or remove stitches once patients have travelled home. Sometimes they appear to employ other agents based in destination countries, but these are often other self-employed agents or ad hoc workers who are associated with, rather than employed by, the sending agent. Agents tend to operate 'alongside' each other in temporary networks rather than in relationships of employment. Despite their large geographic remit, they are often relatively small companies with a single agent covering, as one we encountered advertised, 'New Zealand and the rest of the world'. One respondent recounted:

> I was a travel agent in Melbourne. I'd been a single mum for many years and … I was 54 … I was bored in my job. I'd been in the same role for four years in the travel agents and I wanted to move and one of my colleagues said to me, 'They don't like old ladies in travel', which is why I came here for the facelift, and then I met the owner of this business back in Melbourne … and about a month later she asked me would I be interested … She was going to create a position because she was about to have her second child and she had a 2-year-old and she needed somebody to take over her role within Australia, so she created a position and I [worked from] a home office. (Naomi, Australia-based MTF)

In this comment we see some of the social and cultural – and highly gendered – complexities around the role of agents. Sole parents are often women, and this role impacts on their earning capacity. 'Old ladies' not being liked in the travel industry is profoundly sexist and ageist. The owner of the business, a woman, needed to take time off work to care for her own children. Thus, a conglomeration of gender-based insults, imperatives and decisions led to a new position for a new agent to be created.

On the lowest level are agents who perform what is sometimes known as a concierge service, checking in on or 'buddying' patient-consumers in their destinations. In Malaysia, for instance, these were mostly locals and expatriates with time on their hands who earned small amounts of cash in hand to look after and 'entertain' people recovering from surgery. These freelancers were sometimes paid directly by hospitals and sometimes by sending agents, to undertake care and companionship work as a sideline to other work; in one Malaysia-based MTF company most of the employees were retired expats or the spouses of those who had relocated to work there. Gita, however, was local:

> When people join us to do this, it is not like it is going to be their job, it is just a sideline, hence why we say that right from the start, because some people need a lot of care and some people don't and they are the kind of people who can go along with that philosophy and understand it and they are fine to do it. Like I have even taken someone home once and I have stayed at the hotel until late at night if someone is on their own. (Gita, Malaysia-based MTF)

These individuals did not have their own websites but rather formed part of a network of people providing support for patients and updates for MTFs based in sending countries. They sent drivers to meet new patients at the airport and provided mobile phones with their numbers keyed in so that patients could contact them at any time. They did not engage in triage or other medical procedures but arranged accommodation on behalf of other MTFs, and accompanied patients on hospital check-ups, tours or shopping trips, and liaised between surgeons and patients:

> Healthcare tourism came into my life when a friend of mine from the UK wrote to me [in 2002] and said, 'I want to have a boob job done. They are too small and I want to enlarge them, so could you please help me find a good surgeon that you would trust yourself to do?' So, my husband is a GP and, yes, he knows doctors and everybody, and he knows colleagues who specialise. So, I told her I would find her the best surgeon, best hospital, best aftercare, and she said, 'Would you mind if I did not stay in your house? Because then everyone will come and look at me.' So, she said, 'How about I stay in a hotel? But you have to come and see me every day.' (Gita, Malaysia-based MTF)

One important feature traded on by many of the MTFs we met is forms of affinity with patients. While the quote above notes an already established friendship, other forms of intimacy are created from agents being former patients themselves, selling and sharing their expertise from an 'insider' perspective.

Beyond this, shared language, cultural proximity and empathy are prized assets for MTFs operating in destination countries, and expats working with patients from their origin countries are ideally positioned for this. In this way, previous expat migrations have produced ethnoscapes onto which cosmetic surgery tourism routes map later. These MTFs work to bridge cultural and linguistic barriers that patients may encounter, as other researchers have also discussed:

> Usually if you visit a country, you've got to adapt to that country's culture when you go there. But when a medical tourist comes, you can't expect them to adapt to your culture. You've got to adapt to their culture because they're sick people that come here. There's just not time for that. So, in Malaysia, people have to learn about other cultures that are coming here. (Malaysia-based MTF, cited in Ormond 2014a)

This bridging work is an important part of the conjuring of IMT that we discussed in chapter three; MTFs clearly understand the distinct needs of their clients, and leverage the skills and forms of capital they have in order to facilitate the patient's surgical journey. Cultural affinity enables these MTFs to undertake forms of care work that they alone can perform – helping them retain a foothold in the industry.

MTFs have thus carved out an important niche in the business landscape of IMT, and at least some also undertake forms of care work for patients, as well as handling logistics:

> If someone wants someone to be with them right through their entire surgery they can actually have someone there who speaks their own language. We had a patient who came and said, 'I am alone here, it would be nice if someone was here to talk to me and help me recover from my surgery', you know, because they were all bandaged up from all the cosmetic surgery. So, it depends, many come with their family members and they don't need anyone, but what happens to those who don't have anyone or don't know anyone? It is always nice to have someone there. (Patricia, Australia-based MTF)

MTFs we met talked about doing emotional work, too – reassuring clients during times of anxiety, especially before deciding to go ahead with the surgery. Some MTFs have a very hands-on approach, beginning with consultations and decision-making with surgeons and in the pre-op assessments – where they try to work through any remaining doubts the clients may have about the surgery – and continuing through recovery and return home. MTFs talked about clients getting 'clingy' or emotional after surgery, especially in the first couple of days. However, as former patients themselves, MTFs often have a very clear idea about what level of support is appropriate and so are able to judge when they feel that patients make unacceptable demands, proffering tough love if patients overstep this mark.

There was sometimes conflict between caring and business roles for MTFs, who had to undertake forms of boundary work with particular patients expressed in the distinction between having needs and being needy. As others have noted too, MTFs can take on forms of 'triage' in shaping patient choices not just about destinations and clinics but also about procedures and likely outcomes. They may also advise about the surgeon; some MTFs develop close relationships with particular surgeons and work to maintain these as a priority. Here, the MTFs can shape choice and provide confidence for patients, drawing on the social and cultural capital built in their personal relationships with particular surgeons (Snyder *et al.* 2011).

The work of converting enquiries into clients can take months, and draws in other forms of warm expertise such as that offered by former, current and prospective patients, connected through social media. This can, however, also be a source of conflict if patients feel as if they are being pushed towards a favoured surgeon (who might have bought that favour) rather than being offered experiential advice from someone who cares about them. MTFs thus have to delicately balance impressions, and recognise the value of 'face work' – direct, personal interactions with clients, whereby forms of care work and emotional labour can be performed – and the right balance struck between caring and business (McDonald 2011), or between the logic of care and the logic of choice (Mol 2008).

MTFs also engage in face work with surgeons, keeping up direct relationships with them, sometimes securing preferential treatment and price reductions for their patients. Social time spent with medical professionals, along with international travel, was a key marker of status and pleasure of the job identified by MTFs we spoke with, who cherished being treated to meals out with surgeons, knowing that these powerful men were reliant on them to bring in business. However, as we discuss in the next chapter, this is also a potentially fraught relationship, as surgeons can feel uneasy about the increasingly entrepreneurial world they are working in – a world embodied by MTFs they find themselves having to wine and dine, despite belonging to very different professional and social (and classed and gendered) worlds.

Precariousness and conflict

From our fieldwork, it became clear that it is the middle level of agents, those with their own companies and online presence, who are the most precarious. As former patients, these MTFs are usually early adopters who have travelled as pioneering patients along a previously untested route. Upon their return, when word gets out about their journeys, they are inundated with requests for information and contacts; on experiencing this deluge, they realise its commercial potential. In our study these MTFs were usually women. They did not have offices, but rather ran their businesses from cafes, hired meeting rooms (where they meet groups of potential patients) or spare rooms, kitchens and bedrooms in their own homes. Their unique selling point is the cultural and social capital that they have accrued from their own journeys and subsequently through building up and maintaining contacts and connections in clinics abroad. However, while this capital is valuable and worthy of a fee to the uninitiated, it quickly becomes available to anyone who follows in these pioneering agents' footsteps, and given that the patients seeking surgeries abroad are often on low incomes, the price of this rapidly accrued expertise can quickly become seen as too much, creating a source of tension between agents and patients. During our fieldwork we came across one such conflict which gave us a very clear insight into why many agents quickly go out of business (studies suggest up to 50 per cent of MTF businesses cease trading within five years; Turner 2011). It is worth discussing this in some detail here.

We met Marie, who was travelling from the UK to Poland for a breast uplift. During pre-surgery checks in her destination it became apparent that her blood pressure was far too high for surgery and the surgeon sent her home with clear instructions on how to lower it so she could return in six months for surgery. Marie was disappointed but returned to the UK, followed medical advice and was ready to resume her treatment at the later date. On her second visit she decided, since she now knew where to stay and how to contact the clinic, to bypass the agent and book the arrangements herself, saving herself the agent's fee. However, she also objected at this point to having paid for previous flights and accommodation for a visit when surgery had, after all, been denied her. As a patient on a very tight budget, she decided to ask the agent for a refund. Initially declining, after mounting pressure from Marie in posts on the agent's Facebook page, and having consulted a solicitor, the agent relented in the hope that 'paying off' her ex-client would be the easiest way to placate the growing volume of Marie's online complaints.

At this point, however, the agent's mother, finding her daughter's predicament unfair, waded into the argument through Facebook. A working-class woman from North East England, she did not choose her words carefully, and Marie perceived her post as a personal threat. Initially happy with the outcome of her breast uplift, Marie subsequently began to complain on Facebook about how the procedure was performed. She claimed to have visited a surgeon in the UK who had criticised not the result but the method of surgery. Having been successful first time around in recovering her travel expenses, she began to demand recompense, this time for the surgery itself. Since the agent did not facilitate this second trip the complaint was passed to the hospital and copied to the MTF who ran the portal on which the agent advertised. Complaints from Marie escalated; she began to say she was unhappy with the outcome of her surgery and eventually to accuse surgeons in the hospital she visited of having surreptitiously harvested organs from patients receiving abdominoplasties (this is a persistent rumour connected to IMT). She contacted newspapers, who were initially interested in a sensational story about the dangers of medical tourism, but after fact checking none of them were keen to pursue it. According to the agent, by the end of our fieldwork Marie had sent thousands of emails discrediting her agent – trolling, as the agent put it. While patient-consumers, both actual and potential, did not accept the veracity of Marie's complaints in their entirety, they talked about there being 'no smoke without fire', and patients in the destination awaiting their surgeries were clearly 'spooked'.

As we demonstrate in chapter six, patients in our study did not trust clinic websites and patient 'testimonials', but they relied heavily upon social media groups because they could talk to other patients in real time without mediation. The agent in this account also posted information about the progress of patients through pre-operative, surgery and post-operative recovery. She would publish Facebook posts along the lines of 'John is going down for surgery now. Everyone wish him luck'. And members of the group, both former and potential patients, would send their good luck wishes to John and await news of his recovery. In this sense it was an active and emotionally invested community.

While this process was designed to allay the fears of potential patients, some also accused the agent of downplaying medical complications. When we first arrived in Poland, for instance, we visited Jason (see chapter one), who the agent described online as having had a 'little bleed' when in fact he had needed three blood transfusions. It would be easy to view this as the downplaying of risk for profit, but we would suggest the scenario is more complex. Patients' feelings and anxieties have to be carefully managed – especially close to the point of surgery, when these are heightened. Adverse Facebook posts at this time can have catastrophic effects for whole cohorts of patients. The portal manager was tempted to remove the agent's ad from his site because bad publicity, even when arising from a single patient, could harm his business.

So, while male MTFs operate portals at some distance from patients, female agents are continuously managing the emotions – anxieties, hopes and jealousies – of patient-consumers in highly stressful situations, often without training and access to the appropriate (middle-class) therapeutic language. The enterprises of agents formed on the basis of small amounts of social and cultural capital are highly precarious and susceptible to failure. As the agent's story we have just recounted shows, MTFs are working on multiple fronts to manage relationships with patients, surgeons and other players in the industry, and this is no easy task.

One thing is clear from the discussion of MTFs, however: they 'play a crucial role in shaping medical tourism as a practice' (Snyder *et al.* 2011: 530), from both an industry and a patient perspective. In many ways they enable IMT to take place, and their curious in-between position also seems to embody how IMT is evolving as a phenomenon. To be sure, IMT could not exist without patient demand and without the supply of medical provision; but MTFs occupy a key role in the IMT assemblage and undertake much of the bridging work that holds IMT together (Chee *et al.* 2017). Yet, as noted above, the businesses are often very small and can be precarious (Turner 2011). While Chee *et al.* (2017) rightly stress the central role of MTFs in assembling medical tourism, we should also remember that the emergent, contingent nature of this assemblage can also create turbulence in the business landscape that MTFs are trying to maintain a foothold in. The 'conjuring' of networks by MTFs that we discussed in chapter three, then, is revealed here to be an ongoing and sometimes fraught activity, testing precisely the flexibility and resilience of MTFs and requiring of them the business skills of horizon scanning, contract negotiation, market analysis and remodelling – at the same time they variously take on forms of care work and emotional labour for patients (and their companions) and engage in networking with clinics and surgeons. Burnout would seem a likely explanation for at least some of the high number of business failures in the medical tourism sector.

Our fieldwork also brought us into contact with various other workers who, while not formally part of healthcare settings, clustered around these and offered tailored services for cosmetic surgery tourists. These included interpreters, drivers, people providing or servicing accommodation and so on. As other studies confirm, IMT opens up new business niches, from food provision aimed at suiting patients' tastes to medical supplies shaped by international medical tourists' post-surgery recovery needs (Howard 2010; McDonald 2011). These workers sometimes played vital roles in the day-to-day care of patients, building close relationships and becoming trusted helpmates (see also Bochaton 2015; Ormond 2015b).

One vexed issue with MTFs concerns the 'M' part – 'medical'. While this should arguably be read only in conjunction with 'tourist' – these are facilitators of medical tourists, after all – there can be slippage around whether MTFs are medically qualified to offer advice on treatments and aftercare (or even to provide hands-on care). Here we see another form of boundary work, with medical staff in facilities keen to distinguish their roles from those of MTFs (and IPCs) who are seen as members of administration at best, and at worst as unaffiliated and pushy hangers-on who are effectively preying on patients. Crucially, for staff in facilities, MTFs should not be confused with medical workers (their 'triage' role thus reconfigured as marketing rather than care work). Uniforms and job titles take on considerable importance in managing these impressions.

Yet the reality of IMT is that MTFs can have close and very direct relationships with patients – often much closer than staff in hospitals and clinics. Many MTFs trade on this, in fact. In this respect, arguably MTFs reflect the increasing consumerisation of healthcare more than anything else: they have enterprisingly inserted themselves into a new landscape that uneasily blends care and commerce, and they constantly negotiate this boundary. So, while they are sometimes dismissed as little more than 'cheerleaders for the industry' (Cohen 2015: 27), we have worked in this chapter to offer a more systematic, sympathetic and nuanced depiction of the work that MTFs do – the work of assembling medical tourism:

> Healthcare on its own is probably the most fragmented industry that there is: insurance groups do their own thing, the pharmacies do their own thing, the clinics do their own thing, the private hospitals do their own thing. All these stakeholders – whether it is a second home, whether it is the hotels, whether it is the airlines, whether it is the government – they are not in sync and everybody turns to people like us to deliver that. (Naomi, Australia-based MTF)

As noted, a key way in which MTFs act as intermediaries is in linking patients to surgeons and other healthcare workers – to whom our attention turns in the next chapter.

Notes

1 We are mindful that in the academic literature, work and labour take on distinct meanings; however, we use both terms here, in part reflecting each term's usage in previous research. For example, emotional labour is often defined as occurring in the paid workplace, whereas emotion work takes place in the private space of the home. These distinctions seem to us to be more blurred than clear cut, and our use of the terms reflects this.
2 For a sketch of the IMT industry, see Cohen (2015).

5

The work of cosmetic surgery tourism II:
health workers and patients

The previous chapter provided an overview of the structure of the cosmetic surgery tourism industry as a prelude to a detailed exploration of the forms of work undertaken by some of the key actors in the cosmetic surgery tourism assemblage. Basing our discussion in sociological debates about 'new' forms of work or labour – care work, body work, emotional labour and aesthetic labour – we showed how informal caregiving companions and MTFs carry out these types of work throughout the patient journey; both groups enable patients to undertake that journey, from its beginning to its end. They are, after all, intermediaries – mediating between supply (healthcare providers) and demand (patients). In this second chapter on work we turn our attention more fully to those workers who are brought together at the heart of the assemblage: nurses, doctors and patients themselves. We argue at the end of the chapter that 'patienting' is a particular and crucial type of work.

Health workers

In the discussion that follows, we focus mainly on what Connell and Walton-Roberts (2016) refer to as 'skilled healthcare workers', though the question of what constitutes skill might make us pause for thought. Another way to draw a line around our focus is to say we are interested here in healthcare professionals, but here too we find uneasiness about who is included and who is excluded from such a definition. As noted in the last chapter, however, some actors in IMT are keen to make a distinction between medical professionals and other workers drawn into the IMT assemblage – with the 'M' of MTFs a particularly contested issue. So, perhaps it is simpler to say that our focus here is mainly on nurses and doctors. We do not, therefore, talk about particular novel forms of work that have emerged in the medical world of IMT, such as commercial surrogates or transnational organ donors (see, for example, Pande [2010] and Scheper-Hughes [2011], respectively, for discussion of these specific areas). And here we separate out those whose work is at the biomedi-cal end of healthcare (on the whole) from those engaged in healthcare man-agement and administration (though we should acknowledge the vital roles played by non-medical staff in healthcare, and indeed by the countless things that circulate through the spaces of IMT – things like medical records, insur-ance policies, travel documents, accreditation certificates, medical devices and so on; Wilson 2015).

Nursing staff

In terms of nurses, there is surprisingly little research situated specifically in the IMT context – surprising given the front-line nature of nursing work and its flexible combination of care work, body work, emotional labour and aesthetic labour. More than anything or anyone else, nurses are engaged in 'the conduct of care' in their daily working lives (Latimer 2000). Staff in IMT facilities are frequently characterised by their 'naturally caring' attrib-utes, assumed as elements of national character – and often assessed favour-ably by patients in comparison with medical care at home. Attentiveness, patient-centredness or customer service, dedication and care are among the positive attributes identified by Canadian international medical tour-ists when receiving care abroad (Crooks *et al.* 2015). From the perspective of critical research on work, we can see how medical staff might be compelled to perform national character in ways that meet the needs of international medical tourists – performing the kind of 'surface acting' that Hochschild (1983) describes among flight attendants. This assumption about caring attributes, as discussed earlier, is used as part of 'national branding' in IMT – for example, Thailand is 'the land of a thousand smiles' – and healthcare workers are clearly on the front line of this, too. The discursive reach of this ideoscape of natural care draws patients into particular cosmetic surgery tourism assemblages.

Note that customer service is a prized aspect of the patient–worker experi-ence according to Crooks and colleagues: making patients into consumers changes the nature of the relationship between patients and staff in both posi-tive and negative ways (see also Mol 2008). For workers, the requirement to embody this new service ethos at the same time as they carry out forms of care, body and emotion work, can place considerable strain on staff like nurses – leading at times to conflict with patients who might be seen as demanding too much or crossing boundaries (Whittaker & Chee 2015). In high-end hospital-hotels, this clash between care and commerce can be especially apparent as the space is reconfigured to meld luxury and indulgence with medicalised care (Bochaton & Lefebvre 2009; Whittaker & Chee 2015). Health workers in such settings are often called upon to selectively perform both strategic essen-tialism (emphasising positive national and natural attributes) and strategic cosmopolitanism (welcoming difference as embodied in medical tourists), changing their workplace identities and the nature of nursing as work. While this issue has been studied in the context of migrant health workers (Dyer *et al.* 2008; Yeoh & Huang 2015), it is equally apparent in instances where patients travel to different national/cultural contexts and health workers are required to adjust their working practices to meet their needs. In fact, these two forces sometimes combine, as job opportunities in hospitals servicing international medical tourists can lead to internal and transnational migration of health workers, and so two ethnoscapes converge (Beladi *et al.* 2015; Connell 2011b). We experienced these multiple mobilities in our own research, as health workers and patients were all on the move, coming together sometimes only briefly as their ethnoscapes converged on a particular cosmetic surgery tourism destination. For example, one clinic we visited in Spain was staffed by an Italian surgeon, Irish and Spanish nurses and an English patient coordinator. These workers assembled for a few days each month to treat around ten UK patients, dispersing again in stages as patients moved along their care convoy, reassembling again the following month (Holliday *et al.*, 'Brief encounters', 2015).

Our research found that nurses could be required to perform forms of aesthetic labour too. In South Korea many of the nurses had undergone the facial surgeries sold to their employers' patients – they modelled cosmetic surgery and embodied the skill of the surgeon. These nurses told us that they preferred to work in cosmetic clinics because the work was interesting and more about assisting surgeons than emptying bedpans. The patients were younger, healthier and less demanding than those encountered in general nursing, and they were also more pleased with their outcomes. Nursing was thus experienced as more enjoyable in the cosmetic surgery clinic than in other healthcare settings, and the requirement to model facial surgery was seen more as a benefit than an imposition.

We also found that international hospitals that have a strong focus on foreign patients employ staff specifically to do emotional work, yet who are differentiated from nurses. At hospitals we visited in Thailand, these were Filipino nurses, university trained in the Philippines but not granted permission to work in nursing roles in Thai clinics. These care workers are employed for their English language and communication skills more generally. Their role involves checking on the patient regularly throughout their stay, making sure they understand what is happening, keeping them company and helping to calm them if they are feeling anxious. Here we see another manifestation of how health worker mobility intersects with new employment opportunities created by the changing global health marketplace (and also how it is limited by regulations in labour markets, such as those that refuse to accept foreign nursing qualifications as fully equivalent to those conferred at home).

Surgeons

Clinicians have, like nurses, also been under-studied in contemporary IMT research. There is some published research by doctors on the supposed dangers of medical tourism and on its costs to home healthcare (Jeevan & Armstrong 2008; Miyagi *et al.* 2012), but these accounts are readable as forms of protectionism as much as anything else, and do not shed any empirical light on the overseas doctors allegedly burdening home healthcare with their 'botched' surgeries and dubious procedures (Gimlin 2014). Beyond this, there is a small body of important work on how medical professionals have had to adapt their professional identities as they have sought to internationalise their patient base, for example about how small-scale private practice doctors in Greece are attempting to enter the IMT marketplace (Skountridaki 2015). This has necessitated working alongside new professionals in the sector, such as MTFs – and doctors have been seen to struggle with these new relationships:

> The very moment these actors [MTFs] fill a void in the new market [of IMT], they threaten to differentiate traditional power balances and potentially forge new dynamics. … Medical professionals experience the leverage of facilitators as perturbing and remain cautious in their collaborations. (Skountridaki 2017: 255)

This caution and perturbation relates to the role of MTFs in aggregating both supply (doctors) and demand (patients) and in their intervention into the doctor–patient relationship. So, while MTFs employ face work to wine and dine with doctors, as discussed in the previous chapter, these interactions can be fraught as both parties struggle for power and work to (re-)establish their professional identities and relationships. While surgeons might happily delegate some tasks involved in IMT to MTFs, from handling the financial side to marketing and promotion, this may at the same time challenge the medic's sense of professional identity and autonomy (Skountridaki 2017). As one interviewee said to us:

> It's also quite difficult to work with patient people [MTFs] who are not from the medical field. They also might not understand the procedures, they only get the feedback from the patient and sometimes they have to have confrontations with the patients. If they have a problem the patient has to go to them first and it's quite difficult. (Dr B, surgeon, Thailand)

Part of the struggle for medical professionals – aside from having to work with new collaborations – is the requirement to change their own professional identity, to marry medical practice with entrepreneurial or enterprising characteristics, and a care and service ethic with business-mindedness (Skountridaki 2015). In countries with at least some healthcare still under public provision, this requirement to reorient the medic's professional identity (and to some extent work practices) can be especially difficult to reconcile. In cases such as the UK, austerity, demographic changes and rising healthcare costs demand new behaviours and ideologies across the health sector, leading to what has been labelled 'public sector entrepreneurialism' (Lunt *et al.* 2015).

Surgeons do make occasional appearances in ethnographic accounts of IMT, and they frequently pop up in patients' recounting of their experiences, where they are evaluated (and usually praised) in ways that echo discussions of overseas nursing care. Here we draw on selected studies that specifically discuss cosmetic surgeons in IMT settings, supplementing our discussion with insights from sociological and anthropological work on surgeons (and cosmetic surgeons) more generally, and from our own empirical data, which included interviews with thirty-six surgeons in nine destination countries.

At the heart of surgeons' work in cosmetic surgery tourism is, of course, the work of surgery, of using surgical skill to alter the body of the patient. So, surgeons engage in a particular form of body work, directly labouring on patients, as our opening visit to a clinic in Bangkok showed (see chapter one). Surgical work is central to surgeons' professional identity and standing, and it is work that needs to be practised. For some surgeons, international patient flows are important as they enable skills to be maintained and even enhanced – if there is an oversupply of doctors relative to the domestic patient load, then working on tourists can become an alternative to becoming a tourist yourself and working abroad. Surgeons we spoke with (as is true in other studies) were keen to emphasise their high skill level – not just as individuals, but at the national scale. Aesthetic surgeons (sometimes the preferred title in the profession) must be both scientists and artists – many we met exhibited their own art, and sometimes they drew comparisons between their surgical work and forms of artistic expression, justifying their choice of surgical specialism in terms of the positive impact on patients of aesthetic transformation:

> I find it interesting that we are able to construct new details [to features]. Also, there is no right answer, as cosmetic surgery is all about making changes. It's not a matter of fixing something definitively, like an illness, but about reconstructing something. As a result, you can to some extent incorporate your own styles to create something new. (Dr V, surgeon, Korea)

> It is a very creative field, where you can try a lot of new things. Since the industry is very dynamic and a lot of new methods are being introduced, it is a very interesting field to work in. Throughout the year it is very rare to perform the same type of surgery – it is always different. So, compared to other branches of medical surgery, where the types of operations you perform are very similar and generic, cosmetic surgery is a lot more fun. (Dr A, surgeon, Korea)

In the above accounts, collected in fieldwork in the Gangnam district of Seoul, we can hear a number of defining characteristics that set cosmetic surgery apart from other medical specialisms: that it is about 'reconstructing' rather than 'fixing' the patient's body after illness, that it is creative and innovative with considerable variety and scope for individual expression by the surgeon – and that it is 'fun'. Another Korean surgeon made the point that it is rarely a matter of life and death – he had been upset by the death of one of his patients earlier in his career, and so welcomed the comparative safety of cosmetic surgery. And below we can see how the notion of the creativity of cosmetic surgery is stitched into Dr Z's biographical narrative:

> I was, you know, kind of fresh from hospital and I wasn't really sure what I wanted to do, so I was tossing up between general surgery or emergency medicine or obstetric gynaecology, and then along the way, someone says to me, 'You know, you're very artistic' – because I sculpt and I paint, and I'm always, you know, doing things with my hands, ceramics or something, you know. I did film production, I did some films so I've always had an artistic side. And someone said to me, 'Look, you know, it seems like you should really go into cosmetic medicine'. Initially I was a bit resistant to the idea, but when I agreed to go and assist a surgeon with his work and I started to see him do the work and I said, 'Well, why don't you do it this way?', and he kept saying to me, 'No, well, this is how it is done'. I said, 'Well, who said?' you know, 'Why don't you do it this way? Have you thought about approaching the subject from this angle, rather than this angle?' And I got really frustrated because he was like, 'No, this is how it is done'. I said, 'Well, fine, I think I need to branch out and I need to actually start playing with this product myself.'

When asked whether moving into cosmetic surgery had allowed Dr Z the opportunity to bring more creativity into his new role, he responded:

> Yes, absolutely, absolutely. I do that every day and then to me it really is just like all of a sudden, I have married my medical degree with an art degree and then I can really just combine the two and I feel like my life has been fulfilled because I've always been a frustrated doctor because I was always looking for artistic stuff to do outside of medicine. And, you know, when I left medicine completely and did film production, and I thought well actually I miss medicine, so I had to come back and then – you know, like most artists, I guess sometimes it's front of you but you can't see it. And then eventually it just falls – you know, it fell in the centre. So yes, I am where I'm supposed to be. (Dr Z, surgeon, Australia)

More succinctly, Dr C, a surgeon in a Polish clinic, said to us that she felt like she was 'a magician! I change ugly things into beautiful ones', and a surgeon in Thailand said that in his work 'I have to paint every patient, and not the same'.

While there are potentially worrying elements of a 'Pygmalion complex' at work here (see Jones 2008a, 2009) – the idea of a man crafting a perfect woman – we found that the situation was generally far more nuanced, with surgeons actively listening to what patients wanted (and the surgeons we met were both men and women and were working on men's as well as women's bodies).

Surgeons, moreover, explained job satisfaction in terms of what their aesthetic transformations did for their patients, and this was normally couched in terms of self-esteem and self-confidence:

> A lot of women change completely their attitude to life after breast enlargement surgery. They feel more confident and more feminine after the surgery. They know that they are more attractive for their partners when they are nude, sometimes also they are more attractive for themselves when they look in the mirror. They have a more positive attitude toward their own body. (Dr J, surgeon, Poland)

> First of all, when the results are good the patients gain self-confidence with their look, so it is also good for their mental health. Rather than just simply getting beautiful, there can be many other benefits such as getting the wanted attention from others, or an enhanced social life. So, from a social point of view there can be benefits too. (Dr N, surgeon, Korea)

These accounts chime with Alexander Edmonds's (2010) discussion of what he calls 'aesthetic health' – a discourse and practice he encountered in clinics in Brazil. Here, surgeons understood their intervention not to be limited to bodily transformation, but also to assist with psychological issues that their patients experienced, such as low self-esteem. In our field sites, a similar discourse is clearly evident, and surgeons understand their work as treating the whole person, even when the surgical intervention is focused on a particular body part. In addition, while the status and position of surgeons and patients in cosmetic surgery is very different, in many ways they share the same pragmatic understanding that 'bodily enhancement makes you happier'. Patients and surgeons speak the same language – a very different language from the cosmetic surgery discourse of pathology that we outlined in chapter two. Patients are happy, for instance, to have their small breasts labelled as 'micromastia' because such medicalisation names their problem and legitimates their surgery. When surgeons occasionally talked about women arriving at clinics trying to hide in their clothes and walking out as 'princesses', the construction was gendered rather than sexist. Surgeons were on the side of their patients, locating surgery as an appropriate response to pressures on women in a sexist culture, albeit an individualised response. Being a princess was associated with strength and independence, the courage to go through surgery in search of a better life – not the kind of princess who lies sleeping and waiting for her prince. Nevertheless, this discourse had nothing but silence to offer the considerable proportion of male patients travelling for cosmetic surgery.

Surgeons' work is not confined to the clinic and the operating table; nor is it confined to the work of surgery itself. As other ethnographic studies have teased out, surgeons in IMT destinations are undertaking various labours. Sara Ackerman's (2010) research in Costa Rica explores the many forms of work carried out by surgeons, who, like the nurses discussed above, contribute to the notion of the Costa Rican nation and its people as 'naturally healing'. For US patient-travellers, being in Costa Rica provides a form of 'medical nostalgia' – a return to earlier times, before rampant privatisation and consumerisation damaged US healthcare. This nostalgia is projected onto doctors as well as nurses, who are all seen to provide forms of patient-centred care unavailable back home (and, it should be noted, which healthcare workers felt unable to provide in public health facilities in Costa Rica – so the workers also experience a kind of medical nostalgia for past, better times).

As Ackerman (2010: 414) recounts, patients she spoke with 'bragged … about their doctors' and nurses' amiability, generosity, and charm in addition to their surgical handiwork. One woman said about her surgeon: "He loves you, he nurtures you, he takes care of you … and he is one of the most brilliant surgeons".' She adds that doctors visited the 'recovery retreats' that patients recuperated in, offering house calls that mixed aftercare with socialising. Doctors here did not make patients feel like 'walking chequebooks', as one of our participants put it regarding the domestic private sector, but deployed forms of emotional labour and care work in order to both help their patients heal and to market Costa Rica as a restorative destination for international medical tourists, relying on word-of-mouth referrals from the patients they were currently lavishing care upon. Medical staff critical of the poor state of public healthcare in their own country argued that working in these privatised settings allowed them to provide more 'Costa Rican' care. The attentiveness of surgeons (and nurses) in IMT resorts is therefore the perfect marriage of job satisfaction and patient-centredness: doctors can do the kind of doctoring they want to, and patients respond very positively to this doctoring (on doctoring, see Mol 2008).

Across our field sites, we routinely heard stories of surgeons 'going the extra mile' and providing personal care services that were contrasted with poor care experienced in domestic healthcare. A patient who travelled from Australia to Thailand for surgery said of her surgeon:

He's gorgeous, lovely, we get along. He took the blame for my infection, but nobody knows when you are going to get it or how you get it. … He feels some of the blame, when I was discharging he took me back into surgery in his own time. That was complimentary. He sewed me up again and unstitched the layers, washed it down and sewed me up again. That was in his own time and he hasn't charged me. He came to see me in hospital every day and he didn't charge me once. (Riri, Australia to Thailand)

This patient also favourably compared her post-surgery scarring with scars her mother was left with following a caesarean section in a domestic hospital. Such home–abroad comparisons often focused on the financial side – Riri kept repeating that she was not charged for follow up visits or revision. Similarly, the patient quoted below contrasts private domestic healthcare with that he encountered abroad:

When I'd had the operation and I was still in the recovery room under anaesthetic, the surgeon … came down to my Mum and said, 'I've done the best I can', he's – you know, he didn't have an interpreter, he spoke broken English. I thought that was really good, because when you go [to a private UK clinic] and they want to charge £150 before they even want to speak to you, [whereas here] the guy who's done the operation, instead of sending a nurse down or somebody else, actually himself came down. (Carl, UK to Poland)

Other patients described non-medical forms of care work undertaken by surgeons, and how this impacted on their sense of the doctor–patient relationship – again, usually in contrast to poor experiences or expectations back home:

That surgeon there, he went out and got me a DVD. Who's going to do that here? He'd seen a DVD that he thought I'd like because it was a comedy and it was funny and he went out and got it for me. … Now, you try and find a surgeon here that will do that. I would imagine they're very rare. … He's a lovely, lovely man. A lovely guy and not just a good surgeon, but a nice guy … Yeah, he was somebody I could have been friends with, you know. (Joe, UK to Poland)

While not expressly articulated in terms of medical nostalgia, this kind of comparing and contrasting is powerfully used to legitimate the choice to travel abroad for treatment – as we discuss below, patients frequently engage in forms of talk that work to justify their treatment (and travel) decisions. Here is a field note from our research in Thailand:

Riri talked a lot about her surgeon and how very impressed she was with him. He seems to have a closer interaction with her as patient than one would expect of a busy surgeon. When he went to visit her in hospital for a check-up and discharge on the day after her surgery, he then drove her back to her hotel. They chatted in the car about Riri's plans to go to medical school, and his former teaching work in Chiang Mai. Riri and her Mum told me at length about how genuine and friendly he is, and how his caring personality is evident in his efforts to take care of patients beyond his responsibilities in surgery and consultation. She was practically bragging about how good he was. (Emily talking with Riri, Australia to Thailand)

The 'bragging' by this patient is clearly part of the ongoing justification talk, and is testimony to the powerful impact that these forms of care work by surgeons have on the patient experience. It is also worth noting that many of our patient-consumers were comparing private healthcare abroad with public healthcare back home. While the US patients discussed in previous studies see surgeons back home as money grabbing, our UK and Australian travellers more often saw them as aloof, uncaring or simply overstretched. Interestingly, when we asked surgeons about this contrast between working in public and private healthcare, while many expressed a preference for private work and the less pressured environment it offered, one surgeon told us: 'There is no difference. In public healthcare they make you work too hard to save money. In private healthcare they make you work too hard to make money.'

It is notable from our fieldwork conversations that patients undergoing cosmetic surgery make aesthetic judgements about the medical staff they encounter, including doctors (see also McDonald 2011). Finding your surgeon handsome seems to inspire confidence in the aesthetic judgements he will deploy in the surgical makeover. So, while many of the patients we met talked about surgeons as caring, some spoke of them as attractive, too. One patient travelling to Tunisia told her MTF before she went that she found her surgeon very sexy and that she intended to sleep with him while she was there. This was not the only example of a surgical encounter tinted by romance and desire when doctors meet patients in cosmetic surgery tourism.

One key site where doctors and patients meet and assess each other is in the space of the clinical consultation. Here both parties are working to reach agreement about the treatment and about the surgeon being the best person to perform it. While these forms of labour might contribute to a positive outcome – in terms of the decision to go ahead with surgery and with that surgeon in particular – surgeons must also work in the consultation to build trust and to manage patient expectations. As one clinician wrote in a medical journal commentary, discussing the consultation, and contra the view of the Polish surgeon we quoted earlier: 'plastic surgeons ... are mere mortals; we perform operations with scalpels, not magic wands' (Rohrich 2002: 1507). The consultation requires performances on both sides, therefore – and the work of managing expectations, generating trust, creating the right impression and understanding each other. In the cross-national encounters of cosmetic surgery tourism, this requires extra effort from both parties.

Previous studies have shown how consultations with cosmetic surgeons can sometimes be sites of power play between doctors and patients (Heyes & Jones 2009; Spitzack 1988). Julien Mirivel (2008) shows how doctors' embodied and discursive activities work to shape a particular outcome, and how surgeons tread a fine line between recommending and selling surgery. This means engaging in emotional labour and care work at the same time as working towards a surgical decision. As one clinician in Mirivel's study said: 'results are not the only thing patients are looking at. Patients are also looking at how they are treated. They want an experience. They want to come here and feel special. They want to feel like they're the only ones that matter and we try to make them feel that way' (156). The consultation is thus a vital step in the patient's treatment journey towards becoming a valuable subject, and doubly so perhaps when that journey involves actual travel. While Mirivel writes that US clinicians do not offer reassurance or support to prospective patients, what we witnessed in our field sites is exactly this form of labour, performed by surgeons (see also Ackerman 2010; McDonald 2011). While many overseas surgeons are seen as possessing good technical skills, and are chosen on this basis, those most in demand by patients are also sophisticated care workers.

In our fieldwork in Seoul, we took time to talk with surgeons about their profession, its history and current form, and also about their careers and the status of cosmetic surgery (Holliday *et al.* 2017; see also DiMoia 2013). One recurring theme in their discussions was national pride – especially in the global reputation of Korean cosmetic surgery. A clinic in Seoul that we visited had a museum of cosmetic surgery in its foyer, which embedded surgical practices in the context of Korean culture and celebrated Korea's world standing in this medical field (figure 5.1). Similar narratives of pride in cosmetic surgeons' expertise have also been described in Brazil (Edmonds 2007, 2010, 2011), where it is likewise yoked to a discourse of national (economic) development and repositioning on the world stage. Surgeons in both countries trade on their fine aesthetic tastes, seeing themselves as artists, and also on their willingness to experiment with new techniques. In the story of the development of cosmetic surgery as a medical specialism in both nations, too, there is a shared emphasis on the domestication and localisation of skills, made to better fit the national body – a fit that later becomes exportable as particular bodily attributes of Brazilianness and Koreanness take on regional (and sometimes global) value.

In the case of Korea, cosmetic surgeons we spoke with expressed pride in the global standing of their profession, but sometimes tempered this with worries about the external perception that they are 'playboys' and with anxieties about the legitimacy and status of their specialism compared with other forms of medical work. So, they couched working in cosmetic surgery as a

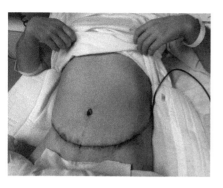

1.1a Jason straight after surgery. Surgeons say results look best 'on the table'

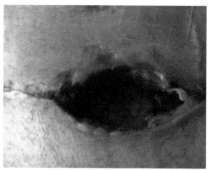

1.1b Jason's complication – a 'little bleed' and ruptured stitches

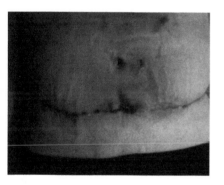

1.1c Jason's infection needed vacuum pump treatment in an NHS facility

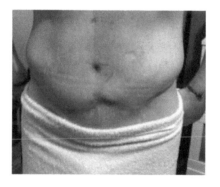

1.1d Jason's final result, front

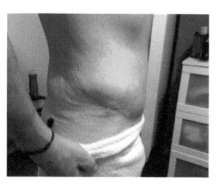

1.1e Jason's final result, side

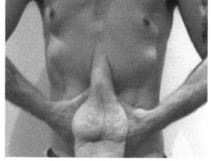

1.2 Neil (UK to Czech Republic and Poland) demonstrating what he called his 'mushroom' after weight-loss surgery but before body contouring

1.3 A bedside table in a Tunisian clinic

1.4a Durian street-seller in front of a budget Bangkok clinic

1.4b Waiting room, budget Bangkok clinic

1.5 Clinic Exterior in Seoul. Sad Rabbit? Or perhaps not a happy bunny?

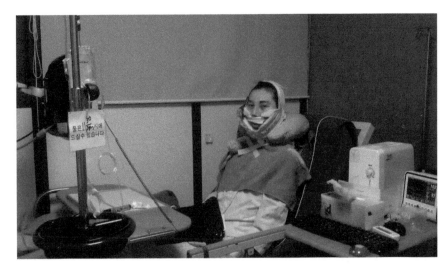

2.1a Hwang, day 1

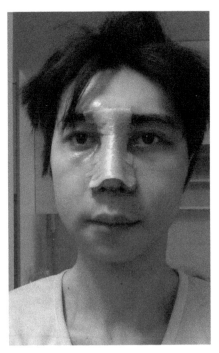

2.1b Hwang, day 2

2.1c Hwang, day 5

2.1d Hwang, day 6

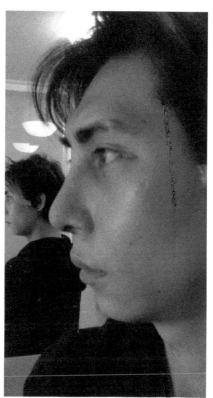

2.1f Hwang, day 7(2)

2.1e Hwang, day 7(1)

2.2a Non-medical silicone being squeezed from a PIP implant

2.2b Ruptured implant silicone should stay in place like a 'jelly baby' but PIP filling seeps through the body

3.1a Advertisement in Apdugeong, Seoul, South Korea

3.1b Advertisement in Gangbeong, Seoul, South Korea

3.1c Advertisement in Tunis, Tunisia

3.1d Advertisement in Marbella, Spain

3.2a Bed in clinic in Itaewon, Seoul, South Korea

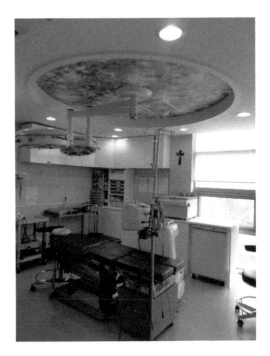

3.2b Operating room in Apdugeong, Seoul, South Korea

3.2c Clinic window, Marbella, Spain

3.2d Clinic registration area, Poland

3.3 Different types of breast implant on desk, Marbella, Spain

4.1 Rollerblading hospital assistant at Yanhee Hospital, Bangkok

According to Korean proverb a tiger leaves his coat after his death, and a patient undergone jaw reduction surgery leaves a piece of bone after his operation.

5.1a Jawbone 'shavings' on display in the BK Clinic's Cosmetic Surgery Museum, Seoul, South Korea

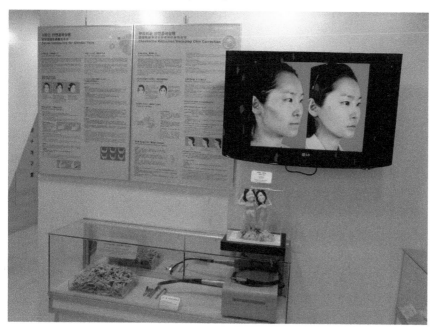

5.1b Display in the BK Clinic's Cosmetic Surgery Museum, Seoul, South Korea

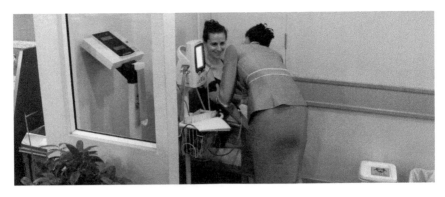

7.1a Sue (Australia to Thailand) consultation, 26 May 2012

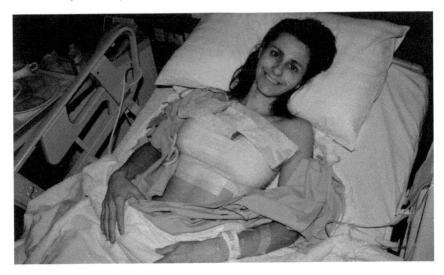

7.1b Sue post-operation, 28 May 2012

7.1c Sue enjoying Thailand (1), 31 May 2012

7.1d Sue enjoying Thailand (2), 1 June 2012

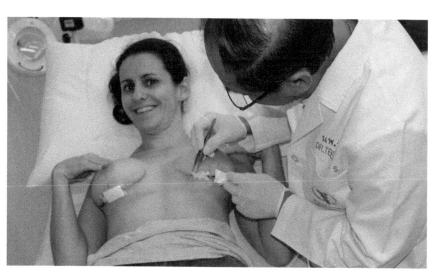

7.1e Sue having her stitches removed, 2 June 2012

7.1f Sue thanking her nurses, 2 June 2012

7.2a Tourist facilities are used out of season by international medical tourists

7.2b A recovering patient taking a photo at her hotel in Tunisia

7.2c Marbella hotels used by medical tourists

8.1a A pile of refuse behind the hospital in Tunisia

8.1b A dog near the hospital in Tunisia: 'All I could hear was what sounded to me like a pack of wolves' (Sally, UK to Tunisia)

8.2a View from taxi on journey from airport to clinic, Tunisia

8.2b Rear-view mirror decoration, Tunisian taxi

way of keeping their surgical skills 'warm', as a way to develop new techniques that might have broader medical use, and in terms of contributing to national pride and profile (Holliday *et al.* 2017), as these two interview extracts show:

> The overall impression of cosmetic surgeons isn't very good. For example, in television dramas and sitcoms we are portrayed in such a stereotype that shows us as rich, extravagant playboys. So yes, not a very good image at all. However, we still hold a sense of pride in that Korea is the number one in the world regarding cosmetic surgery, and we as cosmetic surgeons play a vital part in that, so that may be of some consolation to us. (Dr U, surgeon, Korea)

> I believe Korea is comparatively much more innovative compared to the rest of the world when it comes to cosmetic surgery. I can proudly say that even Europe is impressed at some of the skills we possess. (Dr F, surgeon, Korea)

Our discussion of the clinical consultation, above, focused on the work of the surgeon in steering the patient towards a desired outcome. This might be seen to imply that patients are merely passive recipients of the surgeon's labours – they are worked on, even before their bodies are surgically reshaped. But we want to counter that implication by closing this chapter with a turn to a key but often neglected group of people who are engaged in forms of work along the IMT journey: patients themselves.

The work of patients

To speak of patients as working seems to turn the idea of work on its head: patients are surely on the receiving end of the work of others? They are patients or they are consumers, surely, rather than workers or producers of healthcare? But we would argue that 'patienting' is a particular type of work, which incorporates the four forms of labour outlined above (and much more besides). And it is work that is vital to the IMT assemblage, as patient-travellers undertake work that sits at the interface of tourism and health.

To begin, like other tourists (and like many health consumers), they undertake what we might call the work of choosing and deciding. The patient-traveller's journey starts with information-gathering and decision-making, and this can be both intensive and extensive work. In our study we found that participants had been thinking about surgery for a long time, sometimes five to ten years; researching treatment options, often at home and abroad; weighing up pros and cons, gathering information, talking – to their friends and families, to other patients and would-be patients, to MTFs and to surgeons. Guidebooks, websites, discussion forums and other online resources become vital aids in this information-gathering and decision-making process, and often these texts themselves help to frame patient-tourists in particular ways

– as 'transformative agents [and] independent, self-advocating consumers' (Ormond & Sothern 2012: 938). So, there is identity work going on at this stage: the work of imagining oneself into the identity 'cosmetic surgery tourist'. Given that our participating patients were not worldly, cosmopolitan jet-setters, this identity work could prove uncomfortable and arduous, requiring justification to self and others that undertaking a surgical journey could be aligned with lifestyles not characterised by glamour and luxury.

Here we see the logic of choice at work, as patients mobilise a discourse of choosing as empowerment: as an active and informed practice that gives them agency in the healthcare marketplace. It is important to add that choosing is also about managing risk – this is a significant new form of work that patient-consumers are asked to take on. Here risk is individualised and is carried by the patient who chooses where to travel, what treatments to undergo, which surgeons and agents to use. In public health, as Mol (2008) notes, risk is managed by the institution, embodied by the doctor who we are compelled to trust and whose approach can seem paternalistic and unchallengeable ('the doctor knows best'). Private health patients can use their 'consumer power' to avoid the potential abuses of this approach, but the cost comes in shouldering the work of managing risk personally. One way in which patients work collectively to deal with this work is by providing advice and support to each other: patient communities have formed to help members make informed choices and thereby mitigate risk.

Sociologists such as Beck (1992) and Giddens (1990) argue that the current period of 'Reflexive Modernity' not only produces 'goods' but also many 'bads' by which we are threatened. We encounter these threats to ourselves as risks which we have to reflexively manage in this 'Risk Society'. Expert discourses order the world to make risks seem calculable. Institutions in the risk society make decisions that place citizens at risk but are not made accountable for doing so. We cannot escape risk altogether but must act as individuals to manage our own risk. Risk is made into an individualised, responsibilised choice. But it is important to note that risk is not absolute. Different societies see different activities as risky or not according to different cultural norms and values (Douglas 1992). And individuals are differently positioned in terms of risk–benefit calculations. When we asked a room full of academics at a conference if they would improve their appearance if all they had to do was wave a magic wand, for instance, the vast majority – men and women – said yes (with the exception of a small sub-set of feminists who felt resisting 'lookism' was a political principle). However, when we asked them if they would submit to surgery to improve, very few answered positively.

For a middle-class subject with many other sources of value, the risks of cosmetic surgery outweigh the benefits. This is mitigated somewhat by gender, since women are currently still judged more on their looks than men, especially when women's looks are integral to their income – either from employment or husbands. However, for those with fewer other sources of value, the risk of cosmetic surgery is worth taking. As we showed in chapter two, our patient-consumers' bodies are already commodified for the labour market and their aim is to add value to their bodies or, at least, to limit negative evaluations or devaluations. But again, many of those who would take the risk cannot afford surgery at home, so they opt to take an additional risk of travelling abroad to access it.

Cosmetic surgery tourism patient-consumers believe that risk can be known and managed. They spend considerable time and effort doing their research – exploring clinics, surgeons, agents, destinations, flights, accommodation, aftercare, surgical bandages, breast implants, when and how much to exercise after surgery and so on. Doing research on these factors helps to manage the anxieties of travelling to an unknown clinic in an unknown country to submit oneself, anaesthetised, to surgery in the face of the opinions of surgeons' organisations and the wider public back home that see cosmetic surgery tourism as a dangerous practice engaged in by reckless individuals. Like Ricardo Abadie's (2010) 'professional guinea pigs' making a living by volunteering for clinical trials, cosmetic surgery tourists' 'risk perception... is shaped by their ... experiences and interactions with other [cosmetic surgery tourists]'. As he puts it:

> risk perception is closely related to the socialization of the professional guinea pig. Paid subjects share narratives of which trials represent risk and which do not, and of how to deal with risk. Local knowledge shapes the social construction of risk and the strategies that volunteers use for coping with the risks they perceive. (Abadie 2010: 73)

Cosmetic surgery tourists minimise their perceived risk by doing research on the Internet, scanning for any bad press about a surgeon or clinic and forming communities where they share narratives about good and bad places to go, danger signs to look out for, good and bad experiences and results. These shared experiences and narratives reassure patient-consumers that the risk is worth taking. Unlike Abadie's professional guinea pigs, we encountered very few patients who had become blasé through multiple experiences of travel for surgery. However, patient-consumers were able to amass expertise collectively through shared stories, and crucially through agents, such that their perceptions of risk were far lower than non-cosmetic surgery tourists and society at large. It is worth pointing out that the work of managing risk by doing research as well as giving advice, sometimes over many years, is considerable, and ultimately the value of this work accrues to hospitals and clinics which are largely unregulated and unaccountable for the risks they transfer to patient-consumers.

In addition to research and information-gathering work – the work of choice and of managing risk – international medical tourists also engage in planning and logistical work, preparatory work in advance of their trip and in many cases what Beth Kangas (2002: 59) calls 'funding work': 'finding the money necessary to pay for treatment'. This may involve accessing loans (from banks or from friends and families) or savings, taking out forms of credit or deciding to prioritise surgery over other expenses, diverting expenditure away from things like home improvements or family holidays (and maybe persuading family members of the merits of this change of plan).

As previously noted, our participants were, on the whole, living on fairly modest means and could not simply reach into their pockets to pay for surgery. They had to find the money, and justify spending it in this way – to others and to themselves. In the context of cosmetic surgery tourism, part of the justification that comes into play here is the promised cost saving of travelling for treatment (and, in some cases at least, the promise of a holiday as part of the package). Yet this rationalising was ongoing for many of our participants, given the expense involved: talk about the surgery being 'worth it' continued throughout the journey, both pre- and post-surgery. Our participants continued to 'narrate' their trip and their transformation long after they returned home, whether to advise other would-be travellers or to reaffirm their choices to themselves and those around them. Echoing work by Keri Cameron *et al.* (2014) on patients travelling for joint surgery, we encountered many instances of motivation, justification and normalisation talk and work – respectively, narrating decision-making processes, offering critique of domestic healthcare and coming to identify as a medical tourist. In some cases, this ongoing narration (especially normalisation talk) was used to consider the broader ethics of medical tourism, as a way to voice concerns about healthcare provision at home and abroad, such that medical tourism might be rethought as a form of health activism (Ormond 2015a).

As well as destination choice and funding work, Kangas (2002) outlines forms of 'logistical work' undertaken by the Yemeni international medical tourists she worked with, work we also heard about from our participants. This included gathering further information about the (now chosen) destination and planning the trip itself, arranging travel and fixing dates, deciding who would accompany the patient and how home life would be managed in their absence, and mentally preparing for both trip and treatment. For some of our participating patients this was a totally new experience – leaving their children in the care of their partner for the first time, while they travelled abroad alone – and so the trip required careful preparation for those left behind as well as for the traveller. This preparatory work can be arduous and fraught, ongoing and subject to change. To aid in this logistical task list, international medical tourists frequently engage the services of MTFs, as discussed in chapter four. Emily McDonald (2011) reminds us that pre-surgical patient work includes collecting together things that will be needed later, such as medical supplies required for post-surgical recovery. She notes that the increasing investment (both financial and in terms of talk) builds momentum, making the trip increasingly inevitable. This momentum helps ensure patients overcome any last barriers that might hold them back.

Preparatory work also involves clinical consultation, of course. As already discussed from the doctor's side of the desk, consultation is a vitally important stage in the ongoing process of deciding to undergo surgery. For international medical tourists, the timing and location of initial consultation is less straightforward than for other patients. Some consultations take place in locations in the sending country, with doctors or their representatives renting consultation rooms for limited periods and assessing multiple potential patients – sometimes hiring rooms in prestigious locations, such as London's Harley Street, to add extra credibility. For surgeons, travelling to source countries and offering consultations there is another way to build their names – they may even undertake 'tours' of target countries (Cheung 2015). Other consultations happen on site in the destination country once the patient has arrived, though this can be a more fraught process, given the momentum already gathering thanks to the travel undertaken, which can make managing the doctor–patient interaction tricky for both parties. Many consultations are in fact undertaken virtually, using email, photos or videoconferencing:

> I explained, 'Look, I don't expect to look twenty, I just want to look less tired'. I don't expect to come out and everybody goes 'Oh My God!' I just didn't want to look quite as – as if my face was melting. You know, I was just tired, so I sent him another picture, the worst picture I could have taken of myself. It was horrific, honest. It would have scared children and animals, seriously bad. So, I sent that one off to him and he's like, 'Right, okay, fair enough'. So, I didn't feel the need to go over for a consultation. You know, words are words whether you're face to face or whether it's done by email or, you know. (Syeda, UK to Poland)

Where the consultation happens can have important impacts on how the surgical journey unfolds: whether the patient is able to access the treatment they want, for example. Patients are not just the passive recipients of the doctor's authority in consultations, however, contra some studies showing how cosmetic surgeons 'manage' patients towards particular procedures in the clinical consultation (Mirivel 2008). Patients empowered by the logic of choice come prepared, armed with their own research and their own understanding of the treatment they want. They sometimes have to work to get the surgeon to agree, and make sure both parties are clear about what is wanted and what is possible. Sometimes surgeons work to counter the unrealistic demands of patients, and sometimes patients struggle to articulate their choice – the breast size patients desired, for instance, was frequently larger than their surgeon thought necessary. These issues also emerged in our fieldwork in Seoul, when Korean surgeons met Chinese patients (see Holliday *et al.* 2017).

Of course, cosmetic surgery patient-tourists are undertaking care work, body work, emotional labour and aesthetic labour on themselves, as well as being 'worked on' in all these ways by countless others, as we have shown. But we also found patients helping each other and engaging in care work both on location and afterwards. Sometimes this mutual care is pre-planned, for example in organised group trips such as the 'Boobie Sisters' we travelled with from Australia to Thailand (see chapter six). At other times such practices are emergent, arising out of the particular situation: post-surgery patients are recuperating in the same spaces that pre-surgery new arrivals find themselves in, as Sara Ackerman (2010: 417–418) also found in Costa Rica. Here incoming patients were 'usually greeted by a congenial and bandaged group of guest-patients … These surgical veterans tacitly instruct newcomers in the rites of recovery sociality'. Together with healthcare workers, Ackerman suggests, they produce an 'effervescent hotel sociality' in the recovery retreat (417–418). Similarly, in one town in Poland in which we conducted fieldwork, patients were housed in an apartment block opposite a McDonald's restaurant. The patients met first through the MTF's Facebook group, then in person at the hospital. Many then arranged to meet up in their apartments upon discharge from hospital, or in McDonald's. Patients called on each other to solve problems like lost Internet connections or how to work the TV, and they advised each other on where to shop for groceries or what they could purchase in the market or the mall. Departing patients also passed on items like toilet rolls and washing powder to new arrivals (as pack sizes meant they purchased more than they used).

As discussed in studies of hospitality work, customers are increasingly called upon to perform work – informal, unpaid work that seems to be, in many cases, freely and gladly given (e.g. Lugosi 2009). This work may be seen as compensating for the distancing effects of IMT, which means that familiar/familial networks of care are too far away (Bolton & Skountridaki 2017). At other times, such informal care work is spontaneous, brought about by chance encounters of patients in destinations, or – as we saw in Tunisia – by the convivialities that can arise out of mutual vulnerability in healthcare settings. As we note in chapter eight, it is important to consider this as a form of work, too – convivial labour.

Ackerman (2010) adds that the women she met in Costa Rican recovery retreats were also engaging in 'moral triage' – talking about their own surgeries from a moral perspective, and also passing judgements on others, especially anyone they felt wanted unrealistic or 'excessive' surgeries. In Tunisia we saw this most vividly, as our cosmetic surgery participants were forced to reflect on their own practices vis-à-vis the Libyan Civil War casualties they encountered. Patients were, in general, very scathing of others who they perceived had not done their research properly, or patients that underwent too many procedures at once. Again, making bad choices was individualised and attached to other patients, actual but most usually those appearing on cosmetic surgery disaster TV, against whom our patients defined themselves. This moral triage can be seen as another example of the normalisation talk that Cameron *et al.* (2014) discuss – the work of producing a moral position and self-identity as a patient-consumer who is savvy rather than duped. Someone, in short, who knows how to choose.

Recipients of successful procedures often become advocates of cosmetic surgery (Adams 2010) – and those who have accessed treatment abroad become advocates of cosmetic surgery tourism, specifically. Some patients capitalise on their new 'expert' status by writing guidebooks or blogs, or by setting up as MTFs: one interviewee in our project said that 150 people had contacted her in the first month after her own surgery to ask for advice, which had prompted her to start her own MTF business. Other trailblazing patient-travellers are content to parlay their experiences as forms of warm expertise, informally advising others considering travel for surgery – just as they were themselves advised by previous patients. Social networks are in fact shown to be particularly influential in international medical tourists' decision-making at all stages, and patient-travellers occupy a privileged position in these networks, with valued and trusted experiential expertise (Hanefeld *et al.* 2015; Yeoh *et al.* 2013). As they themselves have travelled for surgery, they can mobilise the 'spatial capital' accrued by travel – perhaps as a form of 'cosmopolitan beginning' – as well as trading on the embodied and aesthetic capital of surgical success (Bochaton 2015; Yeoh & Huang 2015). We turn to the workings of these social networks in chapter six.

Conclusion

Our fieldwork vividly showed us time and again how IMT disrupts normal work roles and hierarchies in medical and healthcare work, and why it does so. The development of the IMT industry has both created new roles and changed existing ones – doctors have to become entrepreneurs while MTFs have to work to match supply with demand in a sometimes-turbulent environment. The forms of work undertaken multiply, and are sometimes taken up by unlikely providers, from patients themselves to people who might seemingly be carrying out only mundane labour, such as the drivers who transport patients around. In fieldwork in Poland we encountered one such driver, Jarek. Rather than a bit-part player in the cosmetic surgery tourism assemblage here, we found Jarek to have taken up a central and valued position – valued for his

English language skills and for his social and caring skills, which he deployed adeptly to ease patients into an unfamiliar place and experience. And Jarek was by no means alone in this. He is just one example of the ways in which care is provided for patients as they move through their surgical journeys. Our aim in these two chapters was to plot out some of the places where care work, body work, emotional labour and aesthetic labour get performed, and to show who does that work. The new landscapes of care that IMT both creates and requires are unsettling established ideas about what work means and who undertakes it, and about what constitutes healthcare.

6

Community and little narratives

In this chapter we explore how cosmetic surgery tourists form communities, sometimes in person but more often on social media and the websites that they use to conduct research, to meet others, and then to navigate, document and narrate their experiences. In addition to this, we show how some people use social media to make and maintain friendships and links connected with their surgical/travel experiences.

One sort of cosmetic surgery tourist stands out in her sociality and in her intent to make cosmetic surgery a social experience at every point. Usually in her twenties (although we have encountered some in their late teens), she travels in a group organised and led by an agent (MTF). The groups (usually of around ten to fifteen individuals) might consist of already established friends or of people who are introduced to each other by the agent. The tourists that we met in this category were mainly seeking breast augmentation and mainly originated in Australia. For them, the socialising, bonding and support that happens within and because of the group is crucial to a positive cosmetic surgery tourism experience. Once such group we spoke with had travelled from Australia to Thailand for breast augmentations and referred to themselves as the 'Boobie Sisters' to reflect the intense bond they felt for each other. If, as Margaret Gibson (2006: 53) suggests, 'as a category of identification and classification, the cosmetically altered body is now a type of social body', then these tourists embody a distinct form of sociality that arises from and in fact constitutes cosmetic surgery tourism.

As explained in chapter one, our approach builds on feminist work around cosmetic surgery that Victoria Pitts-Taylor (2009) has called 'post-essentialist' (see also Fraser 2003; Jones 2008a). A post-essentialist approach refuses 'to valorise an authentic, natural female body or a proper female subjectivity', while insisting that 'we must think of the meanings of bodily practices like cosmetic surgery as neither solely internal nor external but rather as intersubjective' (Pitts-Taylor 2009: 122). Post-essentialist analyses of cosmetic surgery see it as a practice that is formed through interknit actors, including technologies, media, patients, discourses, surgeons and narratives. Crucially, this mode of analysis does not seek to find reasons for cosmetic surgery in the psyches of individuals but rather to examine the complex medical, social, cultural and economic networks in which cosmetic surgery unfolds. It posits a nexus between materialities (of bodies and spaces) and communications. We argue that together these networks create – or assemble – the cosmetic surgery tourism experience (see chapter three). In this chapter we expand this thesis to show that the cosmetic surgery tourism body is not only surgically shaped into existence but is also called forth via new media that provide platforms for 'little narratives' (Poster 2001: 621) as well as caring human relationships and communities that would otherwise not exist.

Cosmetic surgery tourism has grown hand in hand with online media, through which patients contact agents, seek surgical information, view the qualifications and experience of medical professionals, book flights and accommodation, and see pictures of hospitals, locations and the results of procedures (Holliday *et al.*, 'Beautiful face, beautiful place', 2015). Indeed, it has been argued that cosmetic surgery tourism, and medical tourism more broadly, could not exist without the Internet (Cormany and Baloglu 2011). Since the arrival of Web 2.0, the ubiquity of social networking sites like Facebook and YouTube and the growth of blogging means that online media now also provide accessible space for peer-to-peer networking, planning, community building and storytelling between cosmetic surgery tourists. At once paralleling the rise of 'virtual tourism' and of online health-related networks, cosmetic surgery tourism is a densely mediated phenomenon even as it is profoundly embodied.[1]

Rebecca Huss-Ashmore (2000: 29) analysed conversations between cosmetic surgery patients, cosmetic surgeons and associated practitioners, and found that for most patients cosmetic surgery is a positive experience described in terms of 'transformation' and 'healing'. Importantly, she suggests that transformation and healing do not come about because of surgery alone, but also through talking. She notes that language in the clinic is paramount, and she listened to how narratives were created, recreated and performed by patients and medical practitioners, before and after surgeries. Although her research is about at-home cosmetic surgery, and about face-to-face interactions, it is relevant to our arguments below. Huss-Ashmore insists that discursive and corporeal aspects of surgical processes are intertwined and that cosmetic surgery successes therefore occur

> through the creation and acting out of a therapeutic narrative, a lived story in which the 'me I want to be' or the 'me I really am' is brought into being through the linguistic, emotional, and physical experience of surgery and recovery. (Huss-Ashmore 2000: 32)

This language/surgery overlap in cosmetic surgery has also been examined by Carole Spitzack (1988: 38), who describes the surgeon–patient relationship as one in which physical 'imperfection is "cured" through complex and over-lapping mechanisms of confession and surveillance' (see also Gimlin 2013). While Spitzack and Huss-Ashmore concentrate on practitioner–patient inter-actions, we will focus in this chapter on the ways that cosmetic surgery tourists tell their stories to each other and to a wider, sometimes public audience, and in the online interactions they have with their agents, specifically through social media. Rather than analyse face-to-face patient–surgeon narratives, we look at the many stories and interactions that happen outside and around this dyad. In the world of cosmetic surgery tourism most of those happen online. We look at how cosmetic surgery tourists interact through and deploy social media before, during and after travel, and show how social media are part of the network or assemblage that creates both cosmetic surgery tourism and cosmetically altered bodies. In our discussion we take a temporal approach, using the familiar time slices of before, during and after that structure many cosmetic surgery and tourism narratives.

Before travel

Without digital modes of communication, contemporary cosmetic surgery tourism would not exist; interviewees told us these media were central to finding out about procedures and places. Nearly all spoke about beginning their cosmetic surgery tourism experience online, looking at the websites of surgeons, hospitals and agents: 'Well, everyone goes online, right? So, I started online' (Bianca, Australia to Thailand).

As discussed in chapters one and five, when patients make the decision to move away from national health schemes and beyond home-country regu-lations (and as there are still very few regulations or laws about provision of cosmetic surgery to non-nationals), they take on the burden of respon-sibility for their choices of destination, surgeon, agent, recovery and so on themselves. Most cosmetic surgery tourists have researched procedures and places thoroughly, many taking years to do this: 'It's something you need to research, you can't just go "oh yeah, that's cheap, I'll have that". You know, you've got to look into it' (Sam, Australia to Thailand). So, before embarking on cosmetic surgery tourism, prospective patients become online researchers, picking their way through different sources of information and advice.

We are not concerned here with making claims for how cosmetic surgery tourists *should* do their research or whether they are qualified to conduct such research. Rather, we note that many patients feel an imperative to do the best research they can: 'I looked up Bumrungrad and it's like the second-best hos-pital in the world or something … I looked up all the surgeons, couldn't find a bad word about them, absolutely researched everything' (Anna, Australia to Thailand). Most of our participants were confident about the amount of information and knowledge they had accrued prior to surgery and travel, and some strongly defended the adequacy of their own investigations: 'Everyone always thinks the worst and then you hear the horror stories, but they haven't realised how much I've looked into it and researched' (Sam, Australia to Thailand). This research is a central part of the work that patients do, as we explored in chapter five.

There are crucial differences between websites – such as those maintained by hospitals – and social media. Websites are reasonably stable, looking much the same from week to week, with content that has been previously determined by their producers. If reader comment is invited, it can be moderated, removed or edited. Websites therefore tend to be non-interactive and static – they are 'push' media. They are sources of information and knowledge that have been curated by professionals. They also, of course, act as advertisements, and so can be seen as somewhat untrustworthy.[2]

An Australian agency website, featuring pictures of groups of smiling young women, states at the top of its page:

It's a Group Tour So You Will Make New Friends

Further down we read:

Our group tour clients all agree this is a great way to have surgery in Thailand. They all agree that they make new friends and got to go shopping all the great places, not to mention the food :) all these great dinners!

You will be spoiled on a Destination Beauty Group Tour, and our professional team will always be there for you!

It is not until right at the bottom of the page that we read:

There's also a quick stop at the hospital … to make a new you!
We will all go to the hospital for consultation in the morning and have surgery in the afternoon, most people will discharge after 1 or 2 nights, and then check into the luxury boutique downtown hotel, where the shopping begins … or perhaps you will relax by the pool. (Destination Beauty, n.d.)

Clearly, the group experience is a central part of this package. 'New friends' are offered alongside a 'new you': social and surgical are intertwined so that what is elsewhere and otherwise understood as a highly individualistic and self-centred practice (changing the body through cosmetic surgery; see for example Elliott 2008) becomes a group activity. The surgery itself is discursively minimised, written about in the same fun, light-hearted tone as exotic dinners and bargain designer shopping. What is most interesting to us about this is that cosmetic surgery tourism is being sold as a *group* experience, one that is friendly and social. This is an extreme example of perhaps deceptive advertising that actively minimises the surgery in cosmetic surgery tourism. It is important to note that many of our interviewees were very aware of the differences between websites and social media pages, and were far more likely to trust knowledge gained via social media.

Social media pages change from day to day as individuals contribute and comment. Most social media platforms moderate or remove only comments that are illegal or that violate rules about targeted abuse of individuals or groups, and the majority of content in social media is user/consumer generated (Hjorth 2007). Our interviewees tended to use both websites and Facebook or other social media forums in their pre-surgery research:

> I thought 'well, I'm not stupid, I wouldn't jump into something', so I thought I would research other companies as well. I compared, I looked at before and after photos of that doctor and researched his work and then I looked at other surgeons as well ... I'd researched the implants which were meant to be the best. I knew that the way he does things, he's very precise. I'd read lots of testimonials, not just from [the agent's] website but on forums. (Monique, Australia to Thailand)

Monique's research is typical. She saw these two forms of Internet-based research as working in tandem, with neither having more authority than the other. We found that for most cosmetic surgery tourists we spoke with, patient testimonials were very important. One interviewee noted that social media can provide things that are lacking on more formal websites, especially in terms of reassurance and emotional support:

> The fact that there are so many questions on a lot of these message boards and a lot of confusion and anxiety, it just goes to show that there must be loads of surgeons that aren't really providing people with the reassurance with what is normal, what is not normal and what we should be looking out for and all that kind of thing, because that information just doesn't seem to be there. (Michelle, UK to Belgium)

This 'word of mouse' (Yeoh *et al.* 2013) mirrors the offline word of mouth routinely identified as a key decision-making resource for cosmetic surgery patients, including tourists. It is also a building block for forms of affinity and community, as we discuss below.

Armchair travellers

Andre Jansson (2002) argues that user-generated media allow tourists to travel emotionally and cognitively without actually travelling in geographical space. In this way they can become informed armchair travellers, 'experiencing' places before travelling. This is perhaps more important for cosmetic surgery tourists than others. For them, armchair travelling facilitates familiarity and reduces the strain of the unknown. Many had scrutinised photos or videos of previous patients:

> There was a lady on [Facebook] that had a tummy tuck and I thought, 'Yeah, that's what I want'. I knew I wanted a tummy tuck but that particular picture of that particular lady made me say, 'Yeah, I'm going with [this agent] because that result was brilliant'. (Mark, UK to Czech Republic and Poland)

> There are some mainlanders posted something like interview videos about the procedures of plastic surgery. They posted online to let others see if they think the surgery outcome is okay. I found it by accident and later found the link to browse the hospital's website. Then I called to make enquiries. Then everything went well. (Lun, China to Korea)

Thus, in cosmetic surgery tourism it is the *stories* told by previous recipients that are often of most value to those in the anticipatory phases of their journeys. Engaging with others online, chatting or sharing images, helps to remove the element of surprise, helping people feel they are travelling to a more familiar place for a procedure that is also becoming familiar via online discussion. Megan, visiting Thailand from Australia, told us about watching a previous patient's video diaries:

> She put her whole experience on YouTube, the whole thing from start to finish. Even her crappy days. It was there for you to see. She recently put up some more photos up of her trip and that got me excited because it had more of the hospital and the surgeons. It was very useful for me to see others' experiences, just that she was okay I guess, and that she liked the hospital and the care – the care was nothing like you'd probably get here – and the follow up as well. (Megan, Australia to Thailand)

Others gained advice from previous patients about how to prepare for surgery: 'There's one girl who has got a very good YouTube video, she tells you to bring button-down tops, you need to bring from home your own medication' (Cindy, Australia to Thailand).

Jansson (2002: 441) notes that mediatisation 'creates a new potential for mobility in mediascapes, which also involves the naturalisation of images and fantasies of foreign landscapes and socioscapes'. And, writing about the importance of patient testimony for cosmetic surgery patients more generally, Adams (2010: 760) notes that the 'warm expertise' shared between past and future patients helps to make surgery seem 'more familiar, less bizarre, and more understandable'. In other words, social media allow the strange to become familiar before it is experienced.

Buyer beware

Cosmetic surgery tourism is a 'buyer beware' market where the client is increasingly seen as being responsible for their surgery: for knowing its risks, for making the 'right' decisions in relation to technologies, surgeons, hospitals, countries and products. This is of course problematic in terms of health, safety and risk. However, it also comes hand in hand with a sense of patient autonomy, and helps to bring about a re-balancing of the expert/subject surgeon–patient relationship (see chapter three).

While websites played an important role in patients' research, many of our interviewees also emphasised the importance of contact with peers and previous patients via social media. Most made use of Facebook, forums, blogs or YouTube, or at least 'lurked' on them.[3] Cosmetic surgery tourists are generally not content with the singular authority figure of the surgeon, or the advertising of hospitals and clinics; to augment these modes of information, they rely on each other:

> Really, at some point I wanted some idea of his workmanship more than anything else ... I kept asking the girls, 'but how do I know?' So, I would keep getting feedback everywhere and I would trawl online ... and see 'suture work is impeccable', so since scarring is one of the things that I'm most worried about then it's a good thing, but, you know. (Bianca, Australia to Thailand)

Many cosmetic surgery recipients, whether at home or abroad, see cosmetic surgeons as skilled technicians rather than as aesthetic experts (Gimlin 2013; Holliday & Cairnie 2007). However, we have observed that communities of cosmetic surgery tourists often discuss surgical techniques and the results of particular surgeons as a matter of course in their pre-surgical research.

The fact that social media are often populated by communities of peers for the conversational sharing of information rather than made by professionals for pedagogical or promotional purposes also means that they are seen as more trustworthy. As one patient said:

> I would have shared my experience if it had gone bad because, at the end of the day ... it's a true experience. I wouldn't glamorise it, because at the end of the day, if I was in pain, I would have said I'm in pain because I wouldn't want people to think, 'Oh, he's saying he's not in pain and I've been and I've had this and I'm in agony'. What would be the point? It's got to be the truth. It was a truthful account of my experience. If there were any bad experiences, I would have said. But there wasn't. But if there were, I would have said. (Mark, UK to Czech Republic and Poland)

Mark was not merely relaying his own experiences, but actively contributing to a community of online peers that was seen as trustworthy because those peers are not selling anything.

Reversed meetingness

John Urry's (2003: 170) notion of 'meetingness' is useful here.[4] He argues that online communications and real-life meetings are mutually constitutive and that 'networked sociality' (made up of 'weak ties') is far more meaningful when combined at least occasionally with embodied 'co-presence'. Urry observes that face-to-face or eye-to-eye meetings help to imbue digital communications with trust. For Urry, it is in moments of corporeal co-presence that trust is solidified, and then carried back into the networked communications: 'trust is an accomplishment of such meetings ... which facilitate disembedded network sociality sustained in between at-a-distance' (168–169).

Although it is clear that cosmetic surgery tourism is conducted within digital communications and in real life (face to face), for our purposes a reversal of meetingness makes sense. Trust is built up in the online world, with people the cosmetic surgery tourist is never likely to meet. It is this physically disembodied trustfulness that facilitates the corporeal meetings between patient and surgeon, scalpel and flesh, not the other way around. Cosmetic surgery, an utterly spatial and bodily process, is here augmented by digital communications such as email, Facebook and Skype. Trust is vital where surgery and recovery are concerned; it plays a large part in patient satisfaction and in whether operations are seen as successful or not. Trustfulness in cosmetic surgery tourism is partly designed by industry players such as MTFs, surgeons and hospitals, but is also significantly created in online patient-to-patient communications. Although physically disembodied, cosmetic surgery tourists often share bodily experiences and images online. Analysing YouTube videos, Patricia Lange (2009) writes about the role of the body in producing 'affinity' between video poster and audience: modes of performing embodiment online are used to interpellate viewers into a shared social relationship. Lange gathers many different YouTube videos under her banner 'videos of affinity', and cosmetic surgery tourists' YouTube clips certainly work in this way. By narrating and sharing bodily experiences, a sense of commonality or community is produced.

With the availability of new mobile media, previous tourists have input into the planning as well as the actual experiences of future tourists in ways that were previously restricted to agents, guides, experts and suchlike. Gayle Jennings and Betty Weiler (2006) note that tourists interact with each other in order to formulate, understand and mediate their own experiences, and, in turn, to facilitate the experiences of others. This is deliberately performed in cosmetic surgery tourism, with patients like Mark, quoted above, actively documenting their experiences with the express aim of helping others, just as he was helped by previous patient-tourists' posts. Expectations, fears and hopes are negotiated with peers using narratives and scripts based around information-sharing and truthfulness. The pre-surgical research of cosmetic surgery tourists is a mutual endeavour.

Another patient told us of following, via Facebook, a group of cosmetic surgery tourists' surgery and recovery in the weeks leading up to her own trip:

> It's been really helpful. Some have been having a bad time, they've been in more pain than they expected, whereas some of them are out on the back of elephants, so it's good to see how everybody is different, but it's not all … and one girl got, like, an infection, you know. So, it's not showing only the good side of the story. I hope none of this happens [to me]. I'm very excited. (Lisa, Australia to Thailand)

For Lisa, seeing people miserable with infections alongside those well enough to take post-surgery elephant rides gave her confidence. While she hoped she would have a good experience, she was able to moderate that against the possibility that she might not. It was access to others' stories that allowed her to negotiate the various possibilities of cosmetic surgery tourism in ways that were more accessible, and arguably more useful, than the online advice provided by surgeons or hospitals. The truthfulness of these posts gave her confidence that she had seen the reality of the cosmetic surgery tourism experience, and so her decision-making was validated. As defensive subjects who have to work hard to justify their choices, cosmetic surgery tourists are especially keen to show that they are making good choices based on trusted information, not merely being seduced by glossy marketing hype.

Finally, before their operations we found that some patients used social media to perform a devil-may-care attitude and to make light of the surgery while also acknowledging it as a mode of identity-making and a consumable item: 'Before I left I was like "oh, getting my last swims in before I get my new flotation devices installed", so everyone knew' (Kellie, Australia to Thailand). By making such jokes on Facebook, Kellie was celebrating and performing – with and for her peers – the surgical experience before it had happened, anticipating and foreshadowing a successful, happy result.

During travel, having surgery

Women who had been on cosmetic surgery tourism group tours spoke very highly of the experience. They told of support for first time travellers:

> I think it was better being my first time [overseas] … I was going to go over on my own but … I started getting scared and my husband said if I wanted to

pay that extra then I should go, so I went with the group. (Anne, Australia to Thailand)

They also spoke about the comfort of sharing accommodation with people who were undergoing similar experiences:

> It was nice because you've got something in common. One lady had lipo and a tummy tuck, she didn't have her boobs done. She was staying for fourteen days so she was there for the whole time I was there. It was someone familiar that you could interact with every day. You don't have to spend your whole time with them but it's comforting to know you are coming back to somebody. (Jackie, Australia to Thailand)

However, while some of our interviewees travelled in groups or with family and friends, many were sole travellers, and for them social media was a vital form of connectedness that they carried with them on their journey.

Alone but connected

In her discussion of recovery clinics (retreats) for cosmetic surgery tourism in Costa Rica, Sara Ackerman writes that:

> Some travellers arrive with companions, but many travel alone, and retreats offer a temporary surrogate family. Guests (particularly women) find camaraderie with each other, and many people told me that these friendships were critical to their personal, spiritual, and corporeal recovery. (Ackerman 2010: 418)

For many of our interviewees, using social media was a way to access the camaraderie that Ackerman mentions. In the case of the travellers that Ackerman describes, the cosmetic surgery tourism experience is partly built through collective interchange. For many of our interviewees, this shared making of stories was conducted in social media: in this way they were alone but connected. Mark found a community on the Facebook page of his agent:

> You got all this support from all these people that are on Facebook … that are commenting, that's making you feel you're not completely alone. It is nice. It's a lovely thing that … although I couldn't speak to anybody because there was nobody really out and about that spoke English, it was nice being able to go on Facebook and being able to just make comments. (Mark, UK to Czech Republic and Poland)

In addition to providing pre-surgical information, social networking sites are used for ongoing peer-to-peer networking, community building and storytelling while patients are away. Travellers put up pre- and post-surgery images of themselves, write in detail about their experiences and share 'videos of affinity'

(Lange 2009). Social media saturated the experience of many of our interviewees while abroad and were integral to their experience, helping participants to connect with home, check on other patients, narrate surgical stories and make sense of new surroundings. Without portable devices and social software, many of the people we interviewed would have had a significantly different experience: '[Social media] was a big part of it really and you kind of felt that you weren't doing it all alone. You felt like there were people along for your journey' (Mark, UK to Czech Republic and Poland).

Others used social media to celebrate their surgeries. Immediately after her surgery one patient posted a Facebook status update that read: 'Got boobs? Yeah I do now!' (Kellie, Australia to Thailand). Posting on Facebook was not only a way to let friends and family know that she had made the right decision but also a way to communicate a positive outcome with the rest of the cosmetic surgery tourism community that she had connected with online.

Managing heightened moments

All tourism is about the experience of risk and difference within limits: with cosmetic surgery tourism those limits must be managed extremely carefully. Nelson Graburn ([1989] 2012) suggests that the tourist experience follows a temporal arc from ordinary to heightened and back to ordinary. Heightened moments may be adventurous, unexpected or even frightening, and while they are desirable for many tourist experiences they are less welcome for the cosmetic surgery tourist. While some of our interviewees certainly went looking for exciting moments, for example visiting ping-pong strip shows in Bangkok or going to wildlife parks, none wished for heightened moments to be part of their surgical experience. Communications in social media helped people to manage the temporal arc so that unexpected heightened moments were less likely to occur. A patient told us happily that there had been 'no surprises' on her trip, and attributed this to the way she was in constant communication with a friend at home and with her agent: 'no negatives... [there were no surprises] because my girlfriend had watched me the whole way and I was sending emails to [the agent] left, right and centre' (Cindy, Australia to Thailand).

Some patients used social media to actively manage the future temporal arcs of others. For example, Mark posted Facebook updates throughout his journey:

> I kind of put pictures through my journey, if you will. So, it's like I showed my loose skin and then I had the operation and then pictures through the various stages through the week. I even took pictures of my apartment and the view. I put them on, you know, so people could see what to expect when you go as well. (Mark, UK to Czech Republic and Poland)

Mark's intention was to help others. By showing them what to expect in terms of both his body and the countries visited, he was managing the heightened moments of future patients. In these ways cosmetic surgery tourism narratives serve to construct identity in relation to surgery and to place, and – crucially – to lay foundations for others to do the same; each narrative becomes a script or template upon which others can build their own stories. Mark was also in a sense authenticating the site and process of cosmetic surgery tourism by making a recording of it. This makes sense when we consider Dean MacCannell's ([1976] 1999: 48) and later Nick Couldry's (2005) arguments that tourist sites only become 'authentic' once the first copy has been made – in other words, once the first tourist has been there, taken photos, made drawings or Facebooked. In this way Mark was acting as a pioneer. By creating the first copy, he was making cosmetic surgery tourism available for others. His representations of experience online helped to authenticate his new sense of self but also served to make the surgery 'real' for future travellers.

While away, cosmetic surgery tourists use social media to construct complex and overlapping experiences of place, of identity and of surgery. They create online spaces where virtual meetingness happens, and in these spaces they share knowledge, work out what is realistic in terms of pain and recovery, celebrate decisions and results, and pave the way for future tourists. As we noted in chapter four, some patients capitalise on this pioneering status by becoming agents/MTFs themselves; for others, it is enough to know that they have shared real experiences and in doing so helped others follow their lead. While no one we spoke to attempted to validate this via the usual social media metrics of 'likes' or 'followers', patients posting online clearly felt valued through this sharing, in a sense of 'paying back' to an online community that had been so influential in their own decision-making.

Back home, transformed

The beginning of the rest of my life

Cosmetic surgery tourists use blogs and sites like Facebook and YouTube to tell stories of their experiences after surgery, often summing up the entire process from preliminary enquiries to coming home under headings like 'The beginning of the rest of my life' (All wrapped up 2012) and 'Cosmetic Surgery Thailand – Actual Post Breast Augmentation Testimonial' (cosmeticsurgery-thai 2011). Post-surgical stories might be posted immediately after surgery and are sometimes updated for years afterwards: the YouTube channel of one breast augmentation patient who travelled from Australia to Thailand has around thirty videos about her treatment (TheMrsforman, www.youtube. com/user/TheMrsforman). Online communities created around cosmetic surgery tourism often continue beyond the immediate parameters of before/

during/after. How long they might last, and whether relationships built up during cosmetic surgery tourism continue, is something only a longitudinal study would be able to answer.

Patients often share and compare their transformations and recoveries on social media immediately after surgery, helping to contextualise experiences of pain, complications and healing:

> I feel really good ... [because] I have a Facebook page and a lot of people have video blogged it and stuff, and a lot of the ladies are like, 'I've been bed-ridden' ... it takes to people really differently and I've taken to it really well. ... I wasn't really in agony, I was just in ... a bit of pain and the hardest thing was probably trying to get up out of the bed. (Sam, Australia to Thailand)

Even though it was hard for her to 'get up out of the bed', Sam insisted that she was not 'bed-ridden' like others. We suggest that being able to contextualise one's pain in this way is important in being able to decide what is normal or acceptable – without social media Sam may have perceived her pain as abnormal or unacceptable. Because of social media her pain was not experienced in isolation but in a shared context, and was perhaps therefore more tolerable. Of course, we have no way of proving this, but if, as historian Joanna Bourke (2013: 155) argues, 'pain does not emerge naturally from physiological processes, but in negotiation with social worlds', then we know that Sam's online community had some role to play in how she experienced her pain. Further, Bourke notes that:

> Language does things to bodies. It acts upon them. This is another way of saying that the body-in-pain is not simply an entity awaiting social inscription ... but is an active agent in both creating pain-events and, in turn, being created by them. (Bourke 2013: 173)

For cosmetic surgery patients, the willingness to articulate and share experiences of pain with others who have undergone similar operations invites language in to play a part in the recovery process – to 'act upon' their bodies – to help them actively deal with pain and negotiate its effects.

Boobie birthdays

In some online communities (for both at-home and overseas recipients) 'boobie birthdays' are noted at the anniversaries of breast augmentation surgery:

> It's my boobie birthday today! A year ago I went on a group trip with restore beauty getaways and had a breast augmentation! I have never been happier they look and feel amazing I am so pleased with my results I recommend anyone thinking about doing it to go on a group trip to Phuket!! Thank you so much

for giving me the best care and service you are all amazing!! (Venus Stewart, Facebook post)[5]

In online forums, people who have been on group tours write of bonding, of staying in contact with each other after the trip, and of forming friendships based on the shared surgical experience:

> A girl who got there the same day as me had surgery straight after mine. She was having exactly the same surgery. She was in another apartment, unfortunately, because we just hit it off. She was my boobie buddy and we are still in contact now. (Ann, Australia to Thailand)

Here the 'boobie buddy' is a special sort of friend: one who has shared a life-changing experience and perhaps understands the transformation of cosmetic surgery in ways that nobody else can.

When things go wrong

Given the intimacy shared by cosmetic surgery tourists on social media, it makes sense that these forums are also used to communicate when things go wrong. Some patients who had suffered complications from their surgeries were able to support each other online:

> I just felt, although my story was different to Jane, I wanted to support her a little bit because I know how I felt, although she was ten times worse than me, I didn't know what was going on. I just wanted to let her know that she wasn't alone. (Sharon, UK to Poland)

Michelle, who travelled from the UK to Belgium, found that a US-based forum was the most useful for support:

> I have found [the forum is an] absolute godsend. I mean there are a few, there is this American one … which is really active and it has just been amazing support because I ended up in A&E the day after I got back, because I was just in so much pain. (Michelle, UK to Belgium)

Like Mark, Sharon was keen to provide support to someone she had never met. Michelle felt rescued from her pain by the NHS but equally by an Internet forum that was not even based on her home continent. In this way it is clear once more that spaces of trust and meetingness in cosmetic surgery tourism are likely to be found online.

In addition to surgical complications, sometimes destinations failed to live up to expectations. There was great disappointment when the material realities of place did not match what had been represented (usually on hospital or MTF websites). This is what Jansson (2007: 9) calls 'decapsulation', a state where disjuncture between the represented and the real occurs and upsets the tourist experience: 'decapsulation is most often produced through the inter-play between material and symbolic processes' (see also Couldry 2005). There can be profound dismay when expectations that have been built up via online interactions do not match with actuality. Sally, visiting Tunisia from the UK, found that the guide she had been expecting, Mehdi, had left months earlier:

> Had I known Mehdi wasn't there and had I known that the language barrier would have been a huge problem I would have still gone and had the surgery because I went for surgery – I didn't go for conversation, so I would have still gone but I would have been aware, I would have been prepared ... I still would have gone, had they informed me more I would have still gone, but I would have gone slightly differently. I would have gone with a different outlook, I would have done things slightly differently. (Sally, UK to Tunisia)

Interestingly, when things had gone wrong, patients did not tell us that they regretted their decision to have cosmetic surgery abroad, rather that they had been disappointed by what they generally characterised as a lack of informa-tion. And notably, if Sally had been able to have contact with other patients who were already in Tunisia, she would have 'been aware ... been prepared'. We suggest that it is the lack of social media in this case that caused the unpleasant feeling of decapsulation.

Little narratives and community

Narratives create experience and memory as much as they tell of pre-existing conditions; they also reflect the ideals and desires of the cultures in which they are made (McNay 2002). Accordingly, most cosmetic surgery recipients narrate their surgeries using 'scripts' that fit in with cultural expectations, and deploy different narratives in order to be heard (see Ancheta 2002; Frost 1999; Gimlin, 2002, 2013). The narratives we have examined here are not grand or transcendent, but rather personal, largely unedited stories facilitated through social media – a channel that is 'cheap, flexible, readily available, quick' and therefore not exclusive (Poster 2001: 621). Lois McNay (2002: 83) notes that identity itself is constructed through narrative and that because all narratives are intertwined with others it follows that identity-making is an intersubjec-tive and communal process: 'the idea of narrative is also explicitly relational, that is, it draws attention to the irredeemably intersubjective nature of iden-tity'. In line with this, we suggest that the identity- and body-making that cosmetic surgery tourists conduct happens both corporeally and discursively, and that social media play a large role in the discursive/representational ele-ments of transformation.

Pitts-Taylor (2009: 127) notes that cosmetic surgery discourses are unsta-ble, changing according to mode, speaker and context. Despite this flux, cosmetic surgery patients are 'expected to employ methods of description that make sense to others, thus complying with already scripted codes of meaning that are set out before [them]'. We suggest that part of being a recipient of cosmetic surgery is being able to identify and then position oneself 'correctly' in relation to whichever discourse is appropriate.[6] Among many other possible subject positions, a cosmetic surgery tourist might discursively represent him or herself as adventurer (like Kellie), as pioneer and truth-teller (like Mark) or as caring stranger (like Sharon or the patients in Tunisia we encounter in chapter eight). All positions make it clear that cosmetic surgery tourist identity is constructed through narrative and is not confined to individuals but formed in conjunction with myriad others. The ongoing narrating of cosmetic surgery tourism experiences, in common with other tourist narratives, moves from anticipation to memory, and forms the basis for continued sharing, bonding and 'mattering' – in short, for making community (Heimtun 2007).

Cosmetic surgery tourists thus use 'symbolic-material structures' to make what Jansson (2007: 6) calls 'textures of travel', by mixing online and real-life interactions; in doing so they in fact render this distinction obsolete. Their online communities, with shared vocabularies and discourses, are intricately connected to the very corporeal aspects of actual surgeries. In this way a nexus between material space – of the body and of place – and forms of communication together create the cosmetic surgery tourism experience and validate the subsequent transformation. In turn, this means that cosmetic surgery tourists have something that is different to their stay-at-home counterparts – they have more of a sense of being part of a community. The fact that their corporeal experiences happen off-shore and away from what they know encourages them to connect with strangers, to make community. As one Australian MTF, Yvonne, told us: 'It's just about connecting, it really is about connecting.'

Conclusion

Ackerman (2010: 405) writes of the Costa Rican clinic she researched that 'the labors of local caretakers and social interactions among patients operate on the embodied subjectivities of guests and staff and act as an adjunct to the cuts and sutures performed by surgeons'. Similarly, social media networking augments the work of the scalpel for the people we interviewed. The practices of cosmetic surgery tourists are complex and multifaceted. As Pitts-Taylor (2009: 122) writes about her own cosmetic surgery, it is 'a very personal experience, but it is also incredibly social, public, and semantically unstable, one that is not static but unfolds through various processes of imbuing the body and self with symbolic meaning'. It is not adequate to think of cosmetic surgery tourists as individuals who travel simply because they cannot afford surgery at home. They make up communities, with patterns of behaviour, modes of being, and unique ways of bonding and identity-making.

In the instances of transformation that we are examining in relation to cosmetic surgery tourism, change comes about through a collective rather than through individual subjects. Collectives cannot exist without communication – in this instance via social media. So, transformation of the self or of many selves is actually brought about by and through social media. Here, communicative technologies are far more than conduits for information; they are portals for identities, through which bodies and selves can be refashioned.

Notes

1   For discussion of online patient communities, see, for example, Radin (2006).

2   On tourism websites and trust, see Wilson and Suraya (2004); for a discourse analysis of official tourism websites, see Hallett and Kaplan-Weinger (2010).

3   'Lurking' is the practice of observing but not participating in online forums, and is often viewed negatively.

4   We note that Urry wrote of 'meetingness' before face-to-face online communications platforms such as FaceTime and Skype were commonplace. Thus, while for him one of the differences between real-life meetings and online conversations was the ability to speak face to face, for us the boundaries are a little more blurred.

5   Posted in 2013 on www.facebook.com/RestoredBeautyGetaways/, accessed 1 May 2014 (no longer available).

6   Several feminist scholars have looked at narrative and discourse in relation to cosmetic surgery, especially Brooks (2004), Fraser (2003), Gimlin (2012, 2013), Holliday and Cairnie (2007) and Huss-Ashmore (2000). Debra Gimlin (2012: 64) summarises that 'stories about cosmetic surgery and the surgical process itself are fully intertwined and interdependent'.

7

DECENTRING AND DISORIENTING COSMETIC SURGERY TOURISM

While medical tourism historically has meant wealthy travellers leaving the Global South to seek treatment in the Global North, in the last few decades the direction of patient flows has changed. In academic work, medical tourism has commonly come to be conceptualised in terms of colonialism and orientalism: wealthy westerners exploiting low-wage economies in developing countries and experiencing them through a patronising 'orientalist gaze' – not liking the food, worrying about dirt, treating locals as subservient. Additionally, some writers argue that IMT destinations are enclaves or non-places for recuperation – stripped and sanitised of 'real' local culture so as not to disturb the tourist's recovery (Elliott 2008). IMT patients are here imagined as wealthy, footloose, new service-class members, used to globetrotting for work and leisure, who import their worldly practices and orientations into the medical world in a globalised, consumerised, touristic fashion. This means that discussions of IMT tend to come burdened with assumptions about who is travelling, where to and why – and also with assumed particular negative effects on health services abroad and back home. Selfish individualism wedded to orientalism portrays medical tourists in a negative light, as a prime exemplar of 'bad globalisation'.

Our research challenges many of these assumptions. As we have already discussed, our cosmetic surgery tourists were not wealthy. They were nurses, taxi drivers, hotel porters, shop workers, beauticians, administrators. They were not glamorous and rich members of a global leisure class, frequent fliers or globetrotters, nor were they the celebrity-emulating cosmetic surgery addicts portrayed in the popular media. They were 'ordinary people' who wanted to change one part of their body that they did not like. Our fieldwork enabled us to share their experiences of cosmetic surgery tourism, and these experiences powerfully challenged some of the assumptions in the media and in the academic literature about international medical travel. The photos of Sue's surgical journey capture something of the 'ordinariness' of cosmetic surgery tourism as it was experienced by participants in our study (figure 7.1).

In this chapter we outline some of the experiences that counter the assumed itineraries of the wealthy, footloose, project-of-self-making individual (see also Ormond & Sulianti 2017). To do this, we begin by reviewing work in the field that has overturned the model of IMT as West–East and/or North–South flows of wealthy patients from the developed world accessing low-cost treatment in developing countries. This model has been (at least partially) decentred in three ways: by research exploring (i) South–South IMT, (ii) cross-border travel between neighbouring countries, and (iii) regional flows of patients. In many cases, in fact, these flows are coterminous, and as we found in our project, also evident in the emerging geography of cosmetic surgery tourism. In the second part of the chapter we turn our attention to a central assumption embedded in the West–East, North–South model of IMT: that as well as an exemplar of 'bad globalisation', these tourists carry with them colonialist and orientalist baggage – forms of knowledge about and ways of seeing the world that shape the medical tourism encounter. In the case of the cosmetic surgery tourists we met, we show how the reality of their experiences challenges this view and reveals the disorientations that characterise many of the encounters detailed in our study.

Shifting geographies of international medical travel

While traditionally, 'the flow of health services exports went from North to South, with patients travelling in the opposite direction' (Lautier 2014: 105), today the term 'medical tourism' has come to denote 'the care pursuits by those from the Global North in the Global South … indicative of a perceived significant reversal of global care flows and expertise' (Ormond 2014b: 426). The North-goes-South, West-goes-East model of IMT has for a long time been the dominant critical discourse evident in both media representations and academic research. It has become a common-sense 'truth' due to its repetition across these realms – which have, in fact, coproduced the model, as much academic work has been based on desk research looking at media and marketing materials online, while selected academic research feeds back into the media portrayal of who travels where, and why (especially, in the case of cosmetic surgery tourism, academic research supported and promoted by professional bodies with a stake in stemming the outbound flow of prospective clients). Arguably the dominant visual motif of IMT – the white woman in a bikini, on a beach – circulates across media accounts and also on clinic websites and on the cover of guidebooks, cementing this dominant model (and adding race and gender to the mix). It is important, therefore, to think about the work that these media representations do, as key resources for the broader public conversation about IMT, shaping the perceptions of many of those involved in or interested in the phenomenon, whether as researchers, reporters, providers or consumers (Casanova & Sutton 2013).

In the academic context, to pick one more-or-less representative example, Smith-Morris and Manderson (2010: 334) conclude (unevidenced) that 'while travelling for care is not confined to certain countries and populations, still the primary flows are *from* developed *to* less developed countries', adding that the high-quality facilities these patients access contrast with their immediate surroundings – 'the urban slums and squatter settlements' – which they see as 'a visual reminder of the distributive inequity that private sector healthcare offers at the expense of the public sector, and of its global reach'. Such conclusions are repeated across a large number of accounts, and are used to build a particular critique of IMT as an outworking of (bad) neoliberalisation and (bad) globalisation (e.g. Smith 2012).

Contrary to the above view, and published only one year after Smith-Morris and Manderson's work, Roberts and Scheper-Hughes (2011: 4) argue that what they label 'medical migrants' (to avoid the baggage of the term 'tourist') might 'conjure up an image of affluent westerners taking advantage of the health care resources of poor nations', yet in reality 'many medical migrants today are poor and medically disenfranchised persons desperately seeking life-saving drugs and therapies and corrective surgeries that they cannot get at home'. As Roberts and Scheper-Hughes state, 'medical migrations cannot *presume* the northern exploitation of the global south' (7, our emphasis; see also Thompson 2011). Much of this new wave of academic discussion is underpinned by qualitative, ethnographic fieldwork, capable of producing more attuned accounts of who is actually travelling, where from and to, and why. As one review essay concludes, 'While wealthy patients seeking the best care have always travelled, a new kind of patient is now travelling … This implies a change not only in the purpose of patient mobility but also in the direction of flows' (Glinos *et al.*, 'A typology of cross-border patient mobility', 2010: 1153). This means on the one hand acknowledging flows of Global South international medical tourists, who are more likely to stay local/regional, and on the other hand to see the itineraries and experiences of less wealthy westerners, who may well travel east or south, but along routes, to destinations and with experiences that counter this dominant narrative. Here we briefly highlight selected studies that support this countering, split along the three lines highlighted earlier, though noting again that in practice these three may well be overlapping or coterminous (some examples of regional IMT are by definition cross-border, some are South–South, and so on; see Lunt *et al.* 2016).

South–South IMT

Critical scholarship is beginning to correct the 'Northern bias' in research on IMT. This bias is rightly shown to have 'foreshortened our perception of the dimensions and complexities of international medical travel's diverse contexts and directionalities' (Ormond & Sulianti 2017: 96). Reviewing IMT into South Africa, for example, Jonathan Crush and Abel Chikanda (2015) conclude that the bulk of journeys are either from within the southern African region, or are broader South–South movements. Aggregate data quantifies this: between 2003 and 2008, some 2.2 million patients came to South Africa from the Global South, almost all of these from Africa and the Middle East; by contrast, 281,000 patients came from the Global North – 122,500 from the UK and 41,000 from the US. The South–South travellers can be divided into three main groups: middle-class African international medical tourists, those travelling thanks to government agreements within the Southern African Development Community and those Crush and Chikanda name 'medically disenfranchised' travellers – people mostly from bordering countries not included in formal agreements. This important research contests other accounts that highlight high-end 'Surgeon and Safari' tourism to South Africa (e.g. Mazzaschi 2011).

Marc Lautier's (2014) discussion of South-Mediterranean providers also flags the importance of South–South flows and of regional demand (movements between countries such as Tunisia, Libya, Jordan) as well movements from the north to the south of the Mediterranean region. His data confirms that South–South IMT is an important and growing segment in this region, a finding backed up by many studies reviewed in an essay by John Connell (2016: 543), which maps patient flows with a keen eye on the three routeways we discuss here. As Connell writes, 'South–South intra-regional medical travel is ever-more banal … and it is becoming increasingly visible'. These flows represent, Connell suggests, a form of 'bottom-up transnationalism', not driven by the industry and its marketing hype, but by the real needs of patients travelling relatively small distances that do not bring them into contact with the strange and exotic, nor with luxury. A clearer picture of such 'banal' medical travel is emerging across the Global South, revealing regional connections and multiple cross-border journeys – which we attend to next.

Cross-border IMT

Connell's (2016: 543) exhaustive review, cited above, shows clearly that 'multiple local border crossings rather than globalization characterize medical travel'. Here, too, a growing strand of research documents experiences of local, proximate, cross-border journeys, some formally sanctioned (by bilateral agreements, for example) and others informal, at times clandestine. Audrey Bochaton (2015) charts the movement of Laotians to Thailand, for example, while Meghann Ormond (2015b) focuses on the experiences of Indonesians travelling to Malaysia. Both studies attend in detail to the practices of travel, to the actual business of crossing a national border in search of healthcare, and both show the surprising array of actors enrolled in the journey. Far away from the glamorous life of jet-set international medical tourists imagined in media (and some academic) accounts, their stories detail mundane travels in minibuses, taxis and borrowed cars, while also highlighting the role of social networks in facilitating travel (giving advice, lending money), and the countless forms of informal care experienced along the way.

In the cases described by Bochaton and Ormond, the majority flow is one-way, creating what Connell (2016) describes as an 'asymmetry' across the border. Other cases suggest bidirectional flows, though the make-up of the two moving populations might be somewhat different. Glinos *et al.* ('A typology of cross-border patient mobility', 2010: 1151), for example, note that across the USA–Mexico border, 'patient flows go both ways', with an important diasporic element (as Mexicans working in the US travel back home for healthcare; see also Horton & Cole 2011) matched by US patients, often from proximate southern states (especially Texas), going south seeking cost savings (linked to health insurance limitations) (Su *et al.* 2011). The mobilities evident in cross-border travel are largely undocumented and under-researched, meaning that such movements have by and large failed to 'filter through medical tourism's broader discursive formation' (Solomon 2011: 109).

As noted, cross-border IMT can be informal – initiated by patients themselves, though often with the pull of destinations helping to stoke demand – but it can also be the result of formal agreements, either between facilities on either side of the border (see Glinos & Baeten 2014) or by nation-states or sub-national regions entering into bilateral or multilateral agreements (on the latter, see Volgger *et al.* 2015). The EU directive (2011/24/EU) on patient mobility aims at facilitating such movements across the European Union (Cohen 2015), and many other such agreements have been brokered by neighbours, as in the case of the Libya–Tunisia agreement that we discuss later. Concluding their survey of research in this area, Glinos *et al.* ('A typology of cross-border patient mobility', 2010: 1153) summarise that 'border-regions are home to intense patient flows … Such flows are visible on all continents'. And in many cases, over time, such flows solidify into the formation of (formal or informal) 'health regions' (Connell 2016).

Regional IMT

Formal agreements for regional medical travel are evident around the world, developed through state or supra-state agreements, for example among Gulf Cooperation Council (GCC), Association of South East Asian Nations (ASEAN) or European Union (EU) members (Glinos *et al.*, 'Purchasing health services abroad', 2010; Kangas 2002; Ormond 2013a; Ormond & Sulianti 2017). These health regions seek to formalise and regulate cross-border patient flows, and to streamline bureaucratic processes such as health insurance remuneration. Regionalising healthcare in this way has been, in some cases, seen as a way of bolstering public (national) health systems, catering for uneven demand and allowing the sharing of high-cost resources. In some contexts, specialist care is off-shored in order to overcome physical constraints that limit the development of facilities at home, as Eva-Maria Knoll (2017) discusses in the context of mobility for treatment for beta-thalassaemia among Maldivian patients. Here the physical geography and remoteness of the Maldives archipelago, combined with high rates of the condition among the population, has made patient mobility a fact of Maldivian life.

Sometimes regional agreements map onto 'culture regions' that have been bisected by overlain national borders, and where there is greater cultural and linguistic affinity at the regional scale than the national (Connell 2016; Durham & Blondell 2017). At other times, such agreements are one element in broader policy attempts to build supra-national regions, driven by economic development imperatives. Working cooperatively at the regional scale may also be a protectionist policy aimed at preventing 'leakage' of patients (and their money) beyond the region, by ensuring high-quality care is available regionally even when it is not available nationally.

Aside from formally brokered health regions, research has mapped the de facto development of informal regions emerging from consistent border crossings. As Connell (2016: 538) summarises: 'Through … multiple processes of mobility, within familiar cultural and linguistic settings, distinctive, asymmetrical border regions have emerged, characterized by complex bidirectional flows, cheap accommodation and food outlets, and a flourishing informal economy of care … with national boundaries increasingly blurred and erased, where states are permissive and regulation weak.' Such informal health regions 'have appeared in Asia, Latin America, and Africa as places of dynamic social and spatial practices'. Such de facto health regions come into being through time, carved out by patient flows (and responses to those flows by healthcare providers and nation-states on both sides of the border). Standing back from the detail, what we can see emerging here is a clear regional geography of patient mobility: even in the absence of formal health regions, the flows that make up the majority of IMT movements are regional, whether cross-border or within circumscribed geographical regions. As Connell notes, such regions are often characterised by 'familiar cultural and linguistic settings', though this should not be mistaken as meaning that such movements are seamless and unproblematic. Cultural and linguistic familiarity can still get lost in translation, as we will explore now with reference to Chinese cosmetic surgery tourists in South Korea.

Cosmetic surgery tourism to South Korea

Our Korean fieldwork revealed that regional rather than global dynamics have a major part to play in the flows of cosmetic surgery tourists and the development of destinations. Rather than the simplistic, globally homogenis-ing model of medical tourism assumed in much of the literature, the geography operates at a variety of spatial scales, and these scales (local, regional, global) are connected to one another through flows of people, ideas and money. They sometimes piggyback on existing patterns of movement (for example among diaspora), sometimes exploit economics (exchange rates, low cost travel), and sometimes carry along with them stereotypical views about places and people. What we mapped in South Korea were beautyscapes, therefore, on local and regional as well as global scales.

The local understanding of and attitudes towards cosmetic surgery tourists in South Korea were varied, though in some ways they mirror the ambiva-lences in any place that develops a tourist economy, in which various differ-ent forms of othering may be at work. Our fieldwork illustrates this vividly. In Korea cosmetic surgery tourism is seen as a growth industry and one that positions the country at the forefront of medical science in a global market. There has been tacit support of the industry in the past by the Korean state, in the form of tax breaks (though surgeons grumbled that the government could be more supportive, comparing their experiences with those surrounding the 1988 Seoul Olympics, as observed in our field notes in chapter one).

Our fieldwork shed light on the experiences of Chinese patients travelling to South Korea. In opting to travel abroad, these patients were paying more for their surgeries than they would at home, not less, and Korean clinics have been keen to capitalise on the newly wealthy Chinese tourists travelling there. In one part of the now famous Gangnam district of Seoul there are over two hundred clinics on a single street (Figure 1.5). However, despite the warm welcome by clinics, the Korean government continues to treat Chinese patients with a certain degree of suspicion, employing practices to guard against Chinese migration into Korea. One solution is spatial: the develop-ment of a medical tourism resort on Jeju Island, thereby keeping Chinese international medical tourists off the mainland. Another solution has been bureaucratic: to provide medical travel visas which limit the patient-tourist's itinerary (Holliday *et al.* 2017).

Chinese cosmetic surgery tourists were seen in Korea as being of eco-nomic value, but also as somewhat déclassé, and their requests for procedures were often interpreted as reflecting celebrity culture (and in particular the popularity of K-pop and the Korean Wave). Surgeons therefore specialised in giving patients a Korean Look, assuming this is what Chinese patients desired. However, one respondent, travelling for a jaw bone reduction surgery to make her face more symmetrical, was extremely unhappy with the result – the surgery did change her face, but she thought that she now had a 'Korean face', which she did not like. She thought she looked 'cute and sweet' after the surgery, which she associated with girlish femininity, whereas she wanted to look mature and independent. She was very worried about what her parents and friends would say when they saw her, as she had not told them she was travelling for surgery (Holliday *et al.* 2017).

In our Korean fieldwork, we were powerfully reminded of the importance of the regional scale and of regional imaginaries – ways in which East Asia is imagined as a place of both cultural proximity but also forms of difference. We encountered projections of Koreanness and of Chineseness, both in terms of self-representations and as forms of othering – most vividly in the clinical encounters between Korean surgeons and Chinese patients who had travelled for facial procedures. And we found out some of the ways in which contemporary discourses and practices of cosmetic surgery tourism connect to an uneasiness about colonial histories (both US and Japanese colonialism are re-narrated in South Korea's cosmetic surgery industry; see DiMoia 2013), as well as the country's postcolonial present and its position on the world stage. This vantage point enabled us to witness the regional geography of medical tourism, decentring dominant discourses about centres and peripheries, about the directions of travel and about the global nature of IMT. It also drew our attention to the issue of colonial/postcolonial positionality, and to how these histories and current realities play out in the surgical encounter.

Decolonising and disorienting cosmetic surgery tourism

One prominent, often-repeated marketing slogan for contemporary IMT is 'First World care at Third World prices' (Turner 2007). Packed into a few words and a snappy catchphrase is a whole host of geopolitical and ideological baggage. The idea that care is cheaper in the Global South, or that structural economic relations make it so – Third World prices – is offset by the idea that the care offered is 'First World', though here we see restated the idea that the Global North is the home of the best quality care, the gold standard against which others are measured. The promise of being able to access that care at those prices hinges on the traveller's capacity to exploit various global flows – carried by flightpaths, rendered affordable by exchange rates, guaranteed by promises of First World care often embodied in the mobile careers of health professionals and made thinkable by the neoliberal logic of privatised, consumerised healthcare. It has been easy and perhaps understandable that this practice has been read in critical academic accounts as an instantiation of (neo-)colonialism, with international medical tourists often carrying with them an orientalist worldview that projects onto encounters with the Global South everything that the Global North is not (Buzinde & Yarnal 2012).

As famously developed by Edward Said (1978), orientalism is a worldview based on 'Western knowledge of the Eastern world', a powerful discursive formation that consistently represents the Orient and its people as an irrational, psychologically weak, unmodern, feminised, non-European other, negatively contrasted with the rational, psychologically strong, modern, masculine West. Such a hierarchical binary relation (weak East, strong West) derives, according to Said, from the European psychological need to perpetuate an idea of absolute difference between West and East, with such difference embodying 'immutable cultural essences' inherent to Oriental peoples and things (Said 1978: 65–67). At the heart of Said's account is the question of the production of knowledge: the West produces knowledge about the Orient, it claims to know the Orient, and it comes to experience the Orient and its people from the position of knower. The Orient and its people, by contrast, can only ever be the object of that knowledge, positioned as known. Today, the term orientalism is deployed to critique problematic, essentialised representations of and beliefs about places, people and things from across the non-Western world – it is a 'representational assemblage' that powerfully shapes the imaginaries that also motivate and shape travel, including travel for health treatment (Salazar 2011).

Such a theory has obvious appeal for researchers exploring the IMT encounter. Writing about India, for example, Sengupta (2011: 312) credits 'the perceived exotica of the orient' as one key reason why India is rapidly developing as an IMT destination – hot on the heels of Thailand in terms of patient volume (similarly marked by orientalised exoticisation, as we explore below). He adds that colonial legacies such as English language and the familiarity of Indian doctors working in the West have added to India's appeal as a medical tourism destination. This means, he suggests, that India offers a kind of familiar exotic: exotic enough, but not too exotic. This is achieved in IMT destinations by managing the tourist's encounter with the locale – striking a balance between access to the enjoyable exotic and shielding from the more challenging aspects of exotic difference (often shorthanded as associated with being in a Third World country).

A similar fine balance is evident in marketing materials aimed at promoting particular IMT destinations in the Global South to potential travellers from the Global North. Argentina is an interesting case in this regard, also trading on the 'exotic enough, but not too exotic' balance mentioned above – especially in targeting Western tourists (mainly from the US) and in attempting to carve out a niche in a crowded regional marketplace with some very visible and dominant neighbours, especially Brazil. So, Argentina is promoted as 'a "European" and "white" alternative to other "tropical" [Latin American] tourism destinations', and Buenos Aires is marketed as the Paris of South America (McDonald 2011: 485). Argentina, conclude Viladrich and Baron-Faust (2014: 120), is presented as 'both exotic yet comfortable for Western travellers', where Western is assumed to be white – the exotic is here embodied in the natural landscape, in tango and in the bodies of Argentines, especially beautiful women (who are rendered at once naturally beautiful *and* as having enhanced their beauty through cosmetic surgery). Other Global South IMT destinations that might compete with Argentina, including India, are dismissed in Argentine media and marketing materials because they are *too* Third World: India is, in the words of one newspaper article quoted by Casanova & Sutton (2013: 67), 'known for its dirtiness' and therefore not an ideal surgical destination.

Another orientalising cultural stereotype commonly evoked in IMT marketing is that the particular destination and its people are inherently healing or caring. In Costa Rica, for example, Sara Ackerman (2010) describes efforts to link the natural landscapes with the character of the local people. 'Just with the view you will heal' (413), one respondent said to Ackerman, while others commented on the attentive care they received from all the health professionals they encountered. Ackerman productively theorises this as a form of 'medical nostalgia' for US patients longing for more care-full relationships than they currently experience through healthcare at home. Here, the developmental lag between Costa Rica and the US is seen as a positive attribute, slowing the onset of privatised healthcare, which is less associated with care than with profit (even though the US patients are accessing private healthcare in Costa Rica). Something similar is described by Harris Solomon (2011: 106) in his ethnography of US patients in a private Indian clinic. Here he found some Indian doctors promoting medical tourism 'as a form of postcolonial critique', writing how they contended that 'its popularity marks a repair to the imbalance of medical modernity, whereby the hubris of the West has left its citizens sick and stranded, only to be rescued by India's ... ascent'. India is able to avoid the 'hubris' of the West's 'over-development' (which is framed as in fact leaving people 'sick and stranded' and so is not an expression of development at all), and its 'ascent' is virtuous by comparison.

Solomon (2011: 106) quotes the head of international services at the clinic proffering a very familiar cultural stereotype used repeatedly in IMT: 'caring is part of the Indian tradition'. Similar views of caring as either tradition or natural are evident in many IMT destinations' marketing messages. Studies in Thailand of cosmetic surgery tourism and of sex reassignment surgery (SRS) have mapped this construction of 'naturally caring Thais' (Aizura 2010; Enteen 2014). In the case of SRS, Thais are also constructed as naturally embracing of non-normative genders, an idea emblematised by the *kathoey* or 'ladyboy'. As Aren Aizura (2010: 437) notes, it would be relatively simple to see this as evidence of orientalism. And yes, he concludes, orientalist discourses shape the experiences he recounts. But he adds two important qualifiers: first, that such orientalising discourses and practices are evident in mainstream Thai tourist circuits and are not particular to medical tourism; second, that the Thai nation itself selectively reproduces an orientalised imaginary of itself. Meghann Ormond (2014b: 429) writes about 'self-Orientalizing representations of destinations' culturally determined competence in caregiving (e.g. naturally caring Filipinos)', described by some writers as a form of 'strategic essentialism' (Spivak 1988). In this context, selected aspects of orientalism are reappropriated, repurposed and revalued in the service of 'selling' the nation (Buzinde & Yarnal 2012). In this way, at the least, countries of the Global South can be seen to be negotiating (and at times negating) stereotypical views rooted in orientalist perspectives.

One form of negotiation encountered in studies of medical tourism concerns what we might think of as editing or filtering. Solomon (2011: 109) observed in his study that 'institutions … take pride in carefully calibrating how India appears in their halls and encounters' – adding that some international medical tourists were uneasy about the 'globalized, English-speaking, biomedical frame' they experienced in clinics, and 'felt compelled to reconcile it with the vernacular'. And in Costa Rica, Ackerman (2010: 408) comments on how 'surgical recovery facilities are carefully purified of local conditions that are incompatible with the idealized Costa Rican imagery through which they are sold'. The phrasing of these two comments is noteworthy: neither is describing the complete purging of place from the setting; both describe instead selective uses of Indianness and Costa Ricanness, uses framing cultural specificity and valorising it as part of the medical tourism offer. It is here that the 'tourism' label of IMT becomes resonant: tourists realise the value in experiencing the unfamiliar, exotic or other, though often within limits. Medical tourists are subject to the same logic, navigating sameness and difference as they move through their surgical journey.

These comments open up space to critique a further assumption about the experiences of Western international medical tourists that we want to overturn through our own fieldwork findings: enclaving. Anthony Elliott (2008) describes this enclaving as an elite practice, also revealing a colonialist/orientalist disposition: anxiety about the destinations (and especially about their Third Worldness), with medical tourists needing the reassurance and familiarity of international lifestyle trappings. Elliott tags these 'non-places' or 'recuperative comfort zones', offering a kind of 'global privatized enclosure' (104). Yet one thing we did not encounter in our research was this kind of elite experience of placelessness. When the tourists we met did experience something like placelessness, it was because they were not sure where in the world they were, could not speak the language and so felt isolated and disconnected, rather than enclaved in luxury. They were not savvy globetrotters. And we are not alone in this type of discovery: Casanova and Sutton (2013: 70) quote a news interview with two American cosmetic surgery tourists to Buenos Aires – all they knew about Argentina before their visit was 'what we saw in the movie *Evita*'. Similarly, one of Emily McDonald's (2011: 491) respondents in Argentina was unaware of the hemisphere/seasonal crossing of her journey, arriving in Buenos Aires in June and complaining, 'I just can't believe it can be this cold in *summer*'.

Moreover, Solomon (2011) noted that some of the participants in his research felt 'compelled' to reconcile the India they knew was all around them with their insulated experiences in an international clinic. Other studies have highlighted ways in which selective encounters with difference can be woven into the medical tourism package, sold as an authentic experience rather than an enclaved one. Writing about Johannesburg, Andrew Mazzaschi (2011: 309) recounts how one IMT facilitator encouraged her clients to go on a tour of Soweto – billed as an 'urban safari'. While the intent behind this – beyond the accrual of cultural capital – could be read as countering the otherwise insular, elite experience of international medical tourists in international hospitals in South Africa's largest city, Mazzaschi argues that in practice the opposite occurred, with the 'urban safari' serving to enhance the sense of luxury and privilege among the medical tourists, even as some expressed feelings of guilt at their own indulgence in the face of poverty. We did not encounter anything like this in our fieldwork, though some participants did express feelings of guilt (but also of empathy) for the others they met in their journeys (see chapter eight). However, what is more important to note here is that wholesale placelessness was neither desired nor experienced by our participants. Rather, place was a foregrounded aspect of their touristic experience, in intended and unintended ways. Contrasting examples from our fieldwork in Thailand and Tunisia exemplify this vividly.

Notes from the field: Thailand, Tunisia

In Thailand we accompanied patients to a range of hospitals, mostly in Bangkok but also in the seaside resort towns of Pattaya and Phuket. A significant chunk of the Australian market, however, is based on group tours to a budget cosmetic surgery hospital, Yanhee, in Bangkok, which is a very different experience. It is still a functioning Thai hospital treating locals, but has none of the fancy trimmings of the up-market hospitals like Bumrungrad.

Almost all of our participants visiting Thailand talked up the hospitality and genuine kindness of their nurses and surgeons – something widely promoted as an essentially Thai characteristic in marketing materials on Thailand and easy to read as an orientalising construction of Thai nature, as discussed earlier. A respondent in Perfetto and Dholakia's (2010: 405) 'netography' of US medical tourists similarly recounted how at Bumrungrad hospital in Bangkok she received 'the very best care of Thai angels, who heal from within as well as from without'. But similar views of staff were articulated by UK patients about Poland, a country not clearly associated with caring in the British popular imaginary – in fact, in all other destinations we heard similar descriptions of caring staff, making this arguably a product of privatised medicine where service is considered important, rather than a feature of any particular destination.

Some participants visiting Thailand arrived with knowledge of the thriving sex industry as an exciting and exotic curiosity to be observed while recovering. Ping-pong shows were popular with recovering patients. Two who had booked their surgeries together in Pattaya on their agent's recommendation unknowingly landed in Thailand's sex tourism capital, yet they soon began to recount their evenings in Pattaya's red light district as the highlight of their stay, which also featured prominently in the photos they took to mark their holiday. Photos also included images of *kathoeys* seen walking on the street, objectified as tourist exotica and made part of what they described as a holiday game they named 'spot the "he/she"'. Other patients also commented on the presence of *kathoeys*. In the words of one patient, Kellie, the presence of *kathoeys* was evidence that 'if the surgeons here can make a bloke look that sexy, then my boob job will be a breeze for them'. Surgeons themselves also capitalised on this, using images of *kathoeys* in the marketing of feminising surgeries to women, such as breast augmentation and liposculpture. Here we see cosmetic surgery tourism enfolded with other tourist practices and experiences, and not disembedded from local context and culture. These recurring stories about *kathoeys* and sex shows, pampering and shopping, show that cosmetic surgery tourists who we encountered in Thailand had experiences that were very much about being in Thailand itself rather than in the surgical enclaves of their hospitals and hotels. Indeed, one only has to step outside of a hospital like Bumrungrad to be reminded of one's location, encountering Buddhist shrines and street food vendors all around.

Many IMT websites talk at length about the cleanliness of hospitals at the destinations. A critical reading of this might easily point to orientalist anxieties about dirt in Third World countries from Western tourists. However, our research has shown that patients contrast these accounts of cleanliness not with the rest of the host country but with hospitals back home. Many patients remarked on the clean facilities, and the visible cleaning work that they saw struck them as extraordinary when compared with UK or Australian hospitals – though they were most often referring to public hospitals back home:

> Yes, I wouldn't have [any] worries going abroad because I've never known such a clean hospital as what that was where I was. The room I was in, they came in three to four times a day and cleaned that room, you know, I mean the floors and everything, three and four times a day. It was spotless, it really was spotless. (Julie, Australia to Thailand)

However, when Kellie, mentioned earlier, who had made a twenty-hour low-cost trip from Brisbane to Bangkok, was left short of clean clothes as her luggage arrived two days *after* her surgery, she opted to continuously wear her only pair of underwear rather than risk what she thought would be the unhygienic consequences of washing them in the sink of her hospital room. Commentary and actions like Kellie's were, however, extremely rare among our respondents – though perhaps by commenting on the cleanliness of the hospitals there was still a slight hint of orientalist surprise among patients we spoke with that things were even better than back home.

Bolton and Skountridaki (2017: 505) describe how 'medical tourists experience stress and fear. … Anxiety stems largely from being in a foreign environment, often in a developing country'. This anxiety, we would argue, did not stem from a position of colonialism/orientalism among our respondents, but rather from experiences of *disorientation* (see also Kingsbury *et al.* 2012). We see the idea of disorienting as a means to critique some of the most rigidly imagined models of IMT as orientalist. But we are also interested in the ways in which patients experience medical travel as a disorienting experience – a different kind of relationship to place. Language was a recurrent problem in this respect. For instance, Jason, having an abdominoplasty in Poland, asked a nurse if antibiotics were being administered to him through his drip. He asked 'Antibiotic?', and the nurse was able to answer 'No', but could not volunteer further information. Jason was left wondering if he was receiving pain relief or some other drug. Sharon, meanwhile, was told by a nurse to move from her operating trolley onto her bed via hand gestures. Sharon was not sure if she was supposed to move herself or wait for further assistance, but painfully moved herself anyway.[1] In Tunisia, a daughter wanting to speak to her mother to check on her after surgery failed in her attempts because she did not speak enough French to ask the receptionist to put her through to the room.

English-speaking staff were therefore at a premium and central to business operations in the places of our study. For instance, in our Polish field site, patient appointments seemed to be scheduled as much around the availability of Jarek, the English-speaking driver, as around that of the surgeon. Jarek's role was imagined as sharing and extending the job of the patient coordinator – key to the success of the whole operation – not simply being a driver. Patients there were discouraged from taking taxis or using the tram. Across all of our field sites, patients were often poorly prepared to negotiate non-English speaking destinations, though we might suggest this reflects their often relatively low levels of cultural capital and their lack of experience of overseas travel rather than some colonialist presumption of the primacy of spoken English as the global lingua franca.

Yet it would be wrong to suggest we never encountered anything readable as colonialist or orientalist. For example, as introduced in chapter six, in Tunisia we spoke to Sally, who did deploy at times a typical orientalist narrative about her whole trip and who was very distressed by aspects of her experience. We recount the Tunisian fieldwork in detail in chapter eight, but will sketch some pertinent details here: Sally arrived in Tunisia to find that the translator, Mehdi, who she was assured by the agent would be with her at all times, had left two months previously. In addition, a nurse who was fitting her cannula stopped halfway through to answer his mobile phone and did not then wash his hands until she insisted he did so – her sister, a nurse back in the UK, had told her she must make sure that no one touched her without washing their hands first. The anxiety that she experienced escalated, compounded by her inability to communicate, into panic. Sally several times alluded to what might seem like an orientalising narrative, of wild dogs and poor hygiene, but she mitigated this by recognising her own 'paranoia' and the impacts of the procedure and drugs.

Despite their negative experiences and orientation to place, however, Sally and Kellie were both delighted with their surgeries, and said they would recommend the destination to a friend and would return if they needed to in the future. Both blamed agents for not adequately preparing them for their experiences. Other tourists' experiences of place were very varied. Most travelled straight from the airport to the hospital/clinic, having surgery the same or the following day. After a few days in hospital they were discharged to apartments or hotels, returning to the medical facility for check-ups and aftercare, provoking feelings of isolation that were made worse by lack of local language and by limits on their mobility. At times, their visible presence as cosmetic surgery recipients disrupted the experiences of other tourists in the same resorts, while their presence in hospital settings disrupted their own and other users' understandings of patienthood – though these encounters also facilitated new understandings and intercultural exchanges, as we discuss in chapter eight.

Global elites may stay in the best resorts, hotels and hospitals, and their money may insulate them from the surrounding culture, but our tourists' experiences were frequently disruptive – sense of place came crashing back in. Our Tunisian participants in particular were connected not just to their local setting but unwittingly into a set of global conflicts that they had not anticipated and did not understand. For some patients this profoundly impacted on their consciousness, as we further explore in the next chapter. Most participants in Thailand spent some of their time in surgical enclaves but then actively pursued experiences outside them – experiences that, rather than being disruptive as we observed in Tunisia, were seen as fun and novel distractions. Here, in many cases, place was relished for its difference – up to a point – in terms of 'adding value' to the trip. Many respondents took home tales of adventure that could be endlessly retold, supplemented by countless photos and other mementos, lending a touristic narrative to their surgery itself.

Conclusion

In our fieldwork we encountered very little evidence of Elliott's (2008) place-less cosmetic surgery tourism, nor of straightforwardly orientalist forms of host–guest relationship. In contrast, our empirical findings lead us to conclude that place has a profound influence on a person's cosmetic surgery tourism experience. Furthermore, this placefulness that we observed in cosmetic surgery tourism was at times deliberate and managed, as we saw in Thailand, at other times unavoidable and irruptive, as we saw in Tunisia. As others have shown, and as our research makes clear, there are distinctive geographies of cosmetic surgery tourism at different spatial scales. Directions of patient flows are heterogeneous, as cosmetic surgery tourism is assembled in an ongoing, contingent and malleable process. The main motives for travelling for treatment – cost, access, quality and availability (Holliday & Bell 2015) – map onto sending and receiving places and onto the routeways patients follow. Certainly, our findings contest easy readings of cosmetic surgery tourism as West-exploits-East or as bad (homogenising, placeless) globalisation. It is, instead, time to recognise the many decentrings and disorientations that cosmetic surgery tourism produces. And as we show in chapter eight, these disorientations should be seen as potentially productive and transformative (see also Wiles 2011).

Note

1 See Kingsbury *et al.* (2012) on the anxieties surrounding communicating about treatment in IMT.

8

COSMETIC CONVIVIALITIES AND
COSMOPOLITAN BEGINNINGS

In March 2012 we accompanied three women travelling as part of a package arranged for them by a cosmetic surgery tourism facilitator/agent to Tunisia for a variety of procedures. Lorna, who was 27 and from Scotland, worked on a North Sea oil rig and travelled for a breast augmentation and liposuction; 45-year-old Anita, the owner of an up-market hair salon in the south of England, was having a facelift; and Sally, aged 52, was having breast implants replaced, eyelids lifted, eye bags removed, the muscles in her chin and neck tightened, and a neck lift. We also interviewed 47-year-old Jenny, an IT teacher from North East England, who had won a competition run by their agent, Wendy, to have breast surgery.

The hospital we travelled to was established in 2003, and Tunisians make up around 50 per cent of its client base. The other 50 per cent are medical tourists; some are cosmetic surgery patients from the UK and France, like our respondents, but most are from surrounding Middle East and North Africa region countries such as Syria and Libya. The hospital has grown from an initial 80 beds to around 130 and currently employs around four hundred staff, tripling its revenue within ten years of opening. The hospital specialises in neurology, orthopaedics, spinal injuries, cosmetic surgery and rehabilitation, and caters to more than twenty thousand patients a year, only two hundred to three hundred of whom are from the UK. It is a great example of the success of the medical tourism industry, which developed in Tunisia after a policy change separating the public and private medical sectors. The resultant excess capacity in the private sector incentivised hospital managers to seek new markets overseas, and Tunisia has 'exported' its healthcare by attracting patients from two main markets – through a cross-border healthcare agreement with Libya, and medical tourists from Europe. The latter market includes an emerging niche in cosmetic surgery (Lautier 2008).

As was fairly typical in our research, the hospital owner does not have any medical qualifications, but received an MBA in finance from a prestigious US university. The hospital employs four cosmetic surgeons, but these are not permanent members of staff – clinics like this one in Tunisia often rent facilities to surgeons (Lautier 2008). While two of the surgeons are Tunisian and live in the country, two more fly in – one from France and the other from the US, though it should be noted these surgeons are both Tunisian emigrants – to operate largely on European patients. The two who travel to Tunisia come each month for a few days and are paid in cash by the hospital. Surgeons do not need visas to operate in Tunisia. To access the services of these surgeons in their countries of residence would be well beyond the means of our patients, but cheaper hospital costs in Tunisia (30–50 per cent cheaper than domestic prices, according to Lautier [2008]) make their skills accessible to even those with modest incomes. Here we recount the stories of the patients we met on this itinerary of our research journey.

'I was there for pure vanity and that poor guy had lost everything'

After trying many diets and failing to lose weight, Jenny had gastric bypass surgery through the NHS in Britain in 2007, but the resulting weight loss left her totally flat chested. Before winning a competition offered by Wendy – a fairly typical marketing device employed by agents – she had been saving money for a breast augmentation:

> Because I lost all that weight I lost all the fat in my breast tissue, so I was just skin really and it was horrendous for me, because I was in a new relationship and … he never saw me without my bra on … I didn't go massive … I was a 36A and I'm a 36 small D now, so I'm not like Jordan or anything like that, I just wanted to be normal, and feel a lot better in my clothes and a lot better in myself.

When asked if she felt a bit more confident with her partner having undergone the procedure, Jenny responded: 'Oh yes! He calls them the Twins! He says, you know, if we ever split up, he wants custody of one of them!' It would be easy to read her partner's comment through a feminist lens as reflecting men's entitlement to and ownership of women's bodies. However, Jenny recounts it here instead as a light-hearted and jokey compliment on her enhanced and sexier appearance and a way of affirming the durability of her relatively new relationship, through emphasising shared 'assets'. Another important point to note is that Jenny refers primarily here to the materiality of her body as the motivation for surgery.

While Lorna, Anita and Sally had all travelled after Jenny, they were nevertheless familiar with her experience. Winning the competition had come for Jenny with certain strings attached and she had spent time recounting her positive experience and reassuring subsequent patients via Wendy's website, and sometimes in support groups organised by the agent for actual and potential patients. Such activities were vital in selling cosmetic surgery in unfamiliar destinations like Tunisia, about which patients had little geopolitical knowledge. Tunisia was described to patients by the agent as 'in the Mediterranean'.

Jenny recounted the positive experience of being picked up from the airport and driven to the hospital by a local agent, Mariem, and settled in her room by Tunisian nurse Karim:

> When I got to Tunisia itself there was Karim who was the English-speaking Tunisian/Frenchman who looked after me … [he was] absolutely adorable, you just wanted to bring him home with you. I think personally, it's not very PC of me to say this, but I think personally Karim is a gay man that had to get married, if you get what I mean, because of the country he was in. Very, very feminine man, in fact he couldn't do enough for my partner, Ian … my little problem was that I couldn't make other people understand what I was on about. Karim was the main English-speaking one and if he wasn't there it was a bit difficult.

UK patients were placed in the hospital's European ward. This facilitated greater possibilities for friendship, conversation and care between patients, passing their time and alleviating the inevitable boredom of recovery. The grouping of patients also enabled them to share home comforts like tea and hot chocolate between them and, of course, to swap stories of surgery and recovery between old hands who had been in the hospital for a number of days and new patients just arriving.

While Jenny was comfortable on the ward at first, as she recovered she wanted to move further afield. However, the wider hospital proved more challenging for her to negotiate:

> I found the men quite abrupt, a little bit rude in some cases, but not in all … how they talked to you really. I don't know whether they thought that foreign women, maybe we were beneath their women, or something like that, but it could have also been due to the fact that their women are all covered up, whereas European women didn't, so they could have looked on us with less respect. It was hard at the hospital because I like to be on my feet, I'm up and about and I'm walking, and downstairs they had like a cafeteria type bit and that always used to be full of men and if you went down there, you were stared at, you know, you couldn't get past them. That was the only thing. I mean, I never went down without my partner anyway and I made sure that I was fully covered, I didn't have any bare arms and things like that, out of respect for them really, but I found that uncomfortable … but then I had to respect the fact that it was their healthcare as well, so I understood that the European people were put on one floor so we were able to talk to each other and things like that, so it wasn't too bad.

It is worth mentioning that others in the later party had a different experience of the cafeteria, spending time there and striking up conversations to relieve the boredom: 'I could not stay in that room all day, that's why I went to the coffee shop ... I got a lot out of it' (Anita). But for some of the patients, Tunisia represented a culture shock from the beginning, especially when they arrived unaccompanied. As Lorna told us:

> I was absolutely terrified! [*Laughs*] I arrived at the hospital at half past eleven at night, not a soul in sight. I just had the taxi driver take me in, he didn't speak English ... The drive to the hospital itself, it was quite dark, there was a lot of – I don't know if gangs is the right word, but there was a lot of groups of men hanging about and over the side of the road and stuff like that, and when you see Tunis in the daylight it looks like a Third World country. It's quite scary some of it, to imagine that people live like that ... the nurses didn't speak much English ... so I was basically taken to a room and told to be ready to be prepped in the morning, and I was terrified.

Not speaking French was a persistent problem for all the patients we spoke to in Tunisia and resulted in some significant difficulties. In the absence of satisfactory communication, patients often experienced procedures such as inserting or removing cannulas, or administering antibiotics and other drugs as interventions inflicted on their passive bodies rather than as care administered to knowing subjects. Unable to check what was happening to them, and unable build relationships with their carers, they worried they were being given the wrong medications, meant instead for other patients. The lack of English-speaking staff in this hospital was in contrast to larger 'international' hospitals in more popular destinations such as Thailand (see Whittaker & Chee 2015), where English language becomes one of the central markers of internationalness for these supposedly world-class facilities.

While Lorna had expected to have a room to herself, in fact she was placed in a shared room, which turned out to be an advantage. Her room-mate relayed her own positive experience – her mother and sister had also travelled to Tunisia to have surgery with the same surgeon – without which, Lorna said, 'I don't know for definite if I would have gone through with it'. This caring and information-sharing between patients was a persistent characteristic of cosmetic surgery tourism and is discussed at length in chapters five and six.

Lorna was the youngest member of the group and was undergoing a breast augmentation and liposuction after 'finally finding a diet that worked'. She regularly engaged in many other beauty practices – Botox every four months, lip fillers every six to eight months, eyelash extensions every two weeks, a spray tan every week, acrylic nails every two weeks and sometimes hair extensions: 'I spend a fortune! I think I'll be one of those people, I'll never be happy, I'll always be looking to improve.' She talked about how losing weight had resulted in a new relationship, but that it had been a bad one and she was now single again. She also described her early life and the problems she had experienced with her weight:

> Since I was five years old, everybody has had a go at me: my mum's had a go at me for being fat, my dad's had a go at me if I eat certain foods. I used to hide food when I stayed at my dad's … I was put out at 18, I've never really learned to cook properly, so it's an even harder battle to think, 'right, what's in this?' Effectively, I'm now on another diet where I pay about £350 a month, they send you their meals so I don't have to think about it. But then with my lifestyle of working [on oil rigs], between shore and off-shore, when you go off-shore you can't take any food with you – it's a constant battle really.

Lorna had been considering surgery for around five months. The opportunity for it arose when her job was reassessed and she was given a pay rise, backdated for three months after what she described as 'a battle, to say the least'. When we interviewed Lorna some time after her Tunisia trip, she was not happy with the results of her surgery. She had been hoping to drop a dress size but had remained a size 14 despite the liposuction. She was also unhappy with her breast augmentation and felt her breasts were still too small:

> I sort of expected to come back here and show them off, and they just looked the same but slightly bigger, they didn't look like they'd been done or anything. So, not really anybody noticed except for those that knew I was having surgery, which was a bit of a let-down. I mean, I'm not an exhibitionist, but when you go to the expense of paying for that. [*Laughs*]

The size of breast augmentation is a common point of misunderstanding between surgeon and patient, with surgeons frequently recommending smaller implants than patients would like (Heyes & Jones 2009). In addition, Debra Gimlin (2013) shows how the 'obviously augmented breast' is rapidly increasing in popularity. In the past, cosmetic surgery that seemed 'natural' was highly valued, but as it has become democratised, cosmetic surgery has emerged as a way of marking investment in the body. However, these markers are classed, and Holliday and Sanchez Taylor (2006) have shown that the naturalness and 'less is more' aesthetic preferred by the middle classes is not shared by working-class women seeking cosmetic surgery. Lorna is thus disappointed because she does not share her surgeon's taste in breast size. She was later able to negotiate a revision of her surgery so that she had to pay only travel costs to revisit Tunisia for bigger breasts.

Getting her surgery right was all the more important for Lorna since the money for surgery could have gone towards another kind of investment:

> Without being a sob story, I was actually made homeless. So, to be in a position where I've had a really good job and being able to afford this, it really was a

toss-up at that time whether to go and get a mortgage or to go and sort my life out and hopefully feel better with myself.

Lorna's account tells us something about the status of cosmetic surgery in relation to other important investment decisions. She is aware she could have invested her backpay in property, but she nevertheless chose to invest in surgery, which she saw as the path for her to 'sort her life out'. While some might read this as a rather frivolous choice or evidence of poor judgement, for Lorna investing in her body rather than in property meant feeling good about herself, the promise of a relationship, children perhaps, and financial and other struggles shared.

As we described earlier, Lorna's experience of arriving in Tunisia was profoundly unsettling, and her sense of disorientation was compounded by her post-operative experience. Her agent had carefully explained the risks involved in the surgery itself but had not talked about the possible effects of the anaesthetic. This was something Lorna now had to deal with while being unable to communicate with healthcare staff:

> I felt horrible. I don't think the anaesthetic agreed with me at all, I couldn't stop being sick. There weren't any nurses around to start with when I woke up, it was just like I was in a corridor on my own, it was horrible. I think somebody must have come to me after about maybe ten to twenty minutes, took me back up to my room. But they never said previous to that [what it would be like afterwards]. I tried to get fluids down me, which made me be more violently sick. It was – you know, I thought the nurse was going to come as soon as you pressed the buzzer, but it took them maybe ten minutes to come. So, I had to sort of drag myself out of bed and throw up out of the window, either that or throw up on the floor … I was quite embarrassed to be sick on the floor. The nurse came in and said, 'You can't be drinking' – [my roommate] had actually left a bottle of Coke and it was the first thing I could grab, there was nothing else around me, so I chucked that down and chucked it back up again. [*Laughs*] But the nurse came in and was like, 'No, you can't drink fluids for 12 hours', and I felt like I was going to die, I was so thirsty, it was just the most horrible feeling in the world.

After a couple of days Lorna began to feel better – and hungry – but she had also had a problem with the hospital food. Reliant on the kindness of strangers, she came to know another patient in the hospital:

> I couldn't eat the food, I was becoming ill because I couldn't eat, to the point one of the guys along the corridor, his family actually gave me fruit on a daily basis to eat, because I just could not eat the food … I just couldn't put to my mouth, it made me feel like I was going to be sick. I mean, I didn't eat to the point that when I went for my first shower on my own I honestly thought I was going to collapse. I just had no energy at all.

The generous neighbour was Mohammed, who had been hospitalised as a result of the Libyan conflict. He and his family provided Lorna with oranges and other sugary food, a kindness Lorna felt was extra special in the circumstances: 'Considering what he was in for, I think his needs were a lot greater than mine.' These small niceties notwithstanding, Lorna was still delighted to be transferred to the hotel:

> It just felt like such a weight off my shoulders, you know, you could get onto Wi-Fi, speak to people and everybody there was just so accommodating. The food was out of this world, the hotel was out of this world, it was just amazing, a comfy bed and normal TV. [*Laughs*]

While in the hospital, Lorna met another patient, Sally, who had had multiple surgeries and a very difficult recovery. Sally's extreme post-operative suffering scared Lorna – her seemingly uncontrollable pain and distress threatened to engulf her fellow travellers and confirm the popularly perceived folly of their endeavour. Lorna talked about all the people who had dismissed her plan to travel abroad for surgery as reckless or stupid, drawing on reality TV shows that portrayed cosmetic surgery disasters. Sally's pain seemed, for a few days at least, to corroborate Lorna's friends' forewarnings, leaving her feeling helpless and unprotected.

Sally had travelled to Tunisia to have saline breast implants, which she had acquired fifteen years previously in California, replaced as one had deflated. She was also having a breast uplift, eyelids lifted, eye bags removed and a face and neck lift. This was by far the greatest number of procedures of all the women we travelled with. Sally had travelled to Tunisia to save money. She had been talking to a budget clinic at home, but her surgeries were still half the price in Tunisia than they would have been in the UK. She raised the money for her surgery by selling her house:

> [The saline implant bursting] couldn't have come at a better time really, because I was selling my house anyway and I had some equity in the house, and I just thought, 'Do you know what? The kids have all had their bit over the years' – my youngest son is 32 – so, I just thought, 'Do you know what? I am going to do this for me.'

Sally had been talking to her agent, Wendy, for over a year, but her mind was made up when she spoke to Jenny, the competition winner we met earlier in this chapter. Sally's two major concerns about her destination were the language barrier and standards of hygiene, but in addition to Wendy's reassurances – 'Tunisia is MRSA-free', she reassured Sally – Jenny's account of her experiences finally convinced her she was travelling to the right destination. Although Jenny had taken her husband with her, Sally travelled alone, confessing that 'in hindsight, I would have taken someone with me'.

Both Wendy and Jenny had talked about the support of Mariem, the local agent, and Karim, the English-speaking nurse, but in Sally's experience they were both very difficult to get hold of. When Sally's daughter called the hospital to check on her mother's recovery, she could not make herself understood at the switchboard. When Sally called Mariem, Mariem was initially unavailable, then irritated by the call. Karim, meanwhile, appeared to be no longer working at the hospital. To Sally's dismay, there was also no kettle in her room and tea was difficult to come by. As mentioned in chapter seven, Sally's sister works in healthcare and had given her a list of potential dangers to look out for, so she was very unsettled when a nurse answered his phone while changing her cannula and then did not wash his hands before resuming the task. She was also upset that nurses used her drinking glass to rinse her hair while washing it and that ice for her swollen eyes was brought in a rubber glove that she considered unsterile. Sally was clear that she was delighted with her surgery and that she would still have travelled to Tunisia even had she known what the hospital experience would be like, but argued that the agent should have been more honest so she could have been more prepared. She felt Wendy painted too rosy a picture of the hospital so that she would not lose customers.

It should be noted, however, that Sally had by far the worst and most disorienting experience of all the patients we followed to Tunisia. She spent a long time in theatre undergoing multiple procedures and, like Lorna, she experienced an adverse reaction to the anaesthetic.

> I hadn't slept the whole time I was there. I only slept one night, because of the morphine and because of the anaesthetic, and I was hallucinating as well, and I was so uptight and paranoid about the cleanliness … I was so hungry, all I thought was, 'Oh my God, I am going to die of starvation in Tunisia and if I don't die of starvation in Tunisia I am going to die of an infection', and to me, I really, really was.

There was a further issue that none of the UK patients had anticipated. As Marc Lautier (2008) describes, Tunisia has a cross-border healthcare agreement with Libya. This means that Libyans may travel to Tunisia for treatment, and the Libyan government subsequently reimburses Tunisian hospitals. The hospital that Sally, Anita, Jenny and Lorna travelled to in early 2012 was part of this agreement. Late December 2010 saw the beginning of the Arab Spring, a series of demonstrations and conflicts across a number of countries in North Africa and the Middle East, beginning with the Tunisian revolution which ousted long-time president Zine El Abidine Ben Ali in January 2011. (The hospital our British patients travelled to was in fact owned by a member of the Ben Ali family.) In February 2011 a civil war began in neighbouring Libya between the forces loyal to Colonel Muammar Gaddafi and those who wanted to overthrow his government. Gaddafi was finally captured and killed while trying to escape in September 2011 and the war was declared over the following month. Insurgencies continued, however, leading to a second civil war between forces loyal to Gaddafi, the new democratically elected government and Islamic factions. As a result of the cross-border healthcare agreement, casualties from these conflicts were being treated in the Tunisian hospital we were researching, and our British patients were shocked to find they were placed in adjacent wards to Libyan patients who had lost everything. Some stayed in the hospital itself, but others were day patients and occupied local hotels or were attempting to settle in Tunisia. At one point during our visit a Libyan patient began to slash at his wrists and chest in the lobby of the hotel he was staying in, attempting suicide to escape the distress of losing his daughters in the conflict. For others, Tunisia, and the hospital in particular, was a place of safety.

On arriving at the hospital, the British patients were confronted with their close proximity to geopolitical conflicts reported on news programmes they did not watch and in newspapers they did not read. They did not know they were in Africa – which some had understood to be a country, not a continent – as they had been told they were going to 'the Mediterranean'. Their schooling had not furnished them with a good geographical knowledge and they were left with very few facts from which to construct an understanding of the situation in which they now found themselves. Instead of a clinic, which they had imagined as a kind of up-scaled beauty salon, they found themselves in a hospital with a large number of Libyan casualties of war, often marked by severe physical and emotional trauma – people who had lost eyes, limbs, partners, children or parents in the conflict. This was not the facility the British patients expected to be greeted by. Anita explained:

> I have to say I was shocked at the clinic: it wasn't a clinic it was a *hospital*, with the walking wounded from Libya the second you walked in the door. I thought it might be like a medi-spa clinic or something like that. Not a fully fledged war-torn hospital. You arrive there, straight off the plane, late at night and then you go in through A and E and the whole lobby is just full of all these people. It is a bit of a shock. It's a bit shocking.

And Sally's experience was compounded by her reaction to surgery:

> It was so noisy at night, because another thing; the hospital was also being used for the overflow hospitals in Libya for the war-torn. Now, I do have to say Mike [Wendy's husband, sometimes drafted in by her to help with patients] did skim across that with me. When he was talking about cleanliness, he said to me, 'the Libyans use it for the war-torn', but that is how he left it, but maybe they don't know that at night you can hear them screaming in pain. Plus, just outside my window I thought – because I was probably hallucinating – I thought there

were dogs, that was definite, but what I thought was happening was that they were trying to get in to my room, because all I could hear was [*makes a tapping/scratching sound*] constantly and all I could hear was what sounded to me like a pack of wolves, a pack of dogs catching its kill and the kill screaming all night long. But it wasn't … it was a dog had had puppies and the dog was off hunting and it was the puppies crying, but I didn't know that. So, a combination of things that are: I didn't eat, I didn't sleep, I had one eye open every minute, I had had a lot of drugs, I had had a lot of surgery.

Because of her experiences at the hospital, Sally checked out early and went to stay in a local hotel with Anita, who she had met in the hospital. However, the hotel only had a room for two nights, and although staff offered to transfer her to another equivalent hotel, she decided instead to fly home with Anita, which the latter found very stressful.

Although she was aware of Sally's distress, agent Wendy clearly thought that Sally was over-reacting and spent little time with her in the hospital, advocating a tough love approach and choosing to spend time dining with surgeons and exploring new business opportunities instead. She also claimed that hospital staff had been worried about Sally over-medicating with sleeping pills. Certainly, other patients described Sally becoming something of an irritant and seeming like she was 'on drugs' after she claimed to have had a vision of Christ at the end of her bed. As one recounted, 'Sally was like somebody that was on ecstasy, yeah speed, all about her, her, her, her, her, and she was just doing my head in'. At one point the agent claimed that Sally's pain and distress was caused by her visiting a nightclub with Lorna, but this allegation proved unfounded. Despite this, other patients were not unsympathetic with Wendy's position and described Sally as 'quite spoilt'. The local agent, Mariem, was also conspicuously absent, so responsibility for much of Sally's care fell upon her fellow patients, including some of the Libyan casualties in the next ward, but in particular, on Anita.

Anita travelled to Tunisia for a 'mini facelift' and fat transfer from her legs to her face because she was newly single and worried that men her age only wanted to date younger women. As a salon owner, she also talked about the requirements of working in the beauty industry:

I believe it's about self-esteem, it's to do with confidence, it's to do with self-projection. Depending on the industry you work in … mine is very much about the visual.

Shortly before she travelled to Tunisia, her grandmother died and this experience had made her question her decision to have surgery, which she now saw as risky and unnecessary. However, she had already booked her surgery and travel, so somewhat reluctantly proceeded with her journey. In many respects,

Sally's trauma, described above, defined Anita's cosmetic surgery tourism experience. Combined with her existing doubts, witnessing Sally's pain led Anita to withdraw from some of her planned surgery and undergo only the fat transfer procedure. Having had one of the lightest surgeries and therefore suffering few ill effects, Anita became central to Sally's care, arranging for her to be moved to a different room and sitting talking with her for long periods. But Anita also befriended others in the hospital:

> I asked this [nurse] … 'Could I have a cup of tea?' But she was really abrupt and then I thought, 'Don't you get a cup of tea?' … I didn't eat anything on the plane and then they come along and start sticking the ECG monitor on me, but they couldn't make it stick. It was all falling off – it was like a comedy movie, you know. And they were talking over me and all the things were falling off. I thought, 'What the fuck are they doing?' I just got up, I said, 'Look, listen, I'm going, I've made a mistake, I'm going back, I'm checking out'. And they're like, 'Why are you doing that?' And then suddenly they *could* make a cup of tea.

Mohammed, who had also helped Lorna, came along and offered Anita fruit and cigarettes in his room. Anita was surprised they were allowed to smoke on the ward. They began to converse, and Anita recalls the story Mohammed told her:

> He's a young man in Libya, he was parking his car and he was shot through his legs, through the knee caps and they stole his car … And he basically said that, you know, the hospital is amazing and when he arrived there in the ambulance that … his legs were shattered. And they basically rebuilt him.

They were joined in Mohammed's room by Sally.

> I said, 'Look Sal, I'm going, I'm out of here, I'll lose the money' … I thought [I'd] just stay there for five days … It's like, how can you recover if someone can't even make a cup of tea? And then Mohammed said, 'Well, I'm here, I speak good English'.

Mohammed proved to be an asset to both the hospital and the UK patients. His fluent English helped alleviate communication problems, and staying long term – the hospital specialises in rehabilitation – gave him knowledge which soothed the anxieties of the UK patients, helping them to navigate the unfamiliar setting. He provided them with fruit when they found the hospital food unappetising, especially post-surgery. The UK patients were deeply touched by his kindness. As Sally explained:

> I was there for pure vanity and that poor guy had lost everything. Also, down in the open area downstairs we met a lady that had just had a baby and I think she had been shot in Libya, and she couldn't even feed her baby, she couldn't

even lift her baby. And all those things just made me feel so guilty, I was so guilt-ridden while I was there, it was awful, it really was. You know like Mohammed, he had nothing ... it turned out it was him that I could hear screaming at night because they were [adjusting the pins in his legs] at night ... He had to leave; his father drove him seven hours ... to Tunisia. And that poor guy had nothing and yet he gave me his fruit ... I woke up and he was standing there with chocolate saying to me, 'Please eat, you are not eating, you eat', and he was feeding me chocolate.

The gratitude that these patients felt extended beyond the hospital stay: they kept in touch with Mohammed, and also with two Libyan women they met in the hospital and with whom they visited the cafeteria during their stay. They even sent some small funds. For Anita, Mohammed had become more than a fellow patient:

I made friends with Mohammed, and I kept in touch with him ... and will go back to see him ... to give something back, you know. I didn't want to be take, take, take. And we spoke on the phone and ... but he was quite content, you know ... I've been advised [by Mohammed] to read the Quran ... I think it's quite a spiritual awakening. So, that was all really interesting.

Cosmetic convivialities, vulnerabilities and empathies

To begin to unpack some of what occurred in this particular encounter, we draw on the literatures on cosmopolitanism and conviviality. In an under-developed aside while discussing forms of 'capitalist cosmopolitanism', Jan Nederveen Pieterse (2006: 1250) evokes 'cosmetic cosmopolitanism' as producing 'a gloss that overlays local realities'; he allies the term to notions such as 'banal cosmopolitanism' shaped by and reflected in neoliberalism and in the consumption of global brands (whether Nike or Manchester United), and seen by him as a Western-centric model that excludes other forms of cosmopolitanism – forms that he labels as 'emancipatory' since they emerge from 'below'.

This brief comment by Nederveen Pieterse produces a framing of the cosmetic as meaning trivial or shallow. But for us the phrase contains a more productive tension: what meanings does the idea of cosmetic cosmopolitanism take on in the context of our study? How might we understand some of the encounters we document in this book as moments where a kind of ordinary cosmopolitanism is being forged? Certainly, parts of the Tunisia story described above seem amenable to a reading along these lines, not least in Anita's 'spiritual awakening' which ended our account. To explore this possibility, we turn to the emerging literature on convivialities, which, since the early 2000s, has sought to think about how people live together in contexts marked by mobility and difference – often tagged in this literature as 'urban multiculture'. While conviviality is not always yoked to cosmopolitanism in these discussions, we also find productive linkages to work stressing the practices through which something like cosmopolitanism comes into being in moments of encounter (Glick Schiller *et al.* 2011; Noble 2013). As we will show, this notion of 'ordinary' or 'vernacular' cosmopolitanism *as practice* reframes what being cosmopolitan means, showing that it need not be thought of as a classed orientation or disposition, an openness to the world that is at the same time a way of accruing value for the (middle-class) self (Skeggs 2013). In the account above, it is through convivial encounters that we might be seeing 'cosmopolitan beginnings' (Yeoh & Huang 2015) – shifts in worldview that, as we discuss below, can endure beyond their immediate context, born from 'relationships of experiential commonalities despite differences' (Glick Schiller *et al.* 2011: 403).

Conviviality, for us, provides a useful lens through which to explore moments of coming together that have the potential to reorient 'the practices and capacities which people develop for living with difference' (Noble 2013: 163). This can be thought of as an 'actually existing cosmopolitanism' (Robbins 1998), a cosmopolitanism birthed (sometimes contingently or provisionally, sometimes enduringly) in convivial encounters. To reiterate, this is a cosmopolitan sociality or conviviality that is practised and experienced in context, and does not necessarily imply the taking on of cosmopolitanism as a 'universalistic self-definition' – as Glick Schiller *et al.* (2011: 404) clearly argue, 'not all those who practise cosmopolitan sociability claim a cosmopolitan identity'.

What has come to be seen by some scholars as a 'convivial turn' in social research has as its focus 'the challenges of intercultural relations in an increasingly globalised world, and the consequences this has for local relations of living together' (Wise & Noble 2016: 423). The lineage of this turn is usually traced to comments made by Paul Gilroy (2004, 2006), though this is only part of a much longer story (for overviews, see Nowicka & Vertovec 2014; Wise & Noble 2016). Gilroy deploys conviviality (and the related term *convivencia*) to think about how people in urban multiculture settings get along together, and how this getting along together requires constant work – the work of negotiation, friction and conflict. This has led to a body of work exploring the practices of conviviality, the spaces and times of conviviality, and the ways of relating that are produced and sustained in and through these practices, times and spaces – by whom, with what outcomes. The work is therefore heavily contextual and situated: studies remain mindful of the particularities of setting and of the relations that take place there; as Wise & Noble (2016: 426) put it, we need to remember that conviviality is 'done here, by these people in this context, sometimes routinized, sometimes improvisational'.

That last clause is very pertinent to the discussion that follows. Gilroy (2006) similarly notes that 'in many instances, convivial social forms have sprouted spontaneously'; it is this improvisational spontaneity that we see evident in some of the stories we recount here.

At the same time, researchers make connections across these moments, in order to build conviviality into a useful conceptual lens for understanding the question of how people live together. And while the empirical emphasis in much of this work has been everyday spaces in urban neighbourhoods characterised both by 'superdiversity' and by what Doreen Massey (2005: 149) describes as the 'throwntogetherness' of urban life, the focus on conviviality should not be read as meaning 'happy togetherness', nor the end of racism (Gilroy 2006). As noted, instead it places emphasis on negotiation, friction, even conflict, including conflicts around race. The focus on conviviality foregrounds the practices actually involved in living together, which has therefore to be seen as an accomplishment and as a form of work – 'convivial labour' – that takes place in the spaces of everyday life, such as schools, markets, call centres, shops and buses, and in the variegated public and semi-public spaces of our cities, in which are carved out 'small zones of connection' (Wise & Noble 2016: 429). We would add the sites that our cosmetic surgery tourists occupy to this list – clinic and hospital spaces, hotel lobbies, airport lounges, taxis and so on. For some of our respondents, these too become small zones of connection, spaces where convivial labour is enacted, where 'prosaic negotiations with difference through intimate proximity take place and are often compulsory and necessary' (Back & Sinha 2016: 524). Such quotidian spaces are dense with emotion, as our participants recounted in ways resonant with published autobiographical accounts of medical tourism, in which the 'singular spaces' that travellers encounter 'give rise to fleeting yet intense emotional states' (Kingsbury et al. 2012: 367).

The Tunisian stories recounted earlier in this chapter are filled with small acts of convivial labour in zones of connection, in which throwntogetherness is viscerally felt by the British patients who find themselves confronted with geopolitical realities and cultural differences embodied in the 'war-torn' but also in 'gangs' of men on the streets of 'Third World' Tunis or in the cafeteria at the hospital they find themselves in. Gestures of accommodation, such as sharing fruit, take on profound significance in these zones. This is not, to repeat, to say that racism and othering is not also evident in these zones – the international hospitals that international medical tourists inhabit are also sites of forms of racism between patients and staff, and between different groups of patients (Whittaker & Chee 2015). Gestures of accommodation are mirrored by exclusions, anxieties and hostilities, some of them racialised, some gendered, as IMT involves 'an intensely affective reckoning with deep forms of difference' (Solomon 2011: 106; see also Kingsbury et al. 2012). That reckoning can be profoundly uneasy for all parties involved. Nevertheless, as Gilroy (2004) is at pains to make clear, such zones at least contain the *potential* to open up those involved in the encounter to accommodating difference and rethinking their worldview; as Kingsbury *et al.* (2012: 374) conclude in their analysis of published accounts of IMT, 'encounters with Otherness do not necessarily lead to irruptions of anxiety'. Otherness may not be the static, once-and-for-all-ness that some post-structuralists assert.

For researchers this all means being attuned to those 'practices and capacities which people develop for living with difference' that Noble (2013: 163) highlights. These capacities, he adds, are 'acquired in ensembles of social practices and relations' (167). In the spaces of urban multiculture, such small zones of connection are both routine and spontaneous – shaped by 'the "happenstance" of "bumping into alterity" in places marked by the "thrown-together-ness" of culturally diverse settings' (173). The practices involved in doing conviviality include gestures of welcome and inclusion, empathy and understanding, negotiation and accommodation: 'Conviviality is established in different routine practices of giving and taking, talking and sharing, exchanging news and goods and so on … These banal interactions across social and ethnic boundaries give a sense of togetherness' (Nowicka & Vertovec 2014: 346).

Drawing on earlier discussions of hospitality (Bell 2012), we can think of these banal interactions as moments of conviviality, to emphasise their contingency and mutability: the give and take is mutual, the roles shifting, the practices cobbled together in the moment (though, as Noble [2013] makes clear, these can become habitual). As those gestures take place, they also make place – producing spaces as convivial, even if sometimes fleetingly. Convivial spaces are assembled, therefore, as people and things are brought together through the flows of globalisation, though this should not be misunderstood as a seamless flowing, as footloose and unbounded. In our Tunisian story, this assembling involves multiple actors, some unwittingly conscripted into performing conviviality – roommates, those sharing common spaces in the hospital, fellow travellers compelled into caring roles – as well as the many actors formally charged with providing forms of care, medical or otherwise. These relations are not always straightforward; they are marked by frustration (Anita about Sally), guilt (Sally in relation to Mohammed), feelings of being let down (as when Karim was no longer available) and numerous other frictions. Importantly, though, the intersubjective engagements produced in these convivial spaces can travel back home – relationships formed in convivial encounters can be enduring, leading to forms of 'care at a distance' such as the sending of funds by British cosmetic surgery tourists to 'war-torn' Libyans and the sharing of more spiritual forms of wellbeing from Libyans to those bodies most marked as Western and other – ageing, scantily dressed, sexually exuberant and glamorous cosmetic surgery patients.

In their study of urban conviviality, Les Back and Shamser Sinha (2016) outline what they label (after Illich 1973) tools for conviviality, one of which is 'attentiveness to the life of multiculture' (Back & Sinha 2016: 523), a curiosity about one's own social world, sometimes seen 'with the enchanted eye of a tourist'. This comment caught our attention, making us pause to ask: what if the encounter under discussion involves actual tourists, not just a touristic enchantment? Certainly, a different kind of attentiveness is at work here, for the tourist comes to the setting with a particular orientation. Even if, as tourism scholars have reminded us, tourism should not be set apart from everyday life (Edensor 2007), the tourist encounter frames the forms of attentiveness and the moments of conviviality in distinct ways, we would argue. There are spatial and temporal particularities at work here – this encounter is a temporary assemblage out of place – 'abroad' rather than 'at home', and it is time-bound rather than open-ended and ongoing. This might in many cases be a once in a lifetime experience, rather than the routinised encounters that dominate the discussion of convivialities.

Of course, the tourist brings baggage to the encounter, and takes it back with them into their everyday life. We would argue that the particularities of the cosmetic convivialities we describe in our fieldwork stories should be seen in their particularity on the one hand, but should not, on the other hand, be isolated from the ongoing practices and capacities of conviviality that our respondents might be engaged in. Certainly, in some of the cases we describe, the encounter opened up a new sense of living together and of the wider world. While more than a 'passing propinquity' (K. Brown 2012; H. Wilson 2011), the comings-together of cosmetic surgery tourism need to be seen for what they are: brief encounters (Holliday et al., 'Brief encounters', 2015). Nonetheless, beyond the encounter itself lies the possibility of ongoing change, of caring beyond the local (keeping in touch and sending money to Libyans met in the hospital), of reorientations in worldview (Anita thinking about reading the Quran).[1]

We might think of this ongoing change as arising out of experiences of empathy. While empathy has been subject to critique in other transnational contexts, such as the international development profession's 'immersion' practices (Pedwell 2012), we would offer up the encounters we discuss here as 'spaces for thinking and feeling transnational encounters differently' (165), which do more than provide ways for the neoliberal Western subject to accrue value from their experiences in the Third World. As with the critique of cosmopolitanism as a middle-class disposition that is also about accruing value (Skeggs 2013), this critical reading of the 'affective trajectory of empathy' (Pedwell 2012: 165) seems to dismiss empathy too readily, seeing it as unidirectional and appropriative. Of course, our participants are not development professionals, so the transnational politics of empathy at work here need to be read contextually. The emotional intensity and extensivity seen in accounts of IMT (Kingsbury *et al.* 2012) can be seen to produce a more care-full empathy which does not rely on fixing the 'host' as the object of empathy and the 'guest' as the subject of empathetic self-transformation. In convivial encounters, a more generous and reciprocal empathy might emerge (Gibson 2010).

Further, as Nowicka and Vertovec (2014) remind us, conviviality is also socially located. The location of the tourist – in our case, the cosmetic surgery tourist – is socially marked both at home and abroad. This shapes how conviviality gets done, as the social locations of the different actors interact through the practices of being together, if only for a relatively short time. This is in fact one of the important insights of the convivial turn – to shift attention from a cosmopolitan subject imagined as being 'at home in the world' towards different ways in which socially located actors are oriented towards the wider world, or have 'a capacity for worldliness beyond the local' (Back & Sinha 2016: 525). Such a capacity for worldliness needs to be reframed as an accomplishment, as the product of ongoing work, rather than as a predetermined orientation. Convivial encounters are thus pedagogic, in the sense that they (might) open up such a capacity for worldliness (Noble 2013). The pedagogic nature of these encounters offers an important counter to models of IMT that see medical tourists as 'preloaded' with knowledge that is unchanged by moments of encounter – the orientalist framing that suggests that the Western medical tourist sees only what they already expect to see, given the fixity of their orientalist gaze and the enclaving that insulates them from more disruptive difference, as we discussed in chapter seven. We might instead think of these moments as 'cosmopolitan beginnings' (Yeoh & Huang 2015). This does not entail a complete shift towards 'happy togetherness' – as the patients in Tunisia recount, they remained caught up in anxieties that could be read as shaded by orientalist imaginaries: about wild dogs, or gangs of men, or poor hygiene, or inedible food, or being in a 'Third World country' (figure 8.1). But we would want to keep alive the notion that in these convivial encounters, there is at least the *potential* for cosmopolitan beginnings.

For medical tourists, of course, there are other factors to consider, such as the impact of medical procedures on the embodied experience of sharing space and time with others (Ackerman 2010; McDonald 2011). Taking on the pedagogic potential of the encounter with difference that is afforded by cosmetic surgery tourism is no easy task, not least when it is experienced alongside pain, fear, doubt and sometimes 'guilt'. As we have described, the experience can be profoundly disorienting, and this no doubt shapes the ability to take up the 'tools' for conviviality that are presented. Yet, seen from a different angle, the embodied and emotional experiences of IMT produce the potential for ways of relating and ways of caring that stress 'interdependency, and multidirectionality' (Milligan & Wiles 2010: 737). There is something in the shared experiences of vulnerability in particular that seems to create 'openness, susceptibility and receptiveness', and in so doing 'might make broader social and cultural resources available to those who are positioned as vulnerable' (Wiles 2011: 579, 581; see also Fineman 2008). As Janine Wiles concludes:

> the process of recognising and accepting vulnerability may also be a potentially transformative process incorporating collective and individual journeys of change as well as more corporeal and material changes to people, places, and relationships. (Wiles 2011: 583)

So, we would want to place emphasis on the accomplishments of our respondents as 'vulnerable subjects' (Fineman 2008), in terms of reorienting, to a lesser or greater extent, their own subject positions in relation to those co-present in the encounter. In this, they undertake journeys of change, drawing on social and cultural resources because of, not in spite of, their vulnerability. If, as Yeoh and Huang (2015: 250, 256) suggest, we should 'look for cosmopolitan beginnings in unlikely places' and 'amidst the embodied encounters among all manner of people', then we reaffirm our view that the cosmetic surgery tourism encounter can indeed be one such unlikely place – a place made by all manner of people. As Christine Milligan and Janine Wiles (2010: 738) remind us in their discussion of 'landscapes of care', relationships of care 'are affected by *where they take place*' – we would want to add that these relationships also *make place*.

Conclusion: cosmopolitan beginnings?

Yeoh and Huang's (2015) focus is on cosmopolitan beginnings among transnational healthcare workers; they see care work as a 'potential site of cosmopolitan sociability' (252). This is an important intervention, not least for resituating cosmopolitanism in 'interstitial spaces as part of everyday environments where people negotiate their encounter with the rest of the world ... by opening up to, engaging [with] and *caring* for others' (255) – another way of flagging those ordinary, vernacular or actually existing cosmopolitanisms, and for focusing on cosmopolitan practices among non-elite subjects (see also Glick Schiller *et al.* 2011). The focus on care and on care work in Yeoh and Huang's (2015) research is very instructive for our analysis, since it is primarily through relations of care – formal and informal – that the convivialities we describe take shape (though their focus on caregivers needs to be balanced by thinking about the recipients of care, and by seeing these roles as interconnected and at times interchangeable; Wiles 2011). Care in cosmetic surgery tourism is *distributed*: it is proximate and distant, paid for and freely given, and it is practised by countless different people. Wise and Velayutham (2014) refer to key actors in fostering convivialities as 'transversal enablers', described as 'often charismatic people who make people feel welcome by engaging in gift exchange or creating opportunities for the production of care and trust across cultural borders' (Nowicka & Vertovec 2014: 352). For some, this is formal work: for healthcare workers, for agents and other intermediaries. Here, we might see traces of what Meghann Ormond (2013b) describes as 'strategic cosmopolitanism' (in a conscious echo of the discussion of 'strategic essentialism'), often couched in terms of providing 'culturally appropriate care' for targeted IMT populations. As she writes:

> This 'strategic' brand of cosmopolitanism breaks with universalizing conceptions of cosmopolitanism that favour the cultivation of a deterritorialized 'global citizenship' which transcends cultural difference. Rather, it thrives by reifying and commoditizing particular expressions of cultural difference (Ormond 2013b: 197).

As we saw earlier, in our discussion of orientalism, there is a complex, ongoing play of sameness and difference in the IMT encounter. While this might be institutionalised in the performance of 'culturally appropriate care' in the way that Ormond describes, it also emerges informally, in the space of the encounter – the case of Mohammed is clearly readable in this way. Roles are taken on and are exchanged, as guests become hosts and the cared-for become carers, as when Anita assists Sally. This is not to ignore that care interactions in IMT also involve tension and conflict – in fact, these have been seen to be routine aspects of formal care work in international hospitals (Whittaker & Chee 2015).

It is, perhaps, in forms of informal care and in experiences of vulnerability – in opening oneself up to being cared for by others – that conviviality itself opens up. This vulnerability – clearly discernible in the accounts of those we met not just in Tunisia, but across our study – powerfully contests models of IMT that see patients as fully centred consumer-subjects or as possessing an orientalist orientation (or both). Ethnographic engagement with the spaces of IMT enables us to move beyond such unhelpful critique, and to see how moments of conviviality and cosmopolitan beginnings flicker across the cosmetic surgery tourism encounter, at times decentring and disorienting those caught up in the encounter's unfolding, at other times enabling reciprocity, care and transformation to take place. As Noel Salazar (2011: 582) puts it, such encounters have the potential to 'transform all parties involved, changing their conception of who they are, what they know, and how they live in the world'.

Note

1   See Gibson (2010) on this point more generally in tourism encounters.

9

Conclusions

This book has mobilised the often intimate and intricate stories of individual travellers and workers in the cosmetic surgery tourism industry, alongside aggregate data, to illustrate the complex and uneven phenomenon that is cosmetic surgery tourism. Along the way we hope we have robustly dispelled some of the more common stereotypes of rich, vain women or duped young women travelling on a whim without knowledge of or preparation for surgeries in countries with cowboy surgeons and substandard healthcare. Instead, we have attempted to paint a picture of travellers – of all genders – who have informed and prepared themselves as best they can, choosing medical facilities based on the most careful personal research they were able to conduct (albeit usually without understanding the intricacies of medical qualifications and accreditations).

We have shown that online communities of would-be, current and previous patient-consumers equip medical travellers with a demystified form of knowledge more useful to them in practice than unfathomable medical acronyms and memberships. Patient-consumers use this knowledge to identify and access well-equipped, clean and properly staffed, sometimes quite luxurious clinics in the private sector (with the exception of the poorest travellers such as those travelling for gender reassignment surgeries from Laos to Thailand). Nevertheless, these clinics offer significant savings on prices back home (though we found some examples, such as wealthy Chinese patients going to Seoul for facial surgeries, where costs abroad exceeded those at home, and where drivers other than cost, such as safety and quality, were at play). In this conclusion we reiterate the main findings of our research and make suggestions for the future of the industry. We begin by discussing the industry as a significant employer of a whole range of workers, as discussed in more detail in chapters four and five.

Employment in cosmetic surgery tourism

We have demonstrated that cosmetic surgery offers significant opportunities for well-paid and well-respected employment in destination countries. This privileges those who have previously travelled (such as surgeons with experience of working in countries like the US and the UK) who can mobilise experience abroad as valuable capital in the medical tourism industry. Further, we have demonstrated how usually low-paid, low-status workers like Jarek, the driver in Poland, can become important in cosmetic surgery tourism. Jarek's previous experience of language and culture gained through migration for work in the UK was deployed to care for UK patients back home in Poland. He was crucial to the extent that, for patients, fitting around his schedule became even more important than fitting around the surgeon's. This mundane cosmopolitanism comes to hold significant value in the world of international medical travel. Language skills are essential, of course, but a culturally sensitive sense of humour when transporting nervous passengers facing surgery alone in an unfamiliar country makes workers like Jarek lynchpins of their organisations.

The cosmetic surgery tourism industry provides significant opportunities for surgeons too. Surgeons reported higher earnings than were possible working in the public sector or not-for-profit hospitals. However, they also talked at length about the satisfactions of being able to practice medicine in the ways that they had been trained to expect but that they found impossible to in tax-funded basic care sectors (this applied no matter which country they were in) by moving from other specialisms, where surgeries were less varied, into cosmetic surgery. While they certainly valued the variety and creativity of the work they could undertake, and enjoyed working in an environment where a death on the operating table is far less likely compared to other branches of surgery, what seemed to afford them the greatest satisfaction was the more holistic model of 'care for the whole person' that in the private cosmetic surgery tourism sector they had time to mobilise.

Finally, the cosmetic surgery tourism industry offers significant possibilities for agents. While more senior types of MTFs are ideally equipped to combine knowledge of private healthcare with newly developing digital resources, happily riding the wave of this rapidly developing industry, at the other end of the scale former patients can create transnational micro-businesses as agents, based on their pioneering experiences. The latter businesses are small and precarious, vulnerable to aggrieved clients who can deploy against them the same digital resources that enable the significant successes of larger MTFs, with sometimes devastating consequences. While agents' positions are precarious, they can also reap rewards – not significant financial ones, but certainly a degree of upward social and professional mobility. Depending on the numbers of patient-consumers they can directly facilitate and care for, they are able to make a living, socialise with surgeons and hospital managers, travel the world, and accrue and deploy valued forms of medical, social and cultural knowledge. Such are the industry's job satisfactions.

Neoliberalisation and responsibilisation in healthcare

We could end this book having outlined a comprehensive picture of the cosmetic surgery industry and the intricacies of its workings, but there is a bigger story to tell. This is the story of the significant and growing movement of patients across national boundaries in search of medical intervention. As developed countries in the Global North and East Asia neoliberalise, they effect four changes. First, they roll back the resources of the state. As Meghann Ormond (2013a) shows, national healthcare is being redefined from an individual human right to a charitable safety net providing basic and emergency care for those who cannot afford to go private. Second, expectations for quality healthcare are being raised through numerous patient-centred interventions such as treatment, practitioner or trial 'choices', by direct marketing by drug and medical device companies and through different types of media representations, especially medical reality TV (see Holliday 2019). Raising expectations while cutting care creates the space for a burgeoning private sector for healthcare. Third, patients are being 'responsibilised' – in the face of healthcare rationing, patients are now required and expected to look after their own health. They are told they should not drink, or smoke, or become overweight; they should eat healthily and exercise, and if they have a medical condition, they should learn about it and direct their own care, accessing trials and feeding back their experiences to drug companies where possible. Being ill is now a job in itself, as Kerr and Cunningham-Burley (2015) argue. Finally, if things become so bad that conventional treatments do not work, patients should never give up, but rather seek experimental technologies in low-regulation countries, as Petersen *et al.* (2017) show. Hope has become an ethic for neoliberal responsibilised patients. And for wealthy patients, this works. We are able to access more and better medical treatments than ever before. Our options are limited only by the depth of our pockets.[1]

Once patients are made into patient-consumers in the neoliberal private healthcare market, cost inevitably becomes a factor and the IMT market is born. This is a problem for domestic private healthcare companies whose profits depend on keeping patients in their home countries with their needs unmet by the state. It is this condition that means that international medical travel becomes a moral panic. On the one hand in the UK, the post-war deal between citizens who agree to pay taxes in return for state-provided healthcare (the NHS) has all but broken down, producing much popular anxiety and pushing citizens towards private medicine. On the other hand, private domestic healthcare companies and their representatives actively emphasise the dangers of medical tourism in an attempt to keep business at home, perpetuating myths about irresponsible patient-consumers, unregulated foreign healthcare and the costs to the taxpayer of patching up casualties of IMT.

We are moving, apparently inexorably, away from a post-war consensus of high taxation and a commitment to care for each other, further and further into the individualising, responsibilising neoliberal agenda of healthcare rationing and private provision. Thus, the relatively small number of international medical tourists (very conservatively sixty to eighty thousand per annum in the UK, twenty to thirty thousand per annum in Australia) is only set to grow as patients who are less well-off are squeezed out of increasingly privatised and expensive domestic markets. In this context, understanding the intricacies of different IMT sectors is vital: as Beth Kangas (2011: 329) writes, 'speaking in generalisations and stereotypes interferes with our abilities to uncover the commonalities and complexities within international medical travel'. Cosmetic surgery is already privatised and, in most cases, considered beyond the duty of state or medical insurance provision. We think, therefore, that cosmetic surgery tourism is an excellent indicator of things to come. It is a glimpse into a future of out-of-pocket medicine involving travel to different destinations, stratified according to the income bracket of patient-consumers. It is a future in which medical professionals move relatively freely from country to country to sell and provide services according to the relative cost of facilities and degree of regulation each country imposes. We should take note!

But why, we might ask, should we worry about this, given that the results of this major study paint a picture of significant satisfaction for both industry workers and patient-consumers (recall that 97 per cent of the latter said they were happy with their surgeries and would recommend their surgeon to a friend)? To begin to answer this question, we take a break in our conclusive arguments here to tell one final important story – about an Australian man who died following multiple cosmetic surgery operations in Malaysia. Some of the points made below may seem to run counter to what we have argued elsewhere in this book, but we strongly emphasise that this case was a dramatic exception. Leigh's extreme level of risk-taking was rarely observed in any of our other patient-consumers who to the best of their abilities, as we have shown, were very careful with research, planning and the sharing of important knowledge.

So, why tell a story about a cosmetic surgery tourism death in this book? Leigh's story is deployed partly to show that cosmetic surgery and cosmetic surgery tourism are always intersubjective: experienced in an individual's personal history as well as, crucially, in networks of technologies, media, discourses, surgeons, clinics and agents. We also aim to show here that one of the most difficult tasks we have undertaken in this project has been trying to reconcile the needs and desires of specific individuals with the socio-cultural, financial and geographic context in which each individual lives. We have shown there are no easy answers to the many questions and dilemmas that circulate around cosmetic surgery tourism: for some countries it generates a place in the global economy, high-tech economies and increased GDP, while for practitioners and providers it creates wealth and job satisfaction. For most patients it is a means to obtain bodies (but maybe not subjects) of value. For Leigh it provided, ultimately, an end to life.

Blame and shame: a cosmetic surgery tourism death

Leigh grew up in a middle-class suburb of Melbourne, a city located on the south-east coast of Australia, with a loving family. As an adult he found it difficult to concentrate or to hold down employment, and he went from job to job with periods out of work. He became obese and was much later diagnosed with severe obstructive sleep apnoea, a condition where the muscular walls of the throat narrow during sleep and interfere with breathing. The condition is associated with poor concentration, daytime sleepiness, hyperactivity, obesity and serious complaints like heart attacks, stroke and diabetes (NHS n.d.). But before Leigh knew about his condition, at age 27, he decided to join the Australian Army. Army life was hard for Leigh. His mother told us:

> It was all abuse, verbally and mentally ... Well, he'd wake up, and someone would be naked in front of him, with his penis right in front of Leigh's face, and saying some words to him. The other thing is they'd call him a fat c-u-n-t, mummy's boy, floppy tits. That continuously, continuously happened – it wasn't just once, it was every day.

Despite the bullying, Leigh had found a sense of purpose in the Army. But the Army decided it did not want him and he had to leave: 'They all stood around me,' he told his mother. 'I had no choice but to sign the release papers.' She recounted:

> He came home and he sat there and he broke down. He was down and out for months, probably a year or two with that. And this [cosmetic surgery] operation was meant to be an end and a beginning, to end everything, to get his body the way he wanted it to be.

One way of framing this bullying and Leigh's subsequent actions is to deploy Raewyn Connell's ([1987] 2005) concept of hegemonic masculinity. She explains how the most idealised and most powerful form of masculinity in Western culture is built around characteristics of financial success, physical strength, stoicism and emotional and physical self-sufficiency. This hegemonic masculinity is so entrenched that deviations from it can lead to social and physical penalties like ridicule, discrimination, violence and even death. Importantly, Connell argues that hegemonic masculinity is intertwined with men's bodies. A hegemonic masculine lens shows proper men's bodies as strong and muscular, healthy and not disabled, and thus able to fulfil what other masculinity theorists have called 'pragmatic embodiment' – an embodiment that allows men to perform normative roles such as worker, sportsman and father (Jackson & Lyons 2012; McCreary *et al.* 2005; Watson 2000). Because of his obesity, Leigh was feminised when he joined the Australian Army, the men around him making it clear that he did not fit any acceptable hegemonic masculine ideal due to his weight and his snoring. He woke daily with an erect penis in his face and he was continually called a cunt: these are forms of harassment designed to ridicule and intimidate but also to explicitly and crudely feminise within a deeply masculine environment.

Leigh was obese, but army life helped him to lose massive amounts of weight. Sadly, this made no difference to his status as other in relation to the rampant masculinity around him. He would phone his mum and say: 'I am so ridiculed here and I'm being bullied all because I've lost weight and when I go swimming my skin's floating ... It's really embarrassing and they're doing things.' He wouldn't tell his mother what these 'things' were. Doing her best, and constrained by her own ideas of what it means to be a real man, his mother explained to us that she told him: 'Leigh you're strong, you can take it, not take it, but just ignore it. You're a bigger man if you just ignore it.' But Leigh told her, 'You've got no idea what they're like'. She told us that 'even the corporal or the sergeant, the man in charge of the platoon, he pushed people to tease Leigh, which was worse'.

Two things are evident here: firstly, his mother, in line with cultural norms, told Leigh to 'take it' and 'be a bigger man', pointing to hegemonic masculinity's emphasis on the stoic ability to endure physical and psychic pain without complaint. Secondly, we see here what Drummond (2010) calls a '*hierarchy of masculinities*', where behaviour is taught and led by those higher up, with correctly performed masculinity leading to promotion or success. In any hierarchy someone has to be at the bottom, and in this case it was Leigh: fat, flabby and snoring.

Phenomenologist Drew Leder (1990) writes about *dys-appearance* versus *disappearance*. If we are not ill or in pain, our bodies 'disappear' in a sense – they may recede into the background of our consciousnesses (this is, of course, much truer for white men than for women or people of colour, for a multitude of social and cultural reasons). However, if in pain or sick, the body does the opposite: it 'dys-appears' – its 'dys' is foregrounded in every experience and it becomes central to experience. Leder expands this 'dys' affect as connected to both the bodily/sensorial and the social/cultural. Our bodies come into the foreground not only when we are ill or injured, but also when we are subjected to othering through cultural gazes and social judgements, such as those suffered by Leigh because of his weight and later his loose skin. Obese men, like men with disabilities or those who are old or ill, are vulnerable because their bodies do not align with hegemonic masculinity, but they bear an added burden, which is that their weight is widely thought to be their own fault, further demonising them as lacking willpower and self-control (Wright & Harwood 2009), two more vital aspects of hegemonic masculinity.

Like many people who lose vast amounts of weight, Leigh was left with flaps of loose skin, including an 'apron' that hung down past his groin. His mother told us: 'He looked fantastic and I said to him, "Let me pay for your operation, get the apron done".' She was referring to paying for a 360-degree or circumferential apronectomy/abdominoplasty, but it was unaffordable via the private system in Australia. Leigh joined a waiting list to have it done through Medicare, only to be told two years later that the operation had been re-classified as elective and taken off the list of procedures available (similar reclassifications in the UK have also pushed NHS patients into cosmetic surgery tourism). It seemed the operation would never happen, but in a twist of fate it turned out that Leigh had not been the only person bullied and sexually harassed in the Australian Army at that time, and he was invited to be part of a class action run by a large law firm specialising in workers' rights. Four years after leaving the Army he received a large sum in compensation. His mother explained:

> He got a payout ... he won the case against them [the Australian Army]. And with that money, that was how he spent it, to go to Kuala Lumpur. He was determined, two-hundred per cent determined [to have the operation].

The day after being notified of the success of the compensation claim, he booked his surgery through an agent with whom he had been in contact for a few years. The operation would be affordable in Kuala Lumpur. Leigh did not tell his family doctor of his plans, and he did not tell his family the whole truth about several other operations he planned to undergo. And so, it came that he travelled to Malaysia and underwent a 360-degree apronectomy, as well as liposuction, blepharoplasty, a thigh lift ('leg tuck'), lip augmentation and some sort of chest surgery (his mother was not clear what this had been).

Despite having being bullied for being seen as less than masculine, the risk taking and active performing of willpower and fearlessness that Leigh showed in travelling for such a dramatic set of surgeries were distinctly 'masculine' traits (Robertson 2007). In rushing off to Kuala Lumpur, in booking in for multiple operations, in not telling his family or his GP the truth, in spending all his newly acquired money, we suggest that in fact Leigh was performing a very masculine, although wildly contradictory, set of acts: he was demonstrating independence, and he was doing so through risky behaviour.

Things did not go well in Kuala Lumpur. Leigh's mother told us:

> Three days before he came back, he collapsed. I've got horrific photos of all the blood on the sheets [in the hotel] and all the blood in the car [that took him back to the clinic]. His stitches were opening up and bursting like that. And every couple of days they'd burst and the agent would take him back to the hospital to get stitched up again.

He told her on the phone that he was in a lot of pain and could not walk, but still did not confess as to how many procedures he had actually undergone. It was not until he got home, in fact, that his mother realised how many operations he had had and how long he had been under general anaesthetic:

> He was twelve hours for the 360 op. They had to turn him over. Then he went on to having more operations! Liposuction on the thighs and somewhere else, a leg tuck, and something to do with the chest. He had his lips done! I don't know what he had done. And his eyelids. He had that fixed. So, one, two, three, four, five ... five [operations] in four weeks he had.

Leigh came off the plane in a wheelchair. His mother described his shocking appearance:

> His tube hole was quite big when he was here. I could see into it. On the side. It didn't heal at all ... [his abdomen] was all distended. It was all swollen. And I could smell the infection on him. Or was I smelling death, because his organs were beginning to shut down? I don't know what it was.

When they got home from the airport, he told his mother that he had major regrets over having had the surgeries. His regret was tragically to prove well founded. His mother described his death that night in harrowing detail – below is a small portion of what she told us:

> I tucked him in [that night] ... he was drowsy ... [then at] quarter past six in the morning I just heard a big thump and I came running out, looking in his room and he was lying on the floor, and I said, 'Leigh, what's the matter?' I was trying to help him up and he said, 'I can't breathe' ... He was so clammy and sweaty. I said, 'Oh my God, he's having a heart attack'. I was saying 'breathe, breathe, breathe', and he was saying 'I can't, I can't', and he was bashing his chest.

An ambulance arrived, CPR was performed, defibrillator pads were used, but eventually the paramedics told her that her son was dying:

> Two more ambos [paramedics] came, they worked and worked on him. They all had a go. They got the paddles out, it didn't work. They came to tell me after

twenty minutes that he hadn't responded. Nearly three quarters of an hour went by and they said, 'You need to be prepared' … One of them said, 'Talk to him because their hearing goes last', so I just lay down next to him and I kissed him and just kept talking to him, just telling him he was safe, to let his fears go, and I [told him to] just go in peace as such.

Perhaps the most poignant thing Leigh's mother told us was that his cosmetic surgery operation 'was meant to be an end and a beginning, to end everything, to get his body the way he wanted it to be'. To recall Leder (1990), Leigh wanted his abject, dys-appearing body to be dealt with, to disappear – the operations were in that sense meant 'to end everything', as his mother put it, allowing him to become neutral in terms of pain, ridicule and negative visibility. Instead, what Leigh got was a dramatic heightening of his dys-appearance: the body he died with was worse – in every sense – than it had ever been and was hugely foregrounded in terms of pain, function and appearance. Even in death, Leigh remained abject, the subject of a re-opened coroner's case and much media attention. Leigh's dys-appearance, his desperation to be fixed and the self-responsibilisation that he enacted by taking his problems into own hands parallels many of the other stories that make up this book. His decision to spend hard-won money, to travel and to willingly undergo physical pain were all things that, for most other cosmetic surgery tourists, lead to surgical success (however each individual might define that).

We have shown in this book that examining cosmetic surgery tourism only through the binary relationship between patient and surgeon is deeply inadequate. Cosmetic surgery tourism is made up of multifarious intermediaries and of intertwined networks that are cultural, personal and social. In this case then, who is to blame for Leigh's death? Who or what killed Leigh? His mother insisted it was not a natural death – that it could not be put down to pulmonary embolism as the first coroner had found. Had the agent been neglectful? Had the surgeon been reckless? Had air travel so soon after an operation, a risk every medical tourist takes, been a factor? Or was it something much more insidious and widespread: was it being a man, living up to the strict requirements of hegemonic masculinity, that killed Leigh? A web of people, objects and processes created this death, and thus – like all instances of cosmetic surgery tourism – it can only properly be examined through a range of disciplines and scholarly approaches. Leigh's death was a tragic cumulative node in a largely unregulated network fuelled by brutal gender norms, the breakdown of state healthcare, and increasing cultural imperatives for people to take their health and their appearances into their own hands.

This story came to us after the end of our project (Leigh's mother made contact upon hearing about the project in the Australian media). Leigh's death does not count in our statistics from the more than two hundred qualitative interviews we conducted. But nevertheless, we have included it here because it serves as a stark reminder that things can and do go wrong. Many of the patient-consumers we spoke to – men and women – had suffered some sort of social stigma because of a body part. In this way they were subject to dysappearing bodies. Although none of them told us about suffering intense bullying like Leigh, many were nevertheless experiencing a level of unhappiness because their bodies did not align with certain cultural ideals or selfimage, and sought to rectify this through 'fixing' a body part. So, while Leigh's story shows the dark side of cosmetic surgery tourism and tells of a worst-case scenario, it is also an escalated and disastrous version of other stories. We also note that, although statistics are notoriously difficult to come by, deaths and complications from cosmetic surgery also happen in non-tourist scenarios.

Surgery carries risks both at home and abroad; in cases of elective surgery, many might argue that these risks are not worth taking. Beauty, they would argue, is only skin deep. Bodies should not matter. But the reality is that in a service economy in which the customer encounter is key, people are hired and fired because of their bodies and their looks (Leigh's weight was key to his 'failure' in the Australian Army). Letting oneself go is not an option. Bodies are part of the human capital that corporations sell. Looking after one's body and one's looks is the ethical duty of the corporatised neoliberal subject: having a 'good body' is one of the keys to happiness and fulfilment. Cosmetic surgery patients do not travel abroad on a whim, they travel because selfimprovement is an ethic. Letting go is both a source and sign of shame.

We should not ask why people want cosmetic surgery. This is a question asked only by those with multiple other sources of value. The reason for having cosmetic surgery is obvious: to improve. Having cosmetic surgery carries risks, but as individualised consumers we are asked to calculate risks every day. In the UK, for instance, the PIP scandal (discussed in chapter two) demonstrated that the privatised cosmetic surgery industry is almost entirely unregulated. Indeed, the government review set up to reconsider this situation ultimately decided that surgeons should be self-regulating, despite a further scandal where British surgeon Ian Paterson was jailed for fifteen years for needlessly removing the healthy breasts of suspected cancer patients to increase his income (Campbell 2017). But regulation, they say, is for the 'Nanny State'.

Parting thoughts

Since we want to infer conclusions that are broader than cosmetic surgery, conclusions that could be useful to the growing number of international medical travellers in search of affordable procedures, simply saying 'don't do it' is not good enough. Instead, we hope that this study will join others in calling for the recognition that healthcare is becoming globalised and that we need to make some big decisions about whether or not we want the form of its globalisation left to the invisible hand of the market or whether we want to intervene. At present, what is considered necessary or elective is being hotly disputed in national(ised) healthcare systems that are becoming increasingly financially squeezed, and so definitions are changing in order to accommodate rationing. In our examples the boundary between reconstructive (necessary) and cosmetic (elective) in the UK's NHS and Australia's Medicare is shifting patients who previously had access to procedures such as post-weight-loss body contouring surgery from being able to access it for free (albeit after a wait of up to three years) to having to access it in the private healthcare market. As these boundaries become increasingly tightly drawn, more people are pushed into medical tourism. It seems vital then that we try to make medical tourism itself safer and more transparent for patients, while at the same time noting that healthcare rationing leads to medical tourism and its consequences. We will now turn, then, to some of the problematic issues that our patient-consumers faced on their travels abroad to secure medical services.

First, while healthcare is becoming globalised, medical records are frequently national, and in many countries unavailable to the patients about whom they are written. This causes a number of problems such as patient-consumers being unaware of or withholding information about underlying medical problems that may impact on their surgery or recovery. We met patients with diabetes, high blood pressure, recovering from cancer or other illnesses who had not informed their surgeon and who in some cases only became aware of their condition in pre-surgery checks. In one very dramatic case this underlying condition was not picked up in pre-surgery tests and resulted in the patient needing life-saving blood transfusions after surgery.

Second, because of the stigma of both cosmetic surgery and international medical travel, and because of rules about liability, it is very hard for patients to consult with their GPs or seek their advice before they travel. In addition, GPs can be uncomfortable carrying out minor procedures, such as the removal of stitches, changing of dressings or draining of seromas (fluid) from wounds after patient-consumers return home because they could be made liable if the patient subsequently contracts an infection. For these reasons, and because of the common misconception of both cosmetic surgery patients and international medical travellers as selfish and irresponsible, and of their journeys as highly risky and likely to result in cost to national healthcare back home in times of severe healthcare rationing, relationships between international medical tourists and GPs can be tense, to say the least.

While we recorded a complication rate of 17 per cent and a satisfaction rate of 97 per cent – as reported from the patient-consumers we interviewed – we should stress that these (frequently cited) headline figures are much more complex in practice. First, cosmetic surgery has two different but always inter-linked kinds of outcome – medical and aesthetic. The satisfaction rate some-times included those who had already undergone revisions to their original surgery, for example having larger implants inserted, or seromas or scars from original surgeries corrected. Where these surgeries were offered free of charge, patient-consumers were likely to report very high satisfaction rates, but less so if accessing revisions was difficult or if surgeons played down their concerns about the outcome of the original procedure. So, satisfaction tended to pertain to aesthetic result.

In terms of counting complications, we included a number of very small things that may not even usually be considered – such as the draining of seromas, re-stitching or stitch removal and the treatment of minor infections. These are the issues that were most likely to return patients to the NHS or Medicare, and 9 per cent of our patients needed these kinds of treatments when they returned home. This means that 17 per cent actually represents a fairly low risk rate, especially when we consider that a sizeable group of our cosmetic surgery tourists were having body contouring or abdominoplasty procedures that often carry a revision rate of nearer 50 per cent in the UK. It was this latter group for whom things were most likely to go spectacularly wrong – as they did for Leigh and for Jason, who needed months of NHS treatment and a vacuum pump to heal his wounds (see figure 1.1c). For most though, cosmetic surgery abroad does not seem to be any more risky than cosmetic surgery at home. However, we must be clear that our participants were self-selecting and this was not a randomised, controlled survey. Patients who fared badly may have been more reluctant to participate in our research. Nevertheless, we could also point out how much happier our participants reported being after surgery than they were before, and when calculating the costs to the NHS or Medicare of cosmetic surgery tourism, this should perhaps also be considered. Happier people are often healthier.

Other factors that added to satisfaction were to do with language, culture and geography. Participants in our study (and increasingly international medical tourists more generally) were not wealthy cosmopolitan jet-setters (as Elliott 2008 suggests). Instead, they were people who had been priced out of access to the medicine they sought at home. Staying home is, of course, an easier and more comfortable option because friends and family are on hand should anything go wrong, and doctors, nurses and patients share the same language. Some of our international medical tourists were distressed by the thought of medical staff who did not speak their language administering intra-venous medicines that they were unable to identify. Their relatives struggled to check on their condition after surgery because they could not communicate with switchboard staff. They were unable to get help in hotels and apartments when their Internet connection broke down or they were unable to log on, again limiting communication with loved ones back home. Different cultural conventions meant that international medical tourists struggled with unfamiliar local food while in hospital or recovery hotels, or found themselves unable to access simple home comforts like tea. They also made sharing public spaces in some hospitals uncomfortable. While most patient-consumers expressed nothing but admiration for the facilities they visited, they were sometimes shocked by the general location. They found themselves in countries that were not where they expected and, occasionally, were caught up in conflicts reported on news channels they did not watch. These elements were shocking to our patient-consumers, especially when the high-tech clinics they visited sat in close proximity to local poverty and squalor.

While attempts are being made to regulate healthcare across the European Union, very little cross-border regulation is currently in place for private healthcare. Some, although not many, countries have very highly regulated private healthcare (Belgium, for instance), yet this often only applies to a country's own citizens. In the majority of cases where regulation is needed most – where medicine is practised for profit – it is regulated least. In addition, while healthcare is becoming global, laws and regulations remain largely national, meaning that claiming compensation across national borders can prove extremely difficult. Even if a case of medical negligence is proved for a patient in his or her own country, and the home country's courts accept jurisdiction, there can be no certainty that the clinic's local courts can be compelled to or even be in a position to enforce any judgement if the clinic or surgeon is uninsured and has no assets (see Vick 2012). Some clinics offer guarantees for surgery but it is often impossible to identify who is liable – the surgeon or the clinic – and liability can fall between the two. Few patient-consumers are provided with proper paperwork defining responsibilities if and when problems arise. In addition, because surgeons are so geographically mobile they can easily disappear, even from countries that hold them accountable for shoddy work. But this, of course, might equally be the case in home countries that also employ surgeons from abroad.

With faulty or substandard medical devices, it becomes even more complicated because neither surgeon nor clinic may be liable, but rather the manufacturer, who may be in yet another country: we saw the liability dodged in highly effective ways along similar lines in the European PIP scandal. Some patients we spoke with had purchased insurance policies designed to cover them in the case of problematic outcomes, but even when this covered the cost of revisions to surgery, patients often needed to pay the cost of returning to and staying in their destination country themselves. Even then, insurance policies often ran out a year after surgery, and because surgeons were unlikely to concede that a final result had been achieved without a year's recovery time, costs for revision visits were often not recoverable.

One of the most important points we make in this book is that individuals who choose cosmetic surgery tourism are responding rationally and thoughtfully to their social and cultural environments. As cultural sociologists and geographers, we think that trying to explain cosmetic surgery tourism at the level of an individual's psyche risks ignoring both the complex cultural and social demands that all citizens try to fulfil and the value they accrue from meeting social expectations. Recommendations in the UK by the Nuffield Council on Bioethics (2017) to limit advertising and thereby supposedly erase the desire for cosmetic surgery fail to acknowledge this. Eliminating advertising will not remove the desire to improve oneself, because we do not simply compare our bodies with glossy images, but with other bodies and with our own bodies at different times. As Debra Gimlin (2014) has shown, previous attempts to ban surgeons from advertising have simply resulted in increased protectionism. Diverting patients from surgery to counselling simply transfers the profits from surgeons to therapists.

We assert that cosmetic surgery tourism as undertaken by the people we interviewed is not inherently dangerous. In spite of surgical and medical associations' regular press releases to the contrary, we find no evidence that cosmetic surgery abroad is more risky than cosmetic surgery at home. Indeed, many of our interviewees told us that they felt safer, more listened to, and had better results and better experiences abroad than they could have expected at home. Incidentally, we wonder if the media constructions of irresponsible patients making whimsical and risky journeys would even be possible if cosmetic surgery tourists were not universally represented as women.

Beautyscapes is of course also an intervention into the academic research literature on IMT. By providing a detailed ethnographic discussion of particular assemblages of cosmetic surgery tourism, in particular places and times, it responds to calls to disaggregate discussions of IMT, to reflect that, as Whittaker and Chee (2016: 287) write, 'medical travel is not a singular phenomenon, but one that differs depending on region, country of origin, destination, financial status, type and status of the medical treatment required, legal status of patients, language and cultural affinity, distance travelled and social support'. Through our study we have strengthened this call and others that argue for qualitative empirical study rather than supposition and generalisation. The field of medical tourism studies is maturing, and we welcome its methodological and theoretical developments – to which our own work contributes. Our multi-site study has enabled us to pick out commonalities and differences showing how geography matters, while our focus on experiences and narratives reminds researchers of the importance of talking and listening, recognising that cosmetic surgery tourism is a discursive practice as well as a surgical one.

The focus on cosmetic surgery tourism, meanwhile, has enabled us to rethink entrenched positions regarding cosmetic surgery. We have opened up to critical scrutiny the many forms of work that come together to make cosmetic surgery tourism happen, both extending discussions of paid formal work in healthcare and hospitality, and highlighting the vital work roles taken up informally by carers and by patients themselves. We have turned attention to forms of social relations among patients, either in and around clinics or online. Patients make community, and this work is central to assembling cosmetic surgery tourism. Thinking of cosmetic surgery tourism as an assemblage, finally, enables us to conceptualise both its whole and its parts, to expect contingency and mutability, to be alert to the ways different heterogeneous elements are brought together to enable someone to travel abroad to access treatment to improve their appearance. But this conceptual work only makes sense when it is matched by a commitment to do justice to the narratives and experiences we encountered: as noted earlier, our ethical position is not to be for or against cosmetic surgery tourism, but to ensure that we think with what we were told, to suggest ways in which those who choose to travel for treatment abroad can do so in an environment that supports their choices and decisions, that provides appropriate regulation and potential for redress, without losing sight of the structural transformations and cultural conditions that, in their own ways, bring cosmetic surgery tourism into being.

Note

1 For example, the parents of Ashya King, a 5-year-old British boy with a brain tumour, sold their holiday villa in Spain to access proton beam therapy in the Czech Republic, because without this treatment, available so close to but not in the UK, their child would lose a large part of his brain along with his tumour had he been treated using conventional therapies available at no cost (see Bell *et al.* 2015).

References

Abadie, R. (2010) *The Professional Guinea Pig: Big Pharma and the Risky World of Human Subjects*, Durham, NC: Duke University Press.

Ackerman, S. (2010) Plastic paradise: transforming bodies and selves in Costa Rica's cosmetic surgery tourism industry, *Medical Anthropology: Cross-Cultural Studies in Health & Illness*, 29 (4), 403–423.

Adams, J. (2010) Motivational narratives and assessments of the body after cosmetic surgery, *Qualitative Health Research*, 20 (6), 755–767.

Adams, J. (2013) Medicalization and the market economy: constructing cosmetic surgery as consumable health care, *Sociological Spectrum*, 33 (4), 374–389.

Adkins, L. (1995) *Gendered Work: Sexuality, Family and the Labour Market*, Milton Keynes: Open University Press.

Aizura, A. (2009) Where health and beauty meet: femininity and racialisation in Thai cosmetic surgery clinics, *Asian Studies Review*, 33 (3), 303–317.

Aizura, A. (2010) Feminine transformations: gender reassignment surgical tourism in Thailand, *Medical Anthropology*, 29 (4), 424–443.

All wrapped up (2012) The beginning of the rest of my life [blog], available at http://wrapperharris.wordpress.com/2012/04/19/the-beggining-of-the-rest-of-my-life/, accessed 7 January 2018.

Ancheta, R. (2002) Discourse of rules: women talk about cosmetic surgery, in K. Strother (ed.) *Women's Health: Power, Technology, Inequality and Conflict in a Gendered World*, Boston: Allyn & Bacon, pp. 143–149.

Anderson, B., Kearnes, M., McFarlane, C. & Swanton, D. (2012) On assemblages and geography, *Dialogues in Human Geography*, 2 (2), 171–189.

Anderson, W. (2002) Introduction: postcolonial technoscience, *Social Studies of Science*, 32 (5–6), 643–658.

Appadurai, A. (1990) Difference and disjuncture in the global cultural economy, *Theory, Culture & Society*, 7 (2–3), 295–310.

Aramberri, J. (2001) The host should get lost: paradigms in tourism theory, *Annals of Tourism Research*, 28 (3), 738–761.

Atkinson, S. (2011) Scales of care and responsibility: debating the surgically globalised body, *Social & Cultural Geography*, 12 (6), 623–637.

BAAPS (2011) Cosmetic surgery tourists in breast implant risk [press release], updated

2017, available at www.baaps.org.uk/media/press_releases/1324/cosmetic_surgery_tourists_in_breast_implant_risk, accessed 12 July 2018.

Back, L. & Sinha, S. (2016) Multicultural conviviality in the midst of racism's ruins, *Journal of Intercultural Studies*, 37 (5), 517–532.

Balsamo, A. (1992) On the cutting edge: cosmetic surgery and the technological production of the gendered body, *Camera Obscura*, 10 (1), 207–237.

Beauvoir, S. de ([1949] 2011) *The Second Sex*, trans. C. Borde & S. Malovaney-Chevallier, New York: Vintage.

Beck, U. (1992) *Risk Society: Towards a New Modernity*, London: Sage.

Beladi, H., Chao, C., Ee, M. & Hollas, D. (2015) Medical tourism and health worker migration in developing countries, *Economic Modelling*, 46, 391–396.

Bell, D. (2012) Moments of hospitality, in S. Gibson & J. Germann Molz (eds) *Mobilizing Hospitality: The Ethics of Social Relations in a Mobile World*, Aldershot: Ashgate, pp. 29–46.

Bell, D., Holliday, R., Jones, M., Probyn, E. & Sanchez Taylor, J. (2011) Bikinis and bandages: an itinerary for cosmetic surgery tourism, *Tourist Studies*, 11 (2), 137–153.

Bell D., Holliday R., Ormond M. & Mainil T. (2015) Transnational healthcare, cross-border perspectives, *Social Science & Medicine*, 124, 284–289.

Bell, D. & Valentine, G. (1997) *Consuming Geographies: We Are Where We Eat*, London: Routledge.

Bloxham, A. (2012) Health Secretary vows to sue private clinics who refuse to remove faulty implants, *Telegraph*, 12 January 2012, available at www.telegraph.co.uk/news/health/news/9009103/Health-Secretary-vows-to-sue-private-clinics-who-refuse-to-remove-faulty-implants.html, accessed 12 July 2018.

Blunt, A. & Dowling, R. (2006) *Home*, London: Routledge.

Bochaton, A. (2013) The rise of a transnational healthcare paradigm: Thai hospitals at the crossroad of new patient flows, *European Journal of Transnational Studies*, 5 (1), 54–80.

Bochaton, A. (2015) Cross-border mobility and social networks: Laotians seeking medical treatment along the Thai border, *Social Science & Medicine*, 124, 364–373.

Bochaton, A. & Lefebvre, B. (2009) The rebirth of the hospital: heterotopia and medical tourism in Asia, in T. Winter, P. Teo & T. Chang (eds) *Asia on Tour: Exploring the Rise of Asian Tourism*, London: Routledge, pp. 97–108.

Bolton, S. & Skountridaki, L. (2017) The medical tourist and a political economy of care, *Antipode*, 49 (2), 499–516.

Bordo, S. (1993) *Unbearable Weight: Feminism, Culture and the Body*, Berkeley: University of California Press.

Bordo, S. (1997) Material girl: the effacements of postmodern culture, in R. Lancaster & M. di Leonardo (eds) *The Gender/Sexuality Reader: Culture, History, Political Economy*, London: Routledge, pp. 335–358.

Bourdieu, P. (1984) *Distinction: A Social Critique of the Judgement of Taste*, London: Routledge.

Bourke, J. (2013) What is pain? A history, *The Prothero Lecture, Transactions of the Royal Historical Society*, 23, 155–173.

Briassoulis H. (2017) Tourism destinations as multiplicities: the view from assemblage thinking, *International Journal of Tourism Research*, 19 (3), 304–317.

Brooks, A. (2004) 'Under the knife and proud of it': An analysis of the normalization of cosmetic surgery, *Critical Sociology*, 30 (2), 207–239.

Brophy, J. (2017) Stem cell tourism in China: the dynamics of a moral economy (PhD thesis, Monash University).

Brown, H. (2012) Hospital domestics: care work in a Kenyan hospital, *Space & Culture*, 15 (1), 18–30.

Brown, K. (2012) Sharing public space across difference: attunement and the contested burdens of choreographing encounter, *Social & Cultural Geography*, 13 (7), 801–820.

Brown, W. (1993) Wounded attachments, *Political Theory*, 21 (3), 390–410.

Butler, J. (1990) *Gender Trouble: Feminism and the Subversion of Identity*, New York: Routledge.

Buzinde, C. & Yarnal, C. (2012) Therapeutic landscapes and postcolonial theory: a theoretical approach to medical tourism, *Social Science & Medicine*, 74, 783–787.

Cameron, K., Crooks, V., Chouinard, V., Snyder, J. & Johnston, R. (2014) Motivation, justification, normalization: talk strategies used by Canadian medical tourists regarding their choices to go abroad for hip and knee surgeries, *Social Science & Medicine*, 106, 93–100.

Campbell, D. (2017) Victims of disgraced breast surgeon Ian Paterson granted £37m compensation, *Guardian*, 13 September 2017, available at www.theguardian.com/uk-news/2017/sep/13/victims-of-rogue-breast-surgeon-ian-paterson-to-be-compensated-from-37m-fund, accessed 26 January 2018.

Casanova, E. & Sutton, B. (2013) Transnational body projects: media representations of cosmetic surgery tourism in Argentina and the United States, *Journal of World-Systems Research*, 19 (1), 57–81.

Casey, V., Crooks, V., Snyder, J. & Turner, L. (2013a) Knowledge brokers, companions, and navigators: a qualitative examination of informal caregivers' roles in medical tourism, *International Journal for Equity in Health*, 12 (1), 94.

Casey, V., Crooks, V., Snyder, J. & Turner, L. (2013b) 'You're dealing with an emotionally charged individual…': an industry perspective on the challenges posed by medical tourists' informal caregiver-companions, *Globalization & Health*, 9, 31.

Chee, H., Whittaker, A. & Por, H. (2017) Medical travel facilitators, private hospitals and international medical travel in assemblage, *Asia Pacific Viewpoint*, 58 (2), 242–254.

Cheung, O. (2015) A review of small-scale niche treatment providers, in N. Lunt, D. Horsfall & J. Hanefeld (eds) *Handbook on Medical Tourism and Patient Mobility*, Cheltenham: Edward Elgar, pp. 133–140.

Cohen, G. (2015) *Patients with Passports: Medical Tourism, Law, and Ethics*, Oxford: Oxford University Press.

Collier, S. & Ong, A. (2005) Global assemblages, anthropological problems, in A. Ong & S. Collier (eds) *Global Assemblages: Technology, Politics, and Ethics as Anthropological Problems*, Oxford: Blackwell, pp. 3–21.

Connell, J. (2011a) A new inequality? Privatisation, urban bias, migration and medical tourism, *Asia Pacific Viewpoint*, 52 (3), 260–271.

Connell, J. (2011b) *Medical Tourism*, Wallingford: CABI.

Connell, J. (2016) Reducing the scale? From global images to border crossings in medical tourism, *Global Networks*, 16 (4), 531–550.

Connell, J. & Walton-Roberts, M. (2016) What about the workers? The missing geographies of health care, *Progress in Human Geography*, 40 (2), 158–176.

Connell, R. ([1987] 2005) *Masculinities*, Berkeley: University of California Press.

Cook, P., Kendall, G., Michael, M. & Brown, N. (2011). The textures of globalization: biopolitics and the closure of xenotourism, *New Genetics & Society*, 30 (1), 101–114.

Cooper, C. (2016) *Fat Activism: A Radical Social Movement*, Bristol: Hammeron.

Cormany, D. & Baloglu, S. (2011) Medical traveller facilitator websites: an exploratory study of web page contents and services offered to the prospective medical tourist, *Tourism Management*, 32 (6), 709–716.

cosmeticsurgerythai (2011) Cosmetic Surgery Thailand – Actual Post Breast Augmentation Testimonial [YouTube video], available at www.youtube.com/watch?v=uBA4oeq5x88, accessed 15 November 2018.

Couldry, N. (2005) On the actual street, in D. Crouch, R. Jackson & F. Thompson (eds) *The Media and the Tourist Imagination: Converging Cultures*, London: Routledge, pp. 60–75.

Crooks, V., Casey, V., Whitmore, R., Johnston, R. & Snyder, J. (2015) 'They go the extra mile, the extra ten miles…': examining Canadian medical tourists' interactions with health care workers abroad, in N. Lunt, D. Horsfall & J. Hanefeld (eds) *Handbook on Medical Tourism and Patient Mobility*, Cheltenham: Edward Elgar, pp. 451–460.

Crooks, V., Ormond, M. & Jin, K. (2017) Reflections on 'medical tourism' from the 2016 Global Healthcare Policy Management Forum, *BMC Proceedings*, 11 (Supplement 8), 6–9.

Crush, J. & Chikanda, A. (2015) South–South medical tourism and the quest for health in Southern Africa, *Social Science & Medicine*, 124, 313–320.

Dalstrom, M. (2013) Medical travel facilitators: connecting patients and providers in a globalized world, *Anthropology & Medicine*, 20 (1), 24–35.

Davies, W. (2016) *The Happiness Industry: How the Government and Big Business Sold Us Well-being*, London: Verso.

Davis, K. (1995) *Reshaping the Female Body: The Dilemma of Cosmetic Surgery*, New York & London: Routledge.

Davis, K. (2003) *Dubious Equalities and Embodied Differences: Cultural Studies on Cosmetic Surgery*, Lanham: Rowman and Littlefield.

Department of Health (2013) *Review of the Regulation of Cosmetic Interventions*, London: Department of Health.

Destination Beauty (n.d.) Bangkok plastic surgery group tour [Website], available at http://destinationbeauty.com/bangkok-plastic-surgery-group-tour, accessed 16 August 2017.

DiMoia, J. (2013) *Reconstructing Bodies: Biomedicine, Health, and Nation Building in South Korea since 1945*, Stanford: Stanford University Press.

Donnelly, L. (2012) Cowboy tactics of cosmetic firms to come under fire from MPs, *Telegraph*, 14 January 2012, available at www.telegraph.co.uk/news/health/news/9015050/Cowboy-tactics-of-cosmetic-firms-to-come-under-fire-from-MPs.html, accessed 12 July 2018.

Douglas, M. (1992) *Risk and Blame: Essays in Cultural Theory*, London: Routledge.

Drummond, M. (2010) The natural: an autoethnography of a masculinized body in sport, *Men & Masculinities*, 12 (3), 374–387.

Duncan, T., Scott, D. & Baum, T. (2013) The mobilities of hospitality work: an exploration of issues and debates, *Annals of Tourism Research*, 41, 1–19.

Durham, J. & Blondell, S. (2017) A realist synthesis of cross-border patient movement from low to middle income countries or higher income countries, *Globalization & Health*, 13, 68, https://doi.org/10.1186/s12992-017-0287-8.

Dyer, S., McDowell, L. & Batnitzky, A. (2008) Emotional labour/body work: the caring labours of migrants in the UK's National Health Service, *Geoforum*, 39 (6), 2030–2038.

Edensor, T. (2001) Performing tourism, staging tourism: (re)producing tourist space and practice, *Tourist Studies*, 1 (1), 59–81.

Edensor, T. (2007) Mundane mobilities, performances and spaces of tourism, *Social & Cultural Geography*, 8 (2), 199–215.

Edmonds, A. (2007) 'The poor have a right to be beautiful': cosmetic surgery in neoliberal Brazil, *Journal of the Royal Anthropological Institute*, 13 (2), 363–381.

Edmonds, A. (2010) *Pretty Modern: Beauty, Sex and Plastic Surgery in Brazil*, Durham, NC: Duke University Press.

Edmonds, A. (2011) 'Almost invisible scars': medical tourism in Brazil, *Signs*, 36 (2), 297–301.

Elliott, A. (2008) *Making the Cut: How Cosmetic Surgery is Transforming our Lives*, London: Reaktion.

Enteen, J. (2014) Transitioning online: cosmetic surgery tourism in Thailand, *Television & New Media*, 15 (3), 238–249.

Faria, C. (2014) Styling the nation: fear and desire in the South Sudanese beauty trade, *Transactions of the Institute of British Geographers*, 39 (2), 318–330.

Featherstone, M. (2000) *Body Modification*, London: Sage.

Fineman, M. (2008) The vulnerable subject: anchoring equality in the human condition, *Yale Journal of Law & Feminism*, 20 (1), 1–23.

Foucault, M. (2010) *The Birth of Biopolitics: Lectures at the Collège de France, 1978–1979*, New York: Picador.

Fox, M. & Thomson, M. (2017) Bodily integrity, embodiment, and the regulation of parental choice, *Journal of Law & Society*, 44 (4), 501–531.

Fraser, S. (2003) *Cosmetic Surgery, Gender and Culture*, New York: Palgrave Macmillan.

Frost, L. (1999) Doing looks: women, appearance and mental health, in J. Arthurs & J. Grimshaw (eds) *Women's Bodies: Discipline and Transgression*, London: Cassell, pp. 117–136.

Gan, L. & Frederick, J. (2011) Medical tourism facilitators: patterns of service differentiation, *Journal of Vacation Marketing*, 17 (3), 165–183.

Gibson, C. (2009) Geographies of tourism: critical research on capitalism and local livelihoods, *Progress in Human Geography*, 33 (4), 527–534.

Gibson, C. (2010) Geographies of tourism: (un)ethical encounters, *Progress in Human Geography*, 34 (3), 521–527.

Gibson, M. (2006) Bodies without histories: cosmetic surgery and the undoing of time, *Australian Feminist Studies*, 21/49, 51–63.

Giddens, A. (1990) *The Consequences of Modernity*, Cambridge: Polity Press.

Gilman, S. (1999) *Making the Body Beautiful: A Cultural History of Aesthetic Surgery*, Princeton: Princeton University Press.

Gilroy, P. (2004) *After Empire: Melancholia or Convivial Culture*, London: Routledge.

Gilroy, P. (2006) Multiculture in times of war, *Critical Quarterly*, 48 (4), 27–45.

Gimlin, D. (2002) *Body Work: Beauty and Self-image in American Culture*, Berkeley: University of California Press.

Gimlin, D. (2007a) Accounting for cosmetic surgery in the USA and Great Britain: a cross-cultural analysis of women's narratives, *Body & Society*, 13 (1), 41–60.

Gimlin, D. (2007b) What is 'body work'? A review of the literature, *Sociology Compass*, 1 (1), 353–370.

Gimlin, D. (2012) *Cosmetic Surgery Narratives: A Cross-cultural Analysis of Women's Accounts*, Basingstoke: Palgrave Macmillan.

Gimlin, D. (2013) 'Too good to be real': the obviously augmented breast in women's narratives of cosmetic surgery, *Gender & Society*, 27 (6), 913–934.

Gimlin, D. (2014) National healthcare rhetoric beyond the nation: the materiality of narrative in cosmetic surgery tourism, *Tourist Studies*, 14 (3), 302–318.

Glick Schiller, N., Darieva, T. & Gruner-Domic, S. (2011) Defining cosmopolitan sociability in a transnational age, *Ethnic & Racial Studies*, 34 (3), 399–418.

Glinos, I. & Baeten, R. (2014) Dream vs. reality: seven case studies on the desirability and feasibility of cross-border hospital collaboration in Europe, *Social Science & Medicine*, 117, 18–24.

Glinos, I., Baeten, R., Helble, M. & Maarse, H. (2010) A typology of cross-border patient mobility, *Health & Place*, 16 (6), 1145–1155.

Glinos, I., Baeten, R. & Maarse, H. (2010) Purchasing health services abroad: practices of cross-border contracting and patient mobility in six European countries, *Health Policy*, 95 (2–3), 103–112.

Graburn, N. ([1989] 2012) Tourism: the sacred journey, in V. Smith (ed.) *Hosts and Guests: The Anthropology of Tourism*, 2nd edn, Philadelphia: University of Pennsylvania Press, pp. 17–32.

Grosz, E. (1995) *Volatile Bodies: Towards a Corporeal Feminism*, Sydney: Allen & Unwin.

Haiken, E. (1997) *Venus Envy: A History of Cosmetic Surgery*, Baltimore: Johns Hopkins University Press.

Hall, S. (1973) Encoding/decoding, in S. Hall, D. Hobson, A. Love & P. Willis (eds) *Culture, Media, Language*, London: Hutchinson, pp. 128–138.

Hallett, R. & Kaplan-Weinger, J. (2010) *Official Tourism Websites: A Discourse Analysis Perspective*, Bristol: Channel View Press.

Hanefeld, J., Lunt, N., Smith, R. & Horsfall, D. (2015) Why do medical tourists travel to where they do? The role of networks in determining medical travel, *Social Science & Medicine*, 124, 356–363.

Haraway, D. (1988) Situated knowledges: the science question in feminism and the privilege of partial perspective, *Feminist Studies*, 14 (3), 575–599.

Heimtun, B. (2007) Depathologizing the tourism syndrome: tourism as social capital production, *Tourist Studies*, 7 (3), 271–293.

Hertzell, D. & Moore, C. (2012) Implanting doubts, *New Law Journal*, 26 January 2012, available at www.newlawjournal.co.uk/content/implanting-doubts, accessed 12 July 2018.

Heyes, C. (2007) *Self-Transformations: Foucault, Ethics, and Normalized Bodies*, Oxford: Oxford University Press.

Heyes, C. & Jones, M. (2009) Cosmetic surgery in the age of gender, in C. Heyes & M. Jones (eds) *Cosmetic Surgery: A Feminist Primer*, Aldershot: Ashgate, pp. 1–20.

Hjorth, L. (2007) Domesticating new media: a discussion on locating mobile media, in S. Giddings & M. Lister (eds) *The New Media and Technocultures Reader*, New York: Routledge, pp. 437–448.

Hochschild, A. (1983) *The Managed Heart: The Commercialization of Human Feeling*, Berkeley: University of California Press.

Holehouse, M. (2012) Breast implant scandal: now women with Rofil M-implants 'are at risk', *Telegraph*, 5 January 2012, available at www.telegraph.co.uk/news/health/news/8993738/Breast-implant-scandal-now-women-with-Rofil-M-implants-are-at-risk.html, accessed 12 July 2018.

Holliday, R. (2019) Vagina dialogues: theorizing the 'designer vagina', in G. Griffin & M. Jordal (eds) *Body, Migration, Re/constructive Surgeries: Making the Gendered Body in a Globalized World*, London: Routledge, forthcoming.

Holliday, R. & Bell, D. (2015) Cosmetic surgery tourism, in N. Lunt, D. Horsfall &

J. Hanefeld (eds) *Handbook on Medical Tourism and Patient Mobility*, Cheltenham: Edward Elgar, pp. 421–430.

Holliday, R., Bell, D., Cheung, O., Jones, M. & Probyn, E. (2015) Brief encounters: assembling cosmetic surgery tourism, *Social Science & Medicine*, 124, 298–304.

Holliday, R., Bell, D., Jones, M., Hardy, K., Hunter, E., Probyn, E. & Sanchez Taylor, J. (2015) Beautiful face, beautiful place: relational geographies and gender in cosmetic surgery tourism websites, *Gender, Place & Culture*, 22 (1), 90–106.

Holliday, R. & Cairnie, A. (2007) Man made plastic: investigating men's consumption of aesthetic surgery, *Journal of Consumer Culture*, 7 (1), 57–78.

Holliday, R., Cheung, O., Cho, J. & Bell, D. (2017) Trading faces: the 'Korean Look' and medical nationalism in South Korean cosmetic surgery tourism, *Asia Pacific Viewpoint*, 58 (2), 190–202.

Holliday, R. & Elfving-Hwang, J. (2012) Gender, globalization and aesthetic surgery in South Korea, *Body & Society*, 18 (2), 58–81.

Holliday, R. & Sanchez Taylor, J. (2006) Aesthetic surgery as false beauty, *Feminist Theory*, 7 (2), 179–195.

Hollway, W. & Jefferson, T. (2009) Researching defended subjects with the Free Association Narrative Method, in H. Cook, S. Bhattacharya & A. Hardy (eds) *History of the Social Determinants of Health: Global Histories, Contemporary Debates*, Hyderabad: Orient Black Swan, pp. 296–315.

Horsfall, D. and Lunt, N. (2015a) Medical tourism by numbers, in N. Lunt, D. Horsfall & J. Hanefeld (eds) *Handbook on Medical Tourism and Patient Mobility*, Cheltenham: Edward Elgar, pp. 25–36.

Horsfall, D. & Lunt, N. (2015b) Medical tourism and the Internet, in N. Lunt, D. Horsfall & J. Hanefeld (eds) *Handbook on Medical Tourism and Patient Mobility*, Cheltenham: Edward Elgar, pp. 174–183.

Horton, S. & Cole, S. (2011) Medical returns: seeking health care in Mexico, *Social Science & Medicine*, 72, 1846–1852.

Howard, R. (2010) Urban tourist districts: a taxonomy and a study of a new proposed type, *Tourism & Hospitality Planning & Development*, 7 (4), 415–428.

Huss-Ashmore, R. (2000) 'The real me': therapeutic narrative in cosmetic surgery, *Expedition*, 42 (3), 26–38.

Illich, I. (1973) *Tools for Conviviality*, London: Marion Boyars.

Inhorn, M. & Gurtin, Z. (2011) Cross-border reproductive care: a future research agenda, *Reproductive Biomedicine Online*, 23 (5), 665–676.

Jackson, J. & Lyons, T. (2012) The perfect body: men and women negotiate spaces of resistance against beauty and gender ideologies, *Women's Studies Journal*, 26 (1), 25–33.

Jansson, A. (2002) Spatial phantasmorgia: the mediatisation of tourism experience, *European Journal of Communication*, 17 (4), 429–443.

Jansson, A. (2007) A sense of tourism: new media and the dialectic of encapsulation/decapsulation, *Tourist Studies*, 7 (1), 5–24.

Jeevan, R. & Armstrong, A. (2008) Cosmetic tourism and the burden on the NHS, *Journal of Plastic, Reconstructive & Aesthetic Surgery*, 61 (12), 1423–1424.

Jeffries, S. (2005) *Beauty and Misogyny: Harmful Cultural Practices in the West*, London: Routledge.

Jennings, G. & Weiler, B. (2006) Mediating meaning: perspectives on brokering quality tourist experiences, in G. Jennings & N. Polovitz Nickerson (eds) *Quality Tourism Experiences*, Amsterdam: Elsevier, pp. 57–78.

Jones, M. (2008a) *Skintight: An Anatomy of Cosmetic Surgery*, Oxford: Berg.

Jones, M. (2008b) Makeover culture's dark side: breasts, death and Lolo Ferrari, *Body & Society*, 14 (1), 89–104.

Jones, M. (2009) Pygmalion's many faces, in C. Heyes & M. Jones (eds) *Cosmetic Surgery: A Feminist Primer*, Aldershot: Ashgate, pp 171–189.

Jones, M. (2013) Media-bodies and Photoshop, in F. Attwood, V. Campbell, I. Hunter & S. Lockyer (eds) *Controversial Images: Media Representations on the Edge*, London: Palgrave Macmillan, pp. 19–35.

Jones, M., Bell, D., Holliday, R., Probyn, E. & Sanchez Taylor, J. (2014) Facebook and facelifts: communities of cosmetic surgery tourists, in G. Lean, R. Staiff & E. Waterton (eds) *Travel and Transformation*, Aldershot: Ashgate, pp. 189–204.

Kangas, B. (2002) Therapeutic itineraries in a global world: Yemenis and their search for biomedical treatment abroad, *Medical Anthropology*, 21 (1), 35–78.

Kangas, B. (2007) Hope from abroad in the international medical travel of Yemeni patients, *Anthropology & Medicine*, 14 (3), 293–305.

Kangas, B. (2011) Complicating common ideas about medical tourism: gender, class, and globality in Yemenis' international medical travel, *Signs*, 36 (2), 327–332.

Kemp, C., Ball, M. & Perkins, M. (2013) Convoys of care: theorizing intersections of formal and informal care, *Journal of Ageing Studies*, 27 (1), 15–29.

Kerr, A. & Cunningham-Burley, S. (2015) Embodied innovation and regulation of medical technoscience: transformations in cancer patienthood, *Law, Innovation & Technology*, 7 (2), 187–205.

Kingsbury, P., Crooks, V., Snyder, J., Johnston, R. & Adams, K. (2012) Narratives of emotion and anxiety in medical tourism: on *State of the Heart* and *Larry's Kidney*, *Social & Cultural Geography*, 13 (4), 361–378.

Kinsella, S. (1995) Cuties in Japan, in L. Skov & B. Moeran (eds) *Women, Media and Consumption in Japan*, London: Curzon Press, pp. 220–254.

Kitzinger, J. (2008) Questioning hype, rescuing hope? The Hwang stem cell scandal and the reassertion of hopeful horizons, *Science as Culture*, 17 (4), 417–434.

Knoll, E. (2017) Archipelagic genes: medical travel as a creative response to limitations and remoteness in the Maldives, *Asia Pacific Viewpoint*, 58 (2), 148–161.

Labonté, R. (2013) Overview: medical tourism today: what, who, why and where?, in R. Labonté, V. Runnels, C. Packer & R. Deonandan (eds) *Travelling Well: Essays in Medical Tourism*, Ottawa: Institute of Population Health, University of Ottawa, pp. 6–42.

Lange, P. (2009) Videos of affinity on YouTube, in P. Snickers & P. Vonderau (eds) *The YouTube Reader*, Stockholm: National Library of Sweden, pp. 70–88.

Latham, J. R. (2018) Axiomatic: constituting 'transexuality' and transsexualities in medicine, *Sexualities*, online first: https://doi.org/10.1177/1363460717740258.

Latham, M. (2014) 'If it ain't broke, don't fix it?': Scandals, 'risk', and cosmetic surgery regulation in the UK and France, *Medical Law Review*, 22 (3), 384–408.

Latimer, J. (2000) *The Conduct of Care: Understanding Nursing Practice*, Oxford: Blackwell.

Latour, B. (2005) *Reassembling the Social: An Introduction to Actor-Network-Theory*, Oxford: Oxford University Press.

Lautier, M. (2008) Export of health services from developing countries: the case of Tunisia, *Social Science & Medicine*, 67, 101–110.

Lautier, M. (2014) International trade of health services: global trends and local impacts, *Health Policy*, 118, 105–113.

Leder, D. (1990) *The Absent Body*, Chicago: University of Chicago Press.

Lee, J., Kearns, R. & Friesen, W. (2010) Seeking affective health care: Korean immigrants' use of homeland medical services, *Health & Place*, 16 (1), 108–115.

Lingis, A. (1983) *Excesses: Eros and Culture*, New York: SUNY Press.

Lugosi, P. (2009) The production of hospitable space: commercial propositions and consumer co-creation in a bar operation, *Space & Culture*, 12 (4), 396–411.

Lunt, N. & Carrera, P. (2010) Medical tourism: assessing the evidence on treatment abroad, *Maturitas*, 66 (1), 27–32.

Lunt, N., Exworthy, M., Hanefeld, J. & Smith, R. (2015) International patients within the NHS: a case of public sector entrepreneurialism, *Social Science & Medicine*, 124, 338–345.

Lunt, N., Horsfall, D. & Hanefeld, J. (2016) Medical tourism: a snapshot of evidence on treatment abroad, *Maturitas*, 88, 37–44.

MacCannell, D. ([1976] 1999) *The Tourist: A New Theory of the Leisure Class*, Berkeley: University of California Press.

MacKendrick, K. (1998) Technoflesh, or 'Didn't that hurt?', *Fashion Theory*, 2 (1), 3–24.

Marcus, G. & Saka, E. (2006) Assemblage, *Theory, Culture & Society*, 23 (2–3), 101–106.

Massey, D. (2005) *For Space*, London: Sage.

Mazzaschi, A. (2011) Surgeon and safari: producing valuable bodies in Johannesburg, *Signs*, 36 (2), 303–312.

McCann, E. & Ward, K. (eds) (2011) *Mobile Urbanism: Cities and Policymaking in the Global Age*, Minneapolis: University of Minnesota Press.

McClintock, A. (1995) *Imperial Leather: Race, Gender, and Sexuality in the Colonial Contest*, London: Routledge.

McCreary D., Saucier D. & Courtenay, W. (2005) The drive for muscularity and masculinity: testing the associations among gender-role traits, behaviors, attitudes, and conflict, *Psychology of Men & Masculinity*, 6 (2), 83–94.

McDonald, E. (2011) Bodies-in-motion: experiences of momentum in transnational surgery, in F. Mascia-Lees (ed.) *A Companion to the Anthropology of the Body and Embodiment*, Oxford: Wiley-Blackwell, pp. 481–503.

McDowell, L. (2009) *Working Bodies: Interactive Service Employment and Workplace Identities*, Chichester: Wiley-Blackwell.

McNay, L. (2002) Communitarians and feminists: the case of narrative identity, *Literature & Theology*, 16 (1), 81–95.

Miller, D. (1998) *A Theory of Shopping*, Cambridge: Polity.

Miller, T. (2005) A metrosexual eye on the queer guy, *GLQ: A Journal of Lesbian & Gay Studies*, 11 (1), 112–17.

Milligan, C. & Wiles, J. (2010) Landscapes of care, *Progress in Human Geography*, 34 (6), 736–754.

Mirivel, J. (2008) The physical examination in cosmetic surgery: communication strategies to promote desirability of surgery, *Health Communication*, 23 (2), 153–170.

Miyagi, K., Auberson, D., Patel, A. & Malata, C. (2012) The unwritten price of cosmetic tourism: an observational study and cost analysis, *Journal of Plastic, Reconstructive & Aesthetic Surgery*, 65 (1), 22–28.

Mol, A. (2008) *The Logic of Care: Health and the Problem of Patient Choice*, London: Routledge.

Murphy, M. (2012) *Seizing the Means of Reproduction: Entanglements of Feminism, Health and Technoscience*, Durham, NC: Duke University Press.

Naugler, D. (2009) Crossing the cosmetic/reconstructive divide: the instructive situation of breast reduction surgery, in C. Heyes & M. Jones (eds) *Cosmetic Surgery: A Feminist Primer*, Aldershot: Ashgate, pp. 225–238.

Nederveen Pieterse, J. (2006) Emancipatory cosmopolitanism: towards an agenda, *Development & Change*, 37 (6), 1247–1257.

NHS (n.d.), Overview – obstructive sleep apnoea, NHS [website], available at www.nhs.uk/conditions/obstructive-sleep-apnoea/, accessed 19 November 2018.

Noble, G. (2013) Cosmopolitan habits: the capacities and habitats of intercultural conviviality, *Body & Society*, 19 (2–3), 162–185.

Novas, C. (2006) The political economy of hope: patients' organizations, science and biovalue, *BioSocieties*, 1 (3), 289–305.

Nowicka, M. & Vertovec, S. (2014) Comparing convivialities: dreams and realities of living-with-difference, *European Journal of Cultural Studies*, 17 (4), 341–356.

Nuffield Council on Bioethics (2017) Cosmetic procedures: ethical issues [report], available at http://nuffieldbioethics.org/wp-content/uploads/Cosmetic-procedures-full-report.pdf, accessed 5 August 2018.

O'Bryan, C. (2005) *Carnal Art: Orlan's Refacing*, Minneapolis: University of Minnesota Press.

Ong, A. & Collier, S. (eds) (2005) *Global Assemblages: Technology, Politics, and Ethics as Anthropological Problems*, Oxford: Blackwell.

Ormond, M. (2011) Shifting subjects of health-care: placing 'medical tourism' in the context of Malaysian domestic health-care reform, *Asia Pacific Viewpoint*, 52 (3), 247–259.

Ormond, M. (2013a) *Neoliberal Governance and International Medical Travel in Malaysia*, London: Routledge.

Ormond, M. (2013b) Claiming 'cultural competence': the promotion of multi-ethnic Malaysia as a medical tourism destination, in C. Hall (ed) *Medical Tourism: The Ethics, Regulation, and Marketing of Health Mobility*, London: Routledge, pp. 187–200.

Ormond, M. (2014a) Intermediaries, facilitators, agents, guides: steering international medical travel to Malaysia [conference paper], presented at the 18th ISA World Congress of Sociology, Yokohama, Japan, July 2014.

Ormond, M. (2014b) Medical tourism, in A. Lew, M. Hall & A. Williams (eds) *The Wiley-Blackwell Companion to Tourism*, Malden: Wiley, pp. 425–434.

Ormond, M. (2015a) Solidarity by demand? Exit and voice in international medical travel – the case of Malaysia, *Social Science & Medicine*, 124, 305–312.

Ormond, M. (2015b) En route: transport and embodiment in international medical travel journeys between Indonesia and Malaysia, *Mobilities*, 10 (2), 285–303.

Ormond, M. & Sothern, M. (2012) You, too, can be a medical traveller: reading medical travel guidebooks, *Health & Place*, 18 (5), 935–941.

Ormond, M. & Sulianti, D. (2017) More than medical tourism: lessons from Indonesia and Malaysia on South–South intra-regional medical travel, *Current Issues in Tourism*, 20 (1), 94–110.

Ormond, M. & Toyota, M. (2018) Rethinking care through transnational health and long-term care practices, in V. Crooks, J. Pearce & G. Andrews (eds) *Routledge Handbook of Health Geography*, Abingdon: Routledge, pp. 237–243.

Ouellette, L & Hay, J (2008) *Better Living through Reality TV: Television and Post-Welfare Citizenship*, Malden: Blackwell.

Pande, A. (2010) Commercial surrogacy in India: manufacturing the perfect mother-worker, *Signs*, 35 (4), 969–992.

Pauly Morgan, K. (1991) Women and the knife: cosmetic surgery and the colonization of women's bodies, *Hypatia*, 6 (3), 25–53.

Pedwell, C. (2012) Affective (self-)transformations: empathy, neoliberalism and inter-national development, *Feminist Theory*, 13 (2), 163–179.

Perfetto, R. & Dholakia, N. (2010) Exploring the cultural contradictions of medical tourism, *Consumption, Markets & Culture*, 13 (4), 399–417.

Petersen, A. (2015) *Hope in Health: The Socio-politics of Optimism*, Basingstoke: Palgrave Macmillan.

Petersen, A., Munsie, M., Tanner, C., MacGregor, C. & Brophy, J. (2017) *Stem Cell Tourism and the Political Economy of Hope*, Basingstoke: Palgrave Macmillan.

Petersen, A., Seear, K. & Munsie, M. (2013) Therapeutic journeys: the hopeful travails of stem cell tourists, *Sociology of Health & Illness*, 26 (5), 670–685.

Pitts, V. (2003) *In the Flesh: The Cultural Politics of Body Modification*, Houndmills: Palgrave MacMillan.

Pitts-Taylor, V. (2007) *Surgery Junkies: Wellness and Pathology in Cosmetic Culture*, New Brunswick: Rutgers University Press.

Pitts-Taylor, V. (2009) Becoming/being a cosmetic surgery patient: semantic instability and the intersubjective self, *Studies in Gender & Sexuality*, 10 (3), 119–128.

Pordié, L. (2013) Spaces of connectivity, shifting temporality: enquiries in transnational health, *European Journal of Transnational Studies*, 5 (1), 6–26.

Poster, M. (2001) Postmodern virtualities, in M. Durham & D. Kellner (eds) *Media and Cultural Studies Keyworks*, Oxford: Blackwell, pp. 611–625.

Puig de la Bellacasa, M. (2017) *Matters of Care: Speculative Ethics in More than Human Worlds*, Minneapolis: University of Minnesota Press.

Rabinow, P. & Rose, N. (2006) Biopower today, *BioSocieties*, 1 (2), 195–217.

Radin, P. (2006) 'To me, it's my life': medical communication, trust, and activism in cyberspace, *Social Science & Medicine*, 62 (3), 591–601.

Ramirez de Arellano, A. (2011) Medical tourism in the Caribbean, *Signs*, 36 (2), 289–297.

Robbins, B. (1998) Actually existing cosmopolitanism, in P. Cheah & B. Robbins (eds) *Cosmopolitics*, Minneapolis: University of Minnesota Press, pp. 1–19.

Roberts, E. & Scheper-Hughes, N. (2011) Introduction: medical migrations, *Body & Society*, 17 (2–3), 1–30.

Robertson, R. (1995) *Global Modernities*, London: Sage.

Robertson, S. (2007) *Understanding Men and Health: Masculinities, Identity and Wellbeing*, Maidenhead: Open University Press.

Rohrich, R. (2002) It's only a scalpel, not a magic wand!, *Plastic & Reconstructive Surgery*, 110 (6), 1507–1508.

Rose, N. (2007) *The Politics of Life Itself: Biomedicine, Power, and Subjectivity in the Twenty-first Century*, Princeton: Princeton University Press.

Rose, N. & Novas, C. (2004) Biological citizenship, in A. Ong & S. Collier (eds) *Global Assemblages: Technology, Politics, and Ethics as Anthropological Problems*, Oxford: Blackwell, pp. 439–463.

Ryoo, W. (2009) Globalization, or the logic of cultural hybridization: the case of the Korean wave, *Asian Journal of Communication*, 19 (2), 137–151.

Said, E. (1978) *Orientalism*, Harmondsworth: Penguin.

Salazar, N. (2011) The power of imagination in transnational mobilities, *Identities*, 18 (6), 576–598.

Savage, M., Barlow, J., Dickens, P. & Fielding, T. (1992) *Property, Bureaucracy and Culture: Middle-Class Formation in Contemporary Britain*, London: Routledge.

Scheper-Hughes, N. (2011) Mr Tati's holiday and Joao's safari – seeing the world through transplant tourism, *Body & Society*, 17 (2–3), 55–92.

Sengupta, A. (2011) Medical tourism: reverse subsidy for the elite, *Signs*, 36 (2), 312–319.

Sheller, M. & Urry, J. (eds) (2004) *Tourism mobilities: Places to play, places in play*, London: Routledge.

Shilling, C. (2012) *The Body and Social Theory*, 3rd edn, London: Sage.

Singleton, P., Fawkner, H., White, A. & Foster, S. (2009) Men's experience of cosmetic surgery: a phenomenological approach to discussion board data, *Qualitative Methods in Psychology Newsletter*, 8 October 2009, 17–23.

Skeggs, B. (2013) *Class, Self, Culture*, London: Routledge.

Skountridaki, L. (2015) The internationalisation of healthcare and business aspirations of medical professionals, *Sociology*, 49 (3), 471–487.

Skountridaki, L. (2017) Barriers to business relations between medical tourism facilitators and medical professionals, *Tourism Management*, 59, 254–266.

Smith, K. (2012) The problematization of medical tourism: a critique of neoliberalism, *Developing World Bioethics*, 12 (1), 1–8.

Smith, R., Lunt, N. & Hanefeld, J. (2012) The implications of PIP are more than just cosmetic, *Lancet*, 379, 1180–1181.

Smith-Morris, C. & Manderson, L. (2010) The baggage of health travellers, *Medical Anthropology*, 29 (4), 331–335.

Snyder, J., Crooks, V., Adams, K., Kingsbury, P. & Johnston, R. (2011) The 'patient's physician one step removed': the evolving roles of medical tourism facilitators, *Journal of Medical Ethics*, 37 (9), 530–534.

Sobo, E. (2009) Medical travel: what it means, why it matters, *Medical Anthropology*, 28 (4), 326–335.

Solomon, H. (2011) Affective journeys: the emotional structuring of medical tourism in India, *Anthropology & Medicine*, 18 (1), 105–118.

Spitzack, C. (1988) The confessional mirror: plastic images for surgery, *Canadian Journal of Political & Social Theory*, 12 (1–2), 38–50.

Spitzack, C. (1990) *Confessing Excess: Women and the Politics of Body Reduction*, New York: SUNY Press.

Spivak, G. (1988) Subaltern studies: deconstructing historiography, in J. Culler (ed.) *Deconstruction: Critical Concepts in Literary and Cultural Studies*, vol. 4, London: Routledge, pp. 220–244.

Stone, S. (1991) The empire strikes back: a post-transsexual manifesto, in K. Straub & J. Epstein (eds) *Body Guards: The Cultural Politics of Gender Ambiguity*, New York: Routledge, pp. 280–304.

Su, D., Richardson, C., Wen, M. & Pagan, J. (2011) Cross-border utilization of health care: evidence from a population-based study in South Texas, *Health Services Research*, 46 (3), 859–876.

Swan, E. & Flowers, R. (2018) Lasting impressions: ethnic food tour guides and body work in southwestern Sydney, *Gender, Work & Organization*, 25 (1), 24–41.

Swyngedouw, E. (2004) Globalisation or 'glocalisation'? Networks, territories and rescaling, *Cambridge Review of International Affairs*, 17 (1), 25–48.

Thompson, C. (2011) Medical migrations afterword: science as a vacation?, *Body & Society*, 17 (2–3), 205–213.

Throsby, K. (2008) Happy re-birthday: weight loss surgery and the 'new me', *Body & Society*, 14 (1), 117–133.

Toyota, M, Chee, H. & Xiang, B. (2013) Global track, national vehicle: transnationalism in medical tourism in Asia, *European Journal of Transnational Studies*, 5 (1), 27–53.

Trinh, T. (1989) *Woman, Native, Other: Writing Postcoloniality and Feminism*, Indianapolis: Indiana University Press.

Tsing, A. (2005) *Friction: An Ethnography of Global Connection*, Princeton: Princeton University Press.

Turner, L. (2007) 'First World care at Third World prices': globalization, bioethics and medical tourism, *BioSocieties*, 2 (3), 303–325.

Turner, L. (2011) Canadian medical tourism companies that have exited the marketplace: content analysis of websites used to market transnational medical travel, *Globalization & Health*, 7, 40.

Twigg, J., Wolkowitz, C., Cohen, R. & Nettleton, S. (2011) Conceptualising body work in health and social care, *Sociology of Health & Illness*, 33 (2), 171–188.

Tyler, I. & Bennett, B. (2010) 'Celebrity chav': fame, femininity and social class, *European Journal of Cultural Studies*, 13 (3), 375–393.

Urry, J. (2003) Social networks, travel and talk, *British Journal of Sociology*, 54 (2), 155–175.

Veijola, S. (2010a) Introduction: tourism as work, *Tourist Studies*, 9 (2), 83–87.

Veijola, S. (2010b) Gender as work in the tourism industry, *Tourist Studies*, 9 (2), 109–126.

Veijola, S. & Jokinen, E. (2008) Towards a hostessing society? Mobile arrangements of gender and labour, *NORA – Nordic Journal of Feminist & Gender Research*, 16 (3), 166–181.

Vick, L. (2012) The perils of cosmetic surgery/medical tourism, *AvMA Medical & Legal Journal*, 18 (3), 106–9, https://doi.org/10.1258/cr.2012.012017.

Viladrich, A. & Baron-Faust, R. (2014) Medical tourism in tango paradise: the Internet branding of cosmetic surgery in Argentina, *Annals of Tourism Research*, 45, 116–131.

Volgger, M., Mainil, T., Pechlaner, H. & Mitas, O. (2015) Health region development from the perspective of system theory – an empirical cross-regional case study, *Social Science & Medicine*, 124, 321–330.

Warde, A. (1997) *Consumption, Food and Taste*, London: Sage.

Watson, J. (2000) *Male Bodies: Health, Culture and Identity*, Buckingham: Open University Press.

Weber, B. (2009) *Makeover TV: Selfhood, Citizenship, and Celebrity*, Durham, NC: Duke University Press.

Wegenstein, B. (2012) *The Cosmetic Gaze: Body Modification and the Construction of Beauty*, Boston: MIT Press.

Wegenstein, B. & Ruck, N. (2011) Physiognomy, reality television and the cosmetic gaze, *Body & Society*, 17 (4), 27–54.

Whitmore, R., Crooks, V. & Snyder, J. (2015) Ethics of care in medical tourism: informal caregivers' narratives of responsibility, vulnerability and mutuality, *Health & Place*, 35, 113–118.

Whittaker, A. (2008) Pleasure and pain: medical travel in Asia, *Global Public Health*, 3 (3), 271–290.

Whittaker, A. & Chee, H. (2015) Perceptions of an 'international hospital' in Thailand by medical travel patients: cross-cultural tensions in a transnational space, *Social Science & Medicine*, 124, 290–297.

Whittaker, A. & Chee, H. (2016) 'Flexible bio-citizenship' and international medical travel: transnational mobilities for care in Asia, *International Sociology*, 31 (3), 286–304.

Wiegman, R. (2012) *Object Lessons*, Durham, NC: Duke University Press.

Wiles, J. (2011) Reflections on being a recipient of care: vexing the concept of vulnerability, *Social & Cultural Geography*, 12 (6), 573–588.

Wilson, A. (2011) Foreign bodies and national scales: medical tourism in Thailand, *Body & Society*, 17 (2–3), 121–137.

Wilson, A. (2015) Standards, metrics, and protocols: the regulatory infrastructures of Asian medical mobility [workshop paper], presented at International Medical Travel and the Politics of Transnational Mobility in Asia, Asia Research Institute, National University of Singapore, 26–27 August 2015.

Wilson, E. (2009) *Adorned in Dreams: Fashion and Modernity*, London: I. B. Tauris.

Wilson, H. (2011) Passing propinquities in the multicultural city: the everyday encounters of bus passengering, *Environment & Planning A*, 43 (3), 634–649.

Wilson, T. & Suraya, R. (2004) The tourist gaze goes on-line: Rojak (hybrid) reception theory structures of ludic looking at/from Malaysia, *Tourist Studies*, 4 (1), 69–92.

Wise, A. & Noble, G. (2016) Convivialities: an orientation, *Journal of Intercultural Studies*, 37 (5), 423–431.

Wise, A. & Velayutham, S. (2014) Conviviality in everyday multiculturalism: some brief comparisons between Singapore and Sydney, *European Journal of Cultural Studies*, 17 (4), 406–430.

Wollaston, S. (2012) Breast implant surgeons do not put women first, *Guardian*, 2 January 2012, available at www.theguardian.com/commentisfree/2012/jan/02/breast-implant-removal-cost, accessed 4 January 2018.

Wood, S. & Dovey, K. (2015) Creative multiplicities: urban morpohologies of creative clustering, *Journal of Urban Design*, 20 (1), 52–74.

Woodward, I. (2003) Divergent narratives in the imagining of the home amongst middle-class consumers: aesthetics, comfort and the symbolic boundaries of self and home, *Journal of Sociology*, 39 (4), 391–412.

Wright, J. & Harwood, V. (eds) (2009) *Biopolitics and the 'Obesity Epidemic': Governing Bodies*, London: Routledge.

Yeates, N. (2004) Global care chains, *International Journal of Feminist Politics*, 6 (3), 369–391.

Yeates, N. (2012) Global care chains: a state-of-the-art review and future directions in care transnationalization research, *Global Networks*, 12 (2), 135–154.

Yeoh, B. & Huang, S. (2015) Cosmopolitan beginnings? Transnational healthcare workers and the politics of carework in Singapore, *Geographical Journal*, 181 (3), 249–258.

Yeoh, E., Othman, K. & Ahmad, H. (2013) Understanding medical tourists: word-of-mouth and viral marketing as potent marketing tools, *Tourism Management*, 34 (2), 196–201.

Zuckerman, D., Booker, N. & Nagra, S. (2012) Public health implications of differences in US and European Union regulatory policies for breast implants, *Reproductive Health Matters*, 20 (40), 102–111.

INDEX

9 781526 155818